The Museum in Transition

The Museum in
TRANSITION
A PHILOSOPHICAL PERSPECTIVE

Hilde S. Hein

SMITHSONIAN BOOKS
Washington

© 2000 by the Smithsonian Institution
All rights reserved

Copy editor: Joanne Reams
Production editor: Ruth W. Spiegel
Designer: Janice Wheeler

Library of Congress Cataloging-in-Publication Data

Hein, Hilde S., 1932–
    The museum in transition: a philosophical perspective / Hilde S. Hein
        p. cm.
    Includes bibliographical references and index.
    ISBN 1-56098-371-X (alk. paper)
    ISBN 1-56098-396-5 (pbk.)
    1. Museums—Philosophy. 2. Museums—Educational aspects. 3. Museums—
Technological innovations. 4. Communication and culture. I. Title.
AM7 .H45 2000
069'.01—dc21   00-023058

British Library Cataloguing-in-Publication Data available

Manufactured in the United States of America
07 06 05 04   5 4 3 2

⊖™ The recycled paper used in this publication meets the minimum requirements of the
American National Standard for Information Sciences—Permanence of Paper for Printed
Library Materials ANSI Z39.48-1984.

Contents

Preface   vii

I. Introduction: From Object to Experience   1
2. Museum Typology   17
3. Museums and Communities   37
4. Transcending the Object   51
5. Museum Experience and the "Real Thing"   69
6. Museum Ethics: The Good Life of the Public Servant   88
7. Museums and Education   108
8. The Aesthetic Dimension of Museums   127
9. Conclusion: The Museum in Transition   142

Notes   153
Index   201

Preface

By profession I am a philosopher, etymologically a "lover of wisdom." Philosophers deal with abstract ideas expressed in the medium of words. They tend to be shy of the practical and to treat objects and events irreverently as trivial interruptions of thought. They are suspicious of facts and more at home with theorizing about them, dubious of truth and more hospitable toward the search for it. Things are not accepted by philosophers as complete unto themselves nor as sufficient evidence for anything without the support of theory. Some philosophers are openly distrustful of the material world, while others search beyond embodied phenomena for a transcendent reality that validates the physical world. Most philosophers are fascinated by the relations among ideas rather than by the instantiations of them. Why, then, would a philosopher devote herself to the study of museums, whose preeminent stock-in-trade is the specific, historically circumscribed, and palpable object?

Is it incongruous that I love things as much as ideas and find them equally attractive? I believe these are not incompatible affections; for objects, as I understand them, are ideas reified. From a philosophical perspective, particular things, including embodied structures, physical states, actions, and events, are actualized thought. They figure as exemplary of general claims or constitutive of theoretical explanations. Called the "furniture of the universe," things are whatever we take them to be.

Thinking about things relieves me of the burden of owning them. The world, in all its complexity, appears as a gigantic museum, a treasure house whose content changes continually, reflecting the thought that defines it and inviting its further refinement. Like the world, museums are sites of ideated expression, where things are kept, and the thoughts that inhabit things are transmitted from mind to mind and generation to generation. Museums are places to muse in comparative freedom and security. Inside the museum visitors can contemplate objects imaginatively, partaking of the histories of their creation, function, and meaning.

We may think of museums as enclosures that encapsulate portions of the world—more physical, symbolic, real, or fictional "stuff" than any finite mind can encompass. As such, museums materially accomplish what philosophers do conceptually. Whether we conceive the world as one or many, singular or plural, constant or changing, museums multiply narratives. They are collections of collections—momentary worlds comprising the matter of prior worlds. Philosophers conjecture how worlds are generated out of one another.[1] Museums bring us experientially into the presence of just such alternative ways of world making.

So I make no apology for my apparent defection to the world of things, but I will not linger long with their description or enumeration. Invariably, my visits to museums have catapulted me in thought to new and other worlds, to alternative ways of thinking and feeling. Perhaps that is what museums are good for. Like philosophy, they are an avenue that conducts us outside ourselves. Only slightly constrained by the limits of material representation, museums press continuously against human ingenuity to depict and communicate whatever is expressible. Faced with the knowable, the doable, the possible, the probable, the imaginable—as well as the lovable, fearsome, or despicable—museums are challenged to create through concrete exhibitions anything that can be entertained by philosophical understanding. I suggest that museums may, indeed, be able to advance philosophical understanding.

Can the museum model relations among alternative and ostensibly conflicting world versions that may or may not be ultimately reconcilable? What might be learned from museums or from a philosophical study of them? These are among the questions that motivated me to write this book. I have watched museums change over several decades, adapting to new ideas, new technologies and epistemologies, new generations of people, and newly warranted museum objects. More importantly, I have seen the very notion of what a museum is undergo a process of change whose profundity seems to have escaped ordinary notice. The title of my book reflects my conviction that a conceptual revolution is taking place, one that calls into question the fundamental premises on which museums were grounded. This book is, however, neither a history of museums nor an essentialist analysis of the institution; nor is it a prescriptive treatise intended for the enlightenment of museum administrators, although I am hopeful that some of my insights will prove useful to them. My aim is to elucidate what museums have been and have become, both philosophically and situationally. I understand this to be a critical quest rooted in historical and intellectual contingencies, many of which must be beyond the scope of my investigation.[2] It is not the task of philosophy to give practical advice, but rather to diligently seek out the implicit and often unexpressed thoughts that are hidden in the workings of human institutions and actions. A possible merit of such philosophical reflection is that its attention to and clarification of thinking will permit judicious selection of ends—or at least their intelligent evaluation—and the ordering of practice in conformity with them. I believe that the changes now taking place in museums do have significant consequences. Especially, the shift away from object centeredness to an emphasis on the promotion of experience reveals new ethical, epistemological, and aesthetic horizons whose discovery may shake the museum's foundations.

My own convictions are a secondary matter. I will not elude expressing personal opinion, but this is not a polemical book, and one more partisan voice is not what I think is called for. My aim, rather, is exploratory. I hope to bring to light certain aspects of the metamorphosis that is taking place in the museum world, and whose acknowledgment must affect the configuration of that world.

The challenge that museums face in a time of transition is obscured, on the one hand, by theoretical rhetoric that interprets museums from a distance and ignores their concrete vulnerabilities, and, on the other, by too close a focus on the immediate exigencies of circumstance, which then discourages speculative contemplation. Where one group fixes its gaze on abstract semantic and semiological structures, the other contends on a daily basis with issues of household management and defective communication systems. Partisan commentators at both extremes—the former mostly academics, the latter mostly museum practitioners—have proprietary interests in the survival of the institution. Both sides legitimately profess museological expertise, but there is little communication or common ground between them.[3] From the perspective of some academic disciplines, the museum is a conservative agent of normalization, which, like survey courses and popular anthologies, objectifies things and reifies value.[4] So viewed as legitimating authorities, museums are thought to be de facto dispensers of status, whose power to name and canonize demands deconstruction. An emerging coalition of cultural critics and other museum observers is now poised to carry out that task of historical and hermeneutical exegesis. Meanwhile, a growing cohort of professionally trained museum workers, pragmatically situated and functionally defined, continues independently of the deconstructionists to exercise the skills of collecting, conserving, and managing artifacts according to the programmatic objectives of the several populations within the museum community. The diverse languages these people employ—now abstract, now concrete—convey distinct ontological as well as ideological perceptions of what museums are, what they do, and, more importantly, what are the meanings of the things over which they preside. Museums thus have a part in the philosophical activity of world making that is at once abstract and concrete, theoretical and practical, and that willy-nilly endorses as well as reflects power relations.

Understandably, there is friction among those who would stress one aspect or function of the museum over another; yet they have more to gain from dialogue with each other than from mutual contempt or enmity. In fact, the contenders do inhabit different worlds, which, though focused on the same institution, rarely intersect. In my view, the discrepancies between them mark alternative perceptual shifts rather than altogether distinct worlds, and my aim in this book is to clear a path for their meeting. That path, I will argue, takes the new respect for experience into account and leads to some unexplored territory. I inquire whether museums are, or should be, foremost in the business of producing experiences, and if so, to what extent that aim should preempt the museum's more traditional occupations.

The observation that museums render the world experientially accessible is unlikely to meet with denial or opposition from within the museum world. Is not the richness of their resources and the splendor of their exhibitions what museums have long been about? No doubt, but what follows if these are reconceived for the sake of experience? What is signified by representing objects as instrumental to the "having" of experience? Evidently subjectivity, as the ground of all experience, must occupy a preeminent place within the museum experience; but what, then, is the role of objects? What becomes of the legitimizing power of the professionals who care for them? What valorizes one individual's experience over that of any other?

A contentious struggle over objectivity and the claims to it has lately swept the museum world. Its focus, so far, has been chiefly on externalities, and its effective weaponry has been political. I believe, however, that these debates betide a fundamental reconstruction of the museum's identity. Consistent with a widespread decline of faith in the singularity of reality and the uniformity of truth is the promotion of multivalent plurality. The museum's predisposition to world making, well assorted to the spirit of our times, is vindicated in successful practice, and the authenticity of the worlds thereby created needs only the convincing experience of museumgoers to validate it. Where past representations of museum quality might have given scant notice to what appeared only a by-product, today that production is foregrounded as essential, and the museum's capacity to fabricate experiences (rather than to confirm reality) is celebrated as its raison d'être. The measure of the museum is taken by the intensity of the experience it commands and the degree to which that experience "feels real."

In this book, I begin with a rapid overview of a history that discloses not one but a confluence of several conceptual sources of the institution now designated as the museum. Under the heading "typology," I examine representative institutions in light of their distinct modes of assembling objects and of their association. I suggest that the thematic frameworks defining the institution are brittle and that their spatio-temporal referents are dissolving in a world that affirms the global while denying the universal. Any typology is good only as long as its utility endures, and utility is measured by approximation to perceived ends. As museum objectives change, so must the characteristics by which we classify the institutions.

To truly understand the museum, we ought to study its users as well as its content; and so I consider next the successive collectors and interpreters, inside and outside of the museum premises, who are responsible for its preconditions and multiple meanings. I discuss these under the heading of "museum community," a loose association composed of people linked by bonds of uncommon history and divergent interests. Their functional union would be altogether negated in the absence of the "museum object," an entity whose profoundly contested being is the topic I go on to examine.

The meaning of "museum object" and of the objects it presupposes lies at the center of my analysis. Philosophically and historically this pivotal concept came to identify an autonomous entity positively possessing real meaning and supervenient value. In time, its very objectivity has metamorphosed, leaving behind waves of interpretation, affect, and experience. I argue that such transubstantiation is not without consequences within and without the museum world. Husbanding experience does not resemble caring for things. It calls upon different resources and skills, and it engenders distinct priorities. I turn, therefore, to the question of value; asking first how museums perceived their objectives when couched in terms of cherishing certain things, and second, how that perception is recast when diffused over the potential experiences of the people who make up the loosely limned museum population.

The ethics of deployment must accordingly replace that of amassing, and a simultaneous concern with gratifying a public rather than pleasing individuals must focus attention on the museum's place in a cultural system. Museums are then no longer seen as sites that passively preserve and exhibit received cultural capital. They are active shapers and, indeed, creators of value. Ideally they educate people to become discriminating agents on their own part, learning to learn as a constantly fluctuating world demands. This education, as I represent its ethical function, is aimed at the ripening of experience and becomes no longer a by-product but the central mission of the museum. That is, indeed, the current mantra of the museum world.[5]

I reserve for last the aesthetic dimension of the museum, reflecting in part the fact that aesthetics is that area of philosophy nearest and dearest to my own heart—and therefore, no doubt, what attracted me to the study of museums in the first place. But more to the point, I think that aesthetic theory contains a lesson for the museum more fundamental than the obvious interest that museums must have in aesthetic gratification. Philosophical aesthetics has long dealt with antinomies of the subjective and the universal, the expression of the whole in its parts, and the relation of the cosmic to the microcosm. Aesthetic theory has always concerned the contingencies of experience in the perspicuous consciousness of someone who cares about that which evokes it. Aesthetic interest is not confined to works of art in art museums, whose influence and status, I argue, is excessive. Instead, the aesthetic domain includes the world of all museums and the museum of all the world. It is continuous with and overlaps the ethically obligatory and the cognitively required wherever these are found.

Finally, addressing some doubts I have about the experiential and multiperspectival direction that museums are taking, I question whether this trend simply replaces an old monolithic value with a new one. Focusing on one's own experience in a cultural milieu designed to facilitate that endeavor strikes me as no more (and possibly less) illuminating than contemplating objects presented to us within conventionally imposed cognitive limits. I propose that the overt declaration of those limits would render more poignant, more precise, and more precious the magnitude of our differences and the multitude of our agreements. It would also inspire their deeper exploration.

Museums are struggling now with a multidimensional problem of accessibility, calling for more than signing, handrails, and elevators and representing a recognition of multiple sensibilities and an unwillingness to denounce any of them or to declare any one of them as solely legitimate. It seems an admission of limits that subjectivity is inevitable and experience, therefore, strictly private. One need not insist, however, that to be meaning-ful, experience must be uniform. The experiential experiment in which mu-seums are engaged is by no means completed, and much remains to be learned from it. My caution is directed to a facile readiness to abandon the dialectic of alternate world makings lodged in explicit interpretation of things. Experience is not an isolated goal; it entails a presence that resists the experiencer. Without an anchor in resistant worldliness, experience can only be delusional, regardless of the numbers who share in undergoing it. Massive conformity is not a test of the validity of experience. Whether we agree or disagree with one another in how we experience the world, we must appreciate why and how such agreements are reached. We need to imagine how the world might be differently conceived, and this is not a function of individual experience alone. Things have an important place as markers in conceptualizing the world, and, with museums, philosophers likewise construct a representation of the world with reference to the under-stood presence of things.

My own experience with museum practice and with theorizing about museums has been gained through internships in museums and more than two decades of academic investigation. By following both of these avenues I hope to have found common ground between those who reflect about museums from a cultural perspective and those who know them by work-ing inside. I am grateful for the help of many people who have shared their insights and experience with me.

My fascination with the aesthetics of museums began to take shape in 1976, when I assigned the project of designing a hypothetical museum ex-hibition to a class I was teaching. Coincidentally, a colleague in the Holy Cross Visual Arts Department had been awarded a grant under the auspices of three local colleges and the Worcester Art Museum to mount a series of collaborative exhibitions at the museum. She invited me to curate one of them on the theme of "Art, Science, and Engineering." I was soon hooked by that cross-disciplinary combination. Eight years later, with a similar grant funded by the National Endowment for the Humanities, I mounted another exhibition at the Worcester Art Museum, this one titled "Between Science and Art: Understanding Motion." I am grateful to Professor Vir-ginia Raguin for including me in this program, to the director and staff of the Worcester Art Museum, and to the many other friends, students, and colleagues who advised and assisted me in creating these two exhibitions.

During the same period, Frank Oppenheimer, the founding director of the Exploratorium, invited me to write a series of essays relating to groups of exhibits at that museum. I enjoyed several residencies there between 1977 and 1989, culminating in the publication of my book *The Explorato-*

rium: The Museum as Laboratory, which examines the unique point of view that motivated this influential museum. I thank the many staff members who were my companions and mentors throughout my prolonged visits to San Francisco.

Launched upon this new line of aesthetic exploration, I divided my next sabbatical leave, at the Smithsonian Institution in 1989–90, between an internship with Margery Gordon in the Department of Education at the National Museum of Natural History and a research position with Zahava Doering at the Office of Institutional Studies. I thank them and their colleagues for a very special year. I am grateful also to Lois Brynes and Laura Myers at the Worcester Eco-tarium, formerly the New England Science Center, where I held a summer research appointment in 1993. Between 1994 and 1995, I had the pleasure of working with Wendy Pollock and Caryl Marsh and their colleagues at the Association of Science and Technology Centers on the steering committee of a National Endowment for the Humanities–funded project to teach humanities seminars in science museums. This program introduced me to the innards of a number of science museums, opening new paths for communication and collaboration with museum staff members at all levels.

I am thankful also to my academic colleagues and fellow members of the American Society for Aesthetics, in particular Philip Alperson, Ronald Moore, Arnold Berleant, Carolyn Korsmeyer, Susan Feagin, Barbara Sandrisser, and Robert Tsukuyama, who encouraged my interest in museums, accompanied my visits to many, and paved the way for me to deliver papers, write reviews, and publish articles in an area that our discipline had not previously included. I must also give thanks to Holy Cross College for granting several leaves and a faculty research award in 1995, in addition to repeated subsidies from the Faculty Committee on Research and Publication. Many other friends and relatives, including my immediate family, have shared my museum enthusiasm, enhancing my work by plying me with articles and reference materials, discussing ideas with me, advising, critiquing, and arguing with and humoring me. Among those who have been important in more ways than I can enumerate are Norman Mainwaring, Aleta Ringlero, Jane Roland Martin, Annie Storrs, Robert S. Cohen, Marx Wartofsky, Stephen Weil, Helen Whall, Randy Garber, and Naomi Joshi. I particularly want to thank my copy editor, Joanne Reams, and also Mary Cerasuolo, Gavin Colvert, and Zeyad Moussa, without whose technical assistance I would have been lost. This book has been so long in the making that I have undoubtedly forgotten to mention my indebtedness to many other people who have been helpful to me. I beg their forbearance and forgiveness.

The Museum in Transition

I. Introduction

From Object to Experience

Imagine the following stories:

1. A small natural history museum, located in an environmentally conscientious academic community, meets growing hostility toward its century-old collection of stuffed birds and mammals. Removing them from public display, it replaces the taxidermic mounts with interactive computer kiosks that provide a wealth of biological and ecological information.

2. A textile museum, cramped for exhibition space, displaces cumbersome dioramas that represent home-based, colonial cloth fabrication and labor-intensive, preindustrial tool use with videos in which museum guides, in period costume, demonstrate how felting, spinning, and weaving were done in pre–Revolutionary America.

3. An anthropology museum, finding that sealed glass cases fail to protect certain fragile clay figures against vermin and pollutants, exhibits in place of these sacred objects plastic casts that are visually indiscernible from them.

4. An art museum, upon discovering that some of the objects in its collection are of dubious provenance, proceeds to display these in a special exhibition together with the documents that challenge and support their authenticity. The exhibition

includes scholarly and curatorial correspondence, records of purchase and sale, and other evidence pertaining to the origin of the works, their history of production and ownership, and their accession by the museum.[1]

5. When a prize possession from an art museum's permanent collection is stolen, the museum displays a photograph of the missing item in its former place, together with a printed account of the theft and its impact on the art world.

Do these anecdotes have something in common? All of them refer to the removal of authentic and historically cherished things from exhibition, and the substitution for them of something conceptual. All of them invite reflection on the nature of museums, on their past purpose and functions, their present audiences, and on what they characteristically do and do not include. The cases suggest an institution in transition, influenced by change in physical resources and technology as well as by cultural sensibilities and ideology. The museum is a particularly sensitive barometer of such changes. In recent decades there has been a worldwide explosion in the number of museums and growing interest in museum work as a profession.[2] By and large, however, the museum-going public continues to represent a small percentage of the population, generally of those who are well educated and financially secure.

Among the changes to be contemplated is the endeavor made by museums and their supporters to expand their audience and to reach it in new ways. Museums have striven to become more democratic in their structure and more responsive at all levels to the interests of a broad-based public. This practical reconstruction entails implicit revisions of the fundamental concept of a museum, a concept that, among its early familiars, required no explanation and needed no reform.

Definition

For legal and professional purposes, the concept of the museum has been repeatedly defined. A typical example is the definition adopted by the International Council of Museums (ICOM) in 1974: "a non-profit making, permanent institution in the service of society and of its development, and open to the public, which acquires, conserves, researches, communicates, and exhibits, for purposes of study, education and enjoyment, material evidence of man and his environment."[3]

A similar definition was implemented by the Museum Services Act of

1977: "a public or private non-profit agency or institution organized on a permanent basis for essentially educational or esthetic purposes which, utilizing a professional staff, owns or utilizes tangible objects, cares for them, and exhibits them to the public on a regular basis."[4]

Formal declarations notwithstanding, every element of these definitions is subject to de facto challenge from within and without the profession, and no single feature is viewed as essential by the general public. Disagreement continues not only over the true nature of museums but even as to what sorts of entities are properly to be counted as museums. Many people are surprised to find that zoos and botanical gardens, as well as libraries, are listed among museums in professional and touristic publications; museum workers are equally shocked that visitors are unable to discriminate between museums and theme parks or commercial demonstration sites such as the New York SONY Center. When considering what the objectives of museums are, it is important not to conflate these with the ambitions of all other cultural institutions.

Museums are at once very ancient and very new. Perhaps the oldest sense of "museum" refers to the Pythagorean temple of the muses, a "sylvan grove to which scholars repaired, there to conduct research, amid discourse, and with reference to books or to objects."[5] Although that description of a refined haven for scholarship, comparable to a contemporary "think tank," may be losing its luster, its immense historical power continues to be reflected in metaphorical usages of the word "museum" that evoke conflicting associations with the sacred and the barbarian, the treasury and the trash bin, the orderly assemblage and the chaotic junkpile, as well as the musty and moth-eaten, the rare and precious, the strange and exotic, the desiccated and embalmed. The word "museum" is commonly understood to denote a collection of entities held to have sundry intrinsic worth but whose value is greatly enhanced by the act of gathering and preserving the discrete items as a totality in one place.[6] As museum workers point out, however, the collection of rarities is worthless without additional documentation, a requirement that tends to be underappreciated by the general public.[7] Typically, museum research is conducted using a quantity of individual objects. Although many of these are never exposed to the public, their assemblage in terms of some categorizing or value system is vital to the pursuit of research.

Function

Notwithstanding differences in their choice of priorities, those who venture to define museums have typically concentrated on certain functions and behaviors. These include *collection, preservation, study, exhibition,* and *education.* The condition of *indigence* is wryly appended by some observers, but that seems less a necessary attribute than a contingency whose presence unhappily bedevils the museum's mission of public service. Although museums are not bound by a vow of poverty and would gladly be free of that constraint, they are paradoxically "property rich" and "income poor," a condition owing to their awkward quasi-public, quasi-private situation as fiduciary agents that hold objects in trust for the benefit of the public.[8]

Chief among the activities traditionally attributed to museums is *collection.* Nothing has seemed more central and essential to the very being of a museum than its collection, which is assumed to consist of material objects that can be identified and classified in light of their accrued taxonomic or aesthetic or historical significance.[9] "Whether we excavate, purchase at auction, send out expeditions, receive gifts, ferret in attics, or are the beneficiaries of bequests, we gather the objects of interest and importance to our particular discipline."[10] After the acquisition of objects, the next order of business is conventionally held to be preservation: "It is pointless to gather objects of great beauty, rarity and value and then allow them to deteriorate due to inadequate protection, preservation and restoration."[11]

But there is surprising disagreement as to which objects found in museums are rare, beautiful, or valuable—or even material. Neither is it obvious what would be the optimal state in which to keep an object—the condition in which its original owner(s) acquired or maintained it, or that in which it reached the museum? Most objects found in museums were never intended to be kept there. Many would have been destroyed under conditions of normal use; think of how many potential museum items are thoughtlessly discarded by Americans on rubbish collection day. A tour of suburban curbsides or student residence halls at semester's end invariably unearths abandoned treasures, from antique lamps and buggies to portraits, TV sets, and slightly damaged glass stemware. Moreover, if the cost of preserving objects is excessive, alternatives to preservation have now been perfected that require less expense, labor, and space and are, arguably, as effective educationally. And the public is enthusiastic about them. Everyone loves dinosaurs, for example, but if numbers are a clue, museum visitors are as happy with cleverly engineered models that roar and move as with the carefully researched and reassembled paleobiological specimens found in traditional natural history museums.[12]

Ironically, just as the merit of preserving things in their original state is being questioned, new technologies for doing so are contributing to a renaissance of restoration and conservation.[13] But philosophical questions remain about whether the preservative impulse is properly linked with the primary value of collection, and these doubts threaten to unravel the historic understanding of museums. If museums are not simply storehouses for the protection of cherished objects, other, more innovative museum functions come into focus. Even the traditional commitment to study and research, initially restricted to specialists and scholars, can be mingled with programs to satisfy new educational demands. Likewise, the obligation to interpret objects and to disseminate research in academic presentations fuses with new needs for popular programs. The museum's educational role is being recast and differently performed, addressed to diverse audiences with a variety of cognitive styles. Museums are drawing on the inherently spectacular nature of their resources and presenting themselves in a less linear and more theatrical manner. Display in the service of instruction blends imperceptibly with ceremonial performance and entertainment. Design and spectacle—the semiotics of display—appear increasingly as central elements of museum exhibition, sometimes preempting narrative order, as museums shift their emphasis from preservation and study to dramatic delivery.

Education is merging with public programming in museums, and, combining other museum functions that formerly were kept apart, teaching conflates with exhibition strategy. The increased significance accorded to "outreach" is evident in the fact that exhibition teams no longer execute a plan dictated by curators alone; educators, designers, publicists, and marketing professionals contribute more or less as equals on the team ab initio. As a consequence, exhibitions are becoming more public oriented, more theatrical, and more self-consciously rhetorical. Aesthetically focused to deliver an experience, they underline the museum's unique capacity to teach by showing.

The showing of objects has been the museum's historic mission. Exhibition traditionally put objects "on view," inviting visitors to inspect and contemplate them, guided by the epistemically privileged museum authority. But what is observed in the museum today is no longer unequivocally an object; objects have been reconstituted as sites of experience, and museums increasingly hold themselves accountable for delivering experiences. Paradoxically, the inherent subjectivity of experience weakens the museum's claim to authority over its presentation. Can one any longer guarantee a single "right" way to see an object? Indeed, are objects "seen" at all? Is the object on view one or many? How can certain experiences (of objects) be designated as more legitimate than others? And what are the conditions that validate objective judgment or justify any given interpretation?

To question the status of the object and its interpretation(s) is to challenge the hierarchy of values that sanctions museums and that the visitor is presumed to share. This challenge is implied by the new orientation that museums profess to embrace. Striving to reconcile their historic commitments to collection, preservation, and scholarship with a reinvigorated and self-conscious conception of education and exhibition, contemporary museums are compelled to address questions of identity, objectivity, and privilege that were traditionally obscured. A new museological attitude, more given to asking than to answering questions, contends with metaphysical puzzles (What is an object?) and with epistemological issues (What is truth?). Today's museums proudly accept an amplified educational mandate to stimulate and encourage inquiry. In that environment, the displayed object appears less an end than a means, its function being to generate a museum experience that is illuminating and satisfying.

History

Museums in America have followed a course somewhat different from museums in Europe, where they originated. Most of the latter began as private collections, reflecting the taste and fortunes of their founders, and only subsequently were seized by or bequeathed to the state for the benefit of the public. The major American museums were founded idealistically, often fostered by philanthropic interests and concern for the betterment of humankind. Of course, some entrepreneurs were hucksters, who quickly grasped the recreational potential of museums and made freakshows and spectacles of them, guiding them well along the way toward today's entertainment centers and theme parks.[14]

The American museum movement began in the mid–nineteenth century when private charitable gift giving, testifying to the spirit of individual initiative, played a large part in the country's growth. Perceived as a public benefit, charitable donation was encouraged under subsequent tax legislation and continues to be a primary source of museum income. Most museums are thus quasi-public institutions, incorporated along with hospitals, churches, and various educational and service agencies as nonprofit organizations. In principle, they are thus nominally independent of government supervision, unlike their nationalized European counterparts. In this century, however, most nonprofits have received state financial assistance in the form of grants and subsidies, which enable the government to impose restrictions as a condition of receiving aid. Unable to subsist on exclusively private funds, most museums, like other nonprofit organizations, have reluctantly accepted the compromise and lived uneasily with its consequences.[15]

Today's museums perform their public service by offering themselves as resources and educational institutions, but it remains a matter of debate whether the goods they offer are objects to be valued as cultural treasures and means of education, or, especially in the case of artworks, whether these are sources of original experience (which may, of course, be compatible with further educational programming.) The meaning of "museum experience" may hinge on this apparently abstract and hair-splitting distinction. Is the designated experience of the object exclusively for its own sake, or does the object serve as occasional stimulus for a broader, more encompassing experience? The answer to this question determines whether we must think of museums as "object centered" or "story centered." It affects the architecture and organizational structure of museums as much as the design of exhibitions and programs. Should priority be given, for example, to security, according to the object-centered model, or, assuming that resources are limited, should more effort be expended on visitor-friendly, interactive devices? These concerns lie at the heart of many of the "culture wars" and political confrontations that currently rage inside the professional museum community and also subject it to attacks from outside.

Shifting Priorities

This book is not a history of museums, but it does examine some of the factors that account for the current condition of the institution. It explores such phenomena as the diminishing prominence assigned to collection, not only as a response to changing social and economic circumstances but also as transformatively intended to address the metaphysics and epistemology of objects. If "collection" stands for a deliberative organizational device rather than a physical aggregation of objects demarcated in reality, then the museum's accumulative role is subjectivized and its absolute authority is put in question. The museum's presumed dedication to the "real thing"—the authentic object that is prized and studied—acquires a new and politicized significance when objects cease to be taken as ontological givens and become simply occasions for privatized experience or constellations of assigned meanings.

Directly imperceptible and indefinitely interpretable, museum objects occupy a fictional space that is controlled by the museum. The viewer who engages with a museum object is implicated in a conceptual and cultural metamorphosis that ambiguously preserves the language of material things. A close look at contemporary museum practice exposes this ambiguity and its consequences.

Experiences, unlike things, are not collectibles but rather are quintessentially transient and elusive, strictly located neither in time nor in space. The sense of stability that has long dignified museum collection belongs with an idea of static monumentality and not with fleeting evocations of private experience, however facilitated by the presence of objects. This confusion is compounded by a further mystification of reality—its conjunction with genuineness and authenticity. The claim of an object to be genuine has a connotation altogether different from that of the reality or genuineness of an experience (which might well be initiated by an illusion). Experiential reality is phenomenologically self-contained and divorced from both its causes and consequences. Whatever its stimulus and however great its intensity, no corroborating referent or vindication other than the fact of its presentation matters. In that regard, an electrode stuck in the brain can provide as vivid an experience as a work by Rembrandt. Experience is curiously in the here and now, and there coils the serpent in the museum's garden of fictional delights.

The point at issue is not that museums make false representations or defraud the public, but rather that today's museums are engaged in an entirely new enterprise aimed at eliciting thoughts and experiences in people. That objective is not exclusive of assembling collectibles, but it takes collection seriously as a means rather than an end—and by no means the only means to that end. The end is the achievement of an experience that is genuine, but undergoing such an experience does not depend on mediation by an authentic object.[16] The experience might be triggered by a multitude of devices, not all of which are real, or genuine, or material. Museums today are busily constructing such devices.

We cannot truly appreciate what is happening in museums or recommend what ought to happen there as long as we ignore the changes that are taking place in their conceptual foundation and attend only to the surface. The inconstancy of language (or, more accurately, its misplaced constancy) obfuscates the profound institutional transformations that are actually taking place. It is surely perplexing to find museums still distinguished as establishments that house collections of "material evidence of man and his environment" at a moment when the words "matter," "evidence," "man," and "environment" no longer denote stable ideas.

Forces for Change

Returning to the illustrations with which I began this introduction, we can identify a number of pressures for change at work in different types of museums.

1. Cultural attitudes dictate the removal of "real" objects in some contexts. Popular disapproval of the abuse of endangered species, for example, has influenced some natural history museums not only to eliminate stuffed animals from dioramas but also to exclude from display items manufactured out of their parts—feathered baskets, cloaks, and headdresses, utensils made of bone and horn, snake- and alligator-skin accessories, and fur garments. In their place, interactive computer programs and video or film loops illustrate the banished items and their former uses and also explain the prohibitions against them. Where display of real animals or animal parts is unavoidable, museum labels reassure the public that no living creatures were harmed for the purpose of collection, the exhibited item being a "salvage"—a wounded animal that cannot return to its natural habitat, for example, and that has been rescued by an animal shelter. The public thus receives a double dose of didacticism, learning both the museum's original lesson pertaining to the object and its application while also taking in the humane, environmentally concerned message that exploitation of rare species and causing injury to them, even in the pursuit of knowledge, is not to be tolerated.

2. Space limitation, stringent health and safety restrictions, and inevitable economic pressures on museums conspire against the continuous operation of an inefficient, old apparatus whose work is swiftly accomplished by modern equipment. Although people want information regarding technical procedures and enjoy seeing machines in motion, historic tools tend to be noisy, cumbersome, and sometimes dangerous. Moreover the skill of using them is becoming obsolete. The display of static, inactive tools in glass cases bores people, however, and attracts less attention than film loops and video demonstrations that explain and illustrate the operations that the older machine can perform. Periodic performances by museum staff trained to use antique instruments are sometimes scheduled, but they are

expensive and possibly obtrusive, hazardous, and unsanitary. The equipment's unpredictable performance may be what captivates the visitor's curiosity, but these somewhat unreliable demonstrations are increasingly giving way to prepackaged and scripted lessons that inform the public in standardized, repeatable detail regarding an object's capabilities. Regrettably, video tapes leave little room for independent exploration, but they can easily be replayed.

3. Some institutions, notably London's Victoria and Albert Museum, have displayed casts of famous and immovable works as educational models from their inception—how else could ordinary people ever get close to Trajan's Column or the Ghiberti Baptistry doors? Most twentieth-century museums regarded casts with condescension, however, and relegated them to storage. But certain anthropology and archaeology museums, and even some art museums, have now had a change of heart. Under adverse climate conditions or environmental pollution, the original objects risk deterioration and damage, so for their protection they have been withdrawn from public exposure.[17] Plaster casts are therefore being retrieved for display as well as for educational purposes, as museums are finding that fifty years of automobile exhaust produces far more damage than several thousand years of precombustion machine traffic. The sheer volume of traffic, human and vehicular, also increases the risk of injury to objects from friction and handling, and so, with the exception of scholars and other specialists, visitors are denied access to the oldest and most vulnerable items of museum collections. Ordinary visitors are therefore unable to experience the "aura"—the unique presence in time and space that the museum world venerates as an object's authentic essence, the source of its traditional authority and its place in history.[18] The trade-off for this deprivation is that the replicas made by new reproductive technologies are all but indistinguishable from the originals. The reproductions, moreover, are amply supported by computer documentation, which often permits close-up visualization and manipulations that would be impossible with original objects.[19]

4. Art museums are also contemplating the positive and negative features of electronic reproduction. Digitized images are useful

for educational purposes, historical scholarship, conservation, security, record keeping, and promotion. Computer imaging attains a quality far superior to other reproductive means (e.g., slides or photographs), but there are obvious disadvantages. A practical risk is the museum's loss of control to whoever has the ability to process and reproduce the images. Though it is unlikely that galleries of electronic images will soon take the place of physical paintings and sculpture, their availability raises questions about appropriation, unauthorized reproduction, or other substitutions of accessible images for works of art that are hard to transport and expensive to insure.[20]

Reproductive procedures raise serious philosophical queries, apart from the many legal and practical issues. One concern is the eroding effect upon aesthetic sensibility that comes of substituting a replicated object for an authentic one, even and especially where the difference in immediate aesthetic impact is insignificant. That insensibility, prolonged over a generation of viewers whose experience is limited to surrogates, could undermine the aesthetic foundation that justified the creation of the art museum as institution in the first place.[21] A related doubt probes the troubled philosophical issue known as the *problem of identity of indiscernibles.* Just as the cloned dinosaurs of *Jurassic Park* cannot be identical with their historic predecessors—not least because of their temporal disparity—a molecularly reconstructed *Mona Lisa,* fabricated by nanotechnologists, would not be the same work that Leonardo painted. This must be the case regardless of any differences actually discerned between them and independently of whatever experience each of the *Mona Lisa*s might inspire. A representation is, by definition, a re-presentation and, in virtue of that hyphenated character, differs from what it represents. Neither the accuracy of a reproductive rendering nor its psychological persuasiveness can undo the logical or historical priority of an original.[22]

5. A public weaned on television and computer screens has come to accept simulations as adequate indices of reality. Information *about* a phenomenon is routinely substitutible for the experience *of* it and even thought preferable where some aspects of that experience might be disagreeable.[23] As they are increas-

ingly demanded for the sake of comfort and convenience, simulations are likely to become not merely substitutes for but
displacements of phenomenologically obtuse real things.[24] Today, the boundary between direct sensory apprehension and
cognitively informed recognition has all but disappeared as
technology and the fashion of historical contextualization de-
pose the priority of perception. We can no longer distinguish
between "seeing" and "seeing as" experientially, and contrary
to the teachings of conventional empiricism, there is no breech
between the intake of sensory data and the process of understanding. Surrogates are no less able than originals to trigger
interpretive operations. To the extent that such cognitively
fortified experience is what is wanted of art, the intrinsic aesthetic qualities of an artwork are secondary to its motivational
properties and might even interfere with its mediating role by
calling attention to themselves. A narrative recalling or reconstructing an event can thus take the place of a physical object
that merely stimulated the event's occurrence. The object, it
turns out, was just a placeholder for a story.

In effect, simulacra neither imitate nor replace reality, but rather transfigure
it. "Virtual reality" achieves a degree of realistic precision unmatched by
any prior representational endeavor, but it does not abolish the logic of
representation. Minutely accurate replication in some dimensions can
make fiction seem like reality, but history remains, and if the method of
production is taken into account, confusion is restricted to the phenomenological level. There can be no doubt, however, that every order and level
of experience is real and really does take place. The relation between the
several levels of experiences and their causal dissimilarity is philosophically tantalizing, but museums necessarily have more practical issues to
pursue. From the perspective of practice, the difference between presentation and re-presentation may be insignificant.

Mediating Reality

Having determined that "things are seldom what they seem," museums
have chosen to exalt the seeming at the expense of a once-preeminent reality of being. The examples of current museum practice cited above are typical of the dematerialization and trans-reification that are taking place

throughout contemporary society. Such trends certainly are not confined to museums. Philosophers have long maintained that the world is mediated by language, and the ghost of an accurately representational Ur-language still haunts endeavors to trace the babel of speech back to a common source. Certainty and truth seem imperiled by the relativization that textual pluralism implies. Today's anxiety is augmented by the fact that language is no longer regarded as the sole or primary mediating device. A host of newly destabilized entities now joins the ranks of texts to be decoded. And these nonlinguistic but garrulous things, speaking with increased clamor and insistency, call attention ambivalently to themselves, not only as vehicles, but sometimes as the only accessible reality.[25]

As interpreters of things, museums vie with the best of textual strategists. Freed of the dogma that objects speak for themselves or in a single authoritative voice, museums are nevertheless comfortable with the existence of objects and with the notion that they speak at all. In this respect museums are far in advance of classical philosophy and depart dramatically from the distrust of matter that views it as inimical to understanding. Pivotally placed within an epistemological tradition that elevates subjective consciousness over the apprehended object, museums are unique among cultural institutions in their veneration of objects as bona fide carriers of meaning and value.

Meaning and value are now everywhere under review and everywhere caught in the critical predicament of pluralism. Museums thus find themselves existentially placed at the forefront of a reconstrual of fundamental philosophical concepts whose influence has reverberated throughout the world. Hence museums have a vital investment in reconstructing their own foundations. It is simple to exonerate them before the charge of being "prisons for things," but far more complex to vindicate their emergence as "sanctuaries of meaning."

Mining Meaning

Interpretation, once narrowly defined as a rule-regulated procedure applied to deliberately contrived symbols, has invaded the solid world of matter, mystifying and rendering it transparent. It seems that things never were what they seemed; their fixed identity, whose humble honesty was contrasted with the mendacity of words, turns out to be just another delusion. Things, like words, can indeed tell many stories. They can lie, but even when they are not baldly deceptive, their atomic structure is no more a defense against semantic misleadingness than is the common alphabet of a language protection against its multiple significance and potential for stating falsehood.[26]

What is to be done if the objectivity of objecthood melts into textuality? Museum collections can then no longer be what distinguishes museums from other cultural institutions (which are also charged with the interpretation of texts), nor can museums be differentiated typologically among themselves. Traditional content-based organization collapses if the meaning of the objects museums contain is equivocal. Things that are neither unique nor typical, neither paragons nor specimens of their kind, effectively have no existence at all.[27] "What is it?" is revealed to be an incomplete and inexhaustible question. Posing as a request for substantive information, it demands a decision. Fortunately for museums, this dilemma multiplies presentational opportunities and encourages their exploitation in the form of ingenious design and theatrical techniques.

Museums have elevated to a science the common classificatory compulsion to identify—an imperative that goes beyond mere possession and accumulation. This taxonomic impulse, sometimes pushed to pathological extremes, not only rescues billions of objects (from bottle caps to Vermeers to Lepidoptera) from temporal oblivion but also bestows meaning and value on them and assigns them a place in a quasi-objective order. Collection and the discriminating refinement it fosters make sense of the world and domesticate its "buzzing, blooming confusion." The world making begun by individuals is sanctioned by the institution.[28] As dispensers of coherent order, replacing the contingency and disorder of real time and real events, museums contribute to the production of a secure sense of the world's intelligibility. So understood, museums also play a considerable part in conferring a sense of civic identity on social congregations.

The Politics of Practice

Museum collecting, both cultural and aesthetic, recalls social practices that deploy power and constitute value. Translating these practices into the production of meanings and the dissemination of experiences challenges the common expectation that reality transcends subjective manipulation. To point to these practices and these experiences, however, is not to diminish their reality, but only to expose philosophical perplexities that a simpler, more materialistic reverence for objects did not reveal.

The tendency that I have noted toward dematerialization is oddly incongruous in a world that appears to exalt material values above all others. It extends to aesthetic judgment as much as to legal constructions, in which, for example, private ownership pertains as plausibly to one's reputation, or image, as to one's shoes or plot of land. Indeed, property is reducible to the abstract right to prohibit access to others. What happens under such conditions to the claim that museums house authentic articles? Controversial as the expression "authentic" may have been when applied to material works of art and artifacts, it is yet more obscure when the authenticity of meanings is at issue. We can determine the age and origin of physical objects with some degree of reliability by scientific analysis, and conventional tests exist for the historical authentication of works of art. But meanings are an altogether different matter. How are they authenticated? Meanings are not bound by the laws of physics and have no direct physical or psychological correlates. Unlike things and loosely affiliated with experience, they can occupy several places at once, and a single entity may have a surfeit of meanings—simultaneously or sequentially.

If museums are to remain sites for gathering whatever it is that people believe worthy of collection, preservation, study, and exhibition, they must adapt to an ethos of dislocated meaning—meaning stripped of its usual cushion of active believers and actual belief systems. And so they have done, but the language that describes museums has lagged behind. Still ridiculed as "mausoleums for things" or romanticized as "places to wander and muse," museums are truly more creative than either of these expressions suggests.[29] Serving to catalyze experience in their audiences, museums validate those experiences and celebrate the capacity to have, share, and enjoy experience. These functions are newly ascribed to museums since they are not implied by the conventional, content-focused definitions. They therefore merit attention and investigation that, heretofore, they have rarely received. Delivering experience cannot be taken as just one more activity that museums have undertaken. I will argue that it is especially complex and that it affects whatever museums do in all dimensions.

This book undertakes to investigate museums, beginning with the premise that their description as fundamentally about collections of objects is misleading. It questions the typological system that classifies museums according to the objects they purport to collect and asks instead about the collective thought and action that museum interpretation incorporates. Turning next to the experiential content of museums that, I maintain, now is their stock-in-trade, the book explores appropriate standards of objectivity and public accessibility.

Since the values that museums conserve are traditionally reputed to be somehow embedded in their collections of objects, it is necessary to consider their catalysis of experience. How is value affected in that process? What is the consequence of the shift from ontological to phenomenological value? Are museums obliged to formulate new standards calibrated to the evaluation of experiences rather than of things? Value inquiry has a long ancestry that includes the study of ethics and aesthetics, whose focus on conduct and doing distinguishes these disciplines from theoretical studies chiefly concerned with knowing and contemplation. Museums, however, clearly depend on both types of enterprise. Their work centers as much on cognitive (theoretical) discourse as on practical activity or the production of pleasure. A full assessment of their service would appreciate the integration of these dimensions in museums, while also addressing the merits of their newly elected experiential function. Museums are rightly perceived as world makers and not simply as preservers and propagators of cultural values. A just consideration of that role must examine how experience is disseminated both in museums and elsewhere. It must ask how certain experiences are valorized over others and according to what standards. That inquiry entails reflection upon the educational function that museums have always professed, but have only recently placed at the center of their commitment.

In keeping with their newly espoused focus, museums acquire responsibilities consistent with their prescriptive ability and capacity to canonize. As coauthors of experience understood to be real, museums are competing for the public's allegiance with such manufacturers of illusion as movies, television, theme parks, and advertising. In that light, museums must become as discriminating in the selection of the experiences they purvey as they formerly professed to be solicitous of their collection and care of objects. Confronted with the observation that not all experiences are born equal and that some are more meritorious than others, museums must recast themselves responsibly together with their mission.

2.   Museum Typology

A pair of conflicting ideals has motivated museum collection from its beginnings and remained interlaced throughout its complicated history. On one hand is a fascination with the unique, whose value is perceived to be a result of a thing's rarity, high quality, or unusual history. On the other hand is an interest in the universal, or typical, for which purpose ordinary specimens are wanted, often in great numbers so that their individual differences can be reconciled with their generic oneness. The first approach, although sometimes derided as primitive—the appeal of the shiny pebble to the magpie—is exalted as connoisseurship when eccentric taste devolves into a full-blown aesthetic. The second, generic approach inclines to didacticism, professing an internal coherence among the objects collected that justifies found relationships and rationalizes group affinities with theory. Both tendencies persist in contemporary museums, sometimes harmoniously under the same roof and sometimes in ideological conflict.

The first tendency rewards the idiosyncratic voice of confidence. It exalts arbitrary judgment and, coupled with independent power, naturalizes that judgment to give it objective validity. Museums inaugurated with its assurance have an air of majesty and confidently promise an elite experience. The second tendency is no less authoritative, but its legitimacy stems from a claim to universal agreement. Clarity and self-evidence are its watchwords, and museums committed to this ideal promise community and shared vision. Museums that combine these two tendencies raise incongruous expectations—to provide "an elite experience for everyone" on the one hand; to transcend class and cultural difference on the other.[1] The move toward democratic equality has brought all social practice under the rubric of "culture," writ with a small *c,* thereby dimming the aura that surrounds upper-cased "High Culture." Promotion of "the best that has been thought and said" puts pressure on individuals to at least pretend to cultivated conformity of judgment. Museums are hard pressed to reconcile the contradictory claims of unique superiority and the more egalitarian merits of diversity.

Those institutions now called museums have family resemblances to one another, but they share neither a common history nor a common cause, notwithstanding the emerging professionalism of museum work and the homogenizing discipline of museum studies. The American Association of Museums accepts among its members a staggering array of institutions to which people come for recreation and edification without necessarily attending to a connecting link that purports to join them conceptually.[2]

Like their contents, museums can be classified according to a number of schemes. Taxonomic systems are conceptual devices for ordering masses of data. The ordering system not only reflects a prior intellectual choice but also determines pragmatic decisions regarding a museum's internal organization, acquisition policy, exhibition style, public outreach, and programming. It therefore matters how museums represent themselves to themselves as much as how they are externally identified. Security of precious objects is of highest priority to some museums; to others, user-friendly maintenance is most essential.[3] There is no absolute method of classification, nor are museums irrevocably bound within a single designation. Most are currently experimenting with different models of self-presentation, borrowing procedures from one another, and the categories of classification are being transformed as museums mix and match to fashion new identities for changing circumstances. The convention preserved through popular opinion, recorded by chambers of commerce and tourist bureaus, indexed by telephone directory listings, and implied by the definitions found in professional literature divides museums according to their content. Highly specialized collections persist, of course, and continue to proliferate to the applause of their devotees, but to a great extent these are perceived as the stronghold of eccentricity. They usually have a short life span and are staffed by a single generation of enthusiastic volunteers. Frequently they are open by appointment only, and their location is unknown even to adjacent neighbors.[4]

The primacy of objects appears to be contested, however, as even the architecture of newly constructed museums de-emphasizes their function of collection and preservation and instead stresses public programming and performance.[5] Let us consider some typological prototypes.

Art Museums

The imposing facade of the nineteenth-century art museum seems archetypical to most people when they imagine a museum visit.[6] Although less frequented and less popular than science or historical museums, art museums tend to be considered the museum paradigm. Their content, loosely referred to as "fine art," typically includes not only painting and sculpture but also less exalted aesthetic expressions and even such ambiguously utilitarian items as religious and funerary implements, architectural components, clothing, armor and weaponry, and domestic furnishings. The rhetorical expressions "museum quality," referring to rarity, excellence, and value, and "museum piece," denoting something that is old, unique, and venerable, generally allude to objects that are or should be found in art museums. Fiction often romanticizes childhood hours reverentially spent in museums, although not all reminiscences of such afternoons convey that sentiment.[7] The art museum carries a burden of nostalgia, dignity, and stuffiness not easily counterweighted by the aesthetic gratifications it also provides.

Today's conception of an art museum as a center of exhibition and scholarship, a "symbiosis of collecting, publishing and teaching" whose curatorial staff is both professional and professorial, has roots in private collections that were made public in eighteenth-century Europe. It descends from the Renaissance *Kunstkammer,* itself an offshoot of the earlier medieval *Schatzkammer.* The latter was a heterogeneous collection of treasures, curios, and gifts of natural and artificial origin kept for their individual value. Periodically, items would be removed to be put to their conventional use, as cutlery or chinaware for a banquet, for example, or coins for commercial exchange. Though occasionally shown to privileged guests, these objects were stored for private pleasure and were not essentially on display. The *Kunstkammer* represented a glimmering of a new humanistic consciousness, foretelling an attitude of appreciation toward human artifice seen as skill and mastery. Its collected contents were the counterpart to works of nature. In their universal aspiration, these objects also carried symbolic value, linking the microcosmic human order to the macrocosm of the divinely ordained world.[8]

Through successive generations of collectors, *Kunstkammern* came to reflect the personal aesthetic taste of their possessors, and increasingly, they were separated from collections whose interest was chiefly historical or naturalistic. By the mid–eighteenth century, when Beauty became an ideal of an independent science of philosophical aesthetics, and the ground had been laid for a critical art history, imperial collections were also more segregated in terms of their historical, numinous, or aesthetic value. As the ideals of the Enlightenment (the German *Aufklarung*) trickled down to the bourgeoisie, instruction in drawing was introduced into schools, and the study of original works of art was seen as a means to visual education. Under the reign of "enlightened" monarchs such as the Austrian Habsburgs, Maria Theresa and Joseph II, collections of art were reorganized with didactic objectives, and, for the sake of the people's edification, public access was given free of charge.

An independent public picture gallery, the *Gemaldegalerie* in the upper Belvedere, was opened in 1776. Its collections were placed under the care of a keeper, who cataloged them in accordance with explicit principles of art history, setting a precedent for art museum curatorship that persists unto the present. The ordered exhibition of artworks in their own *Kunsthistorisches* Museum, housed appositely to the Museum of *Naturhistorischewissenschaften*, which likewise organizes its contents according to a sequential pattern of development, has become a standard. This view of art—linking it ineluctably and analogically to the creative power of Nature—is articulated in the aesthetic philosophy of Georg Wilhelm Friedrich Hegel (1770–1831), who regarded human artistic achievement as the incarnation of the Absolute Spirit. According to Hegel, the Absolute, identified with Reason and with God, realizes itself through a graduated sequence of concrete, sensuous expressions that is ultimately destined to self-transcendence—the end of art. The stages of its progress are recorded in the world history of art, which is graphically (and properly) displayed in the structure of the museum and the order of its exhibitions.[9]

At the same time that art museums were dedicated to the uplifting project of tracing the march of the Absolute Spirit through history, they retained a more worldly function of celebrating the taste and refinement of those who would dictate the conditions of culture. The history of this patronage has left an imprint of aristocratic connoisseurship on the art museum and rendered it a symbol of wealth and privilege that the rhetoric of popular revolutions did not erase. Art museums, though now objectively available to all, still maintain the value system of the privileged few. As at their origin, the most prominent among them dictate "cultivated" taste and decree which things are truly beautiful and are rightly to be held as objects of aesthetic appreciation, as distinct from need or mere want or base passion.

From its inception, then, as public institution, the art museum has been something more spiritual than a "depository for aesthetic products of man's creativeness" and more collectively exalted than an "environment for experiencing works of art."[10] It was aggressively designed to transform people into citizens by infusing them with a sense of cultural identity and shared patrimony. "Palaces for the People" no longer has an oxymoronic ring; it designates a civic phenomenon. Yet, as the sociologist Pierre Bourdieu argues, the objective of art museums is not to induce the love of art in everyone but to underwrite existing cultural distinctions by "naturalizing" a stratified culture, so that "cultured people can believe in barbarism and persuade the barbarians of their own barbarity." "Upliftment," as Bourdieu describes it, is not meant for everyone. Only those who are equipped, by education, with the ability to appropriate the works of art are free to enjoy the freedom of free access to them. For the others, the illusion of taste is only further confirmation of their own inferior status.[11]

Contemporary studies of visitor attitudes show that the appellation "secular temple" is not a misnomer. Some people do feel in museums a sensation of awe like that of being in the presence of something sacred. They are inspired with a learned consecration of Culture that preserves distinctions of class and links them with those of taste.[12] The love of beautiful things is not confined to privileged collectors, of course, but the obligation to admire what they admire and to find beautiful what they declare is beautiful continues to be nurtured by art museums, notwithstanding endeavors to make both art and museums more widely accessible.[13]

From a curatorial perspective, the imperative to make art "accessible" poses an odd dilemma. The museum is obliged to collect objects known to be culturally significant, to have been important individually, or, at least, to be typical of a genre that had relevance at the time it was produced or in a later era. But these objects, even when their historic role is correctly assessed, do not invariably appeal to contemporary taste. It is difficult both to satisfy the didactic condition and, at the same time, to acquire objects whose genius or aesthetic merit is spontaneously evident to today's noncollecting museum audience. For this reason, museums tend to be more averse to risk than private galleries in acquiring contemporary art and inclined to augment their holdings only after new work has been recognized through selection by individual private collectors. Some daring curators do follow the idiosyncratic lead of their hearts, but most of them opt for the "safe" representative sample that has been tested by the market. Both options risk ending with what the public sees only as an accumulation of curiosities. In all cases, art museums bank on the reverentially receptive attitude that visitors typically bring to the museum and strive to extend it toward the objects selected for display.

Art museums can work both as anodyne and as stimulus. Ingeniously contrived to rationalize appropriation, they entice the public to take a vicarious and intellectualized part in the delectation of ownership while deflecting their visitors' attention away from the inequities of its denial. The museum's ability to shift attention away from material inequality, and indeed to glorify the displacement of wealth into a symbolic public sphere, has powerful political impact.[14] Vicarious ownership softens the reality of exclusion by creating an illusion of shared history and aspiration. That capacity was not lost on Napoleon, who forced conquered cities and even the Vatican to surrender their treasured artworks as trophies of war. Through the offices of his appointed director of the French museum system, Baron Dominique Vivant-Denon, Napoleon assembled the world's greatest collection of art masterpieces and used it to symbolize and promote the glory of the French nation—in the first instance, to its own citizens.

Collective pride of possession assumes identity of taste, however, and so the educative task of the art museum has been to induce shared pleasure as a means to creating civic unity. Those who lack a good must still be made to see its univocal worthiness if they are to partake of its aura. Cultural authority relies on the ability to control people's wants and pleasures.[15] Art museums thus combine refined recreation with learning. For the past century the cultivation of aesthetic pleasure has been at the center of the museum experience, and this has been depicted as uniquely distinct from all other values. "Art for art's sake," which has no raison d'être apart from itself but exists purely for aesthetic gratification, has been the prize celebrated by modern art museums. The modern art museum professes universality of scope, not on account of an actual community of experience that it evokes but through its appeal to a fundamental human faculty—albeit one "filtered through the taste of generations of connoisseurs."[16] The museum purports to speak to the human condition stripped of the particular and the concrete. Skeptics doubt this universalistic claim and charge the museum with covertly promoting more venal and immediate ends, but the claim that a generic and generalizable experience of beauty can be elicited continues to fuel support both for the production of art and for its exhibition.[17]

Recently the museum's preoccupation with a universal aesthetic has met with serious opposition. At the same time that aestheticians are abandoning essentialist definitions of art and unitary representations of artistic genius, museums are experiencing pressure from "outsiders" who do not find themselves or their work represented in the museum.[18] A new ethical and cognitive consciousness has penetrated the museum world coincident with the shifting tide in art history, theory, and the recast social mission of the museum. We may no longer feel confident as to what is a work of art or who is an artist, let alone which are the good ones, but in sacrificing that false security, the advocates of the new consciousness maintain, we may find fuller aesthetic satisfactions in museums that reach out not only to the heights but also into the depths and varieties of human experience.

Science Museums

Natural History Museums

After art museums, natural history museums are probably closest to the popular museum archetype. This is a paradox, since they are conceptually at the opposite pole, containing mostly natural objects rather than artifacts, and specimens rather than unique creations. Many a scientist recalls the stirrings of scientific enthusiasm sparked by frequent family visits and occasional field trips to these tidy urban oases. And even nonscientists find there a haven of order in the confusion of a noisy world. Many also find excitement in discovering the vastness and the minutiae of the universe and happily lose themselves in the magic of exploration.[19]

Though also consecrated to pleasure, science museums are less ambiguous than art museums in stating their mission to increase and disseminate knowledge. Like art museums in their descent from the medieval *Schatzkammern,* the earliest natural history collections featured the exotic and unusual rather than the regular and orderly. Gradually, however, defying religious prohibitions against excessively probing curiosity, collectors began to observe unexpected patterns in the world and devised systems of classification to describe them.

Initially taken to mirror the divine order of the universe, "cabinets of curiosities" were the pioneers of scientific collection.[20] Collection in the Renaissance grew less idiosyncratic, turning away from personal metaphor and aspiring to encyclopedic completeness. Secular princes and worldly prelates organized expeditions for the sake of gathering far-flung realia that would complete their collections. These contained flora, fauna, minerals, and artifacts from all known continents, as well as drawings and paintings of nonpreservable or nonportable objects. Entire landscapes and social systems were illustrated, supplementing written accounts of geographical, ethnographic, zoological and botanical studies. Princely collectors of the sixteenth to eighteenth centuries vied with one another to perfect collections that would attest to their power and the glory of their dominion. Many maintained scholars and artists in their service, who not only collected but also cataloged and illustrated their discoveries, hoping thereby to explain the natural processes they observed.

By the seventeenth century, sufficiently effective techniques of preservation, display, and communication had been developed, as well as systematic ways of cataloging and recording, so that well-known specimens could be tracked down by scholars who traveled from collection to collection with the express purpose of comparing and compiling. Collections soon found their way into universities and royal households, where they contributed to the beginnings of scientific taxonomy and theory construction. Among the first was that of Ulisse Aldrovandi (1527–1605), a cleric at the University of Bologna, whose collection was assembled to test the (arguably) proto-Marxist environmental theory that social customs are influenced by local availability of raw materials and technologies. His catalog, *Musaeum metallicum,* was not published until 1648, forty-three years after his death.[21]

The first publicly established natural history collection was assembled by the father and son team of John Tradescant, Elder and Younger, landscape gardeners whose gardens were designed to include plant specimens from their worldwide travels. Their collection was given to Oxford University for the benefit of the public by the Tradescants' heir, John Ashmole, in 1678. Ashmole had assisted in cataloging the Tradescants' collection and arranged for its preservation as a semipublic museum of natural history in 1683. The Ashmolean building still exists as a museum, though most of its original collections have been reclassified and dispersed among other museums.[22]

Natural history museums came into their own in an environment inflamed by the desire to amass evidence of God's order and variety. Natural philosophers named the kinds of things they collected by designating ideal types, based on observations of features found to be specific from the study of instances. The museums that kept these collections were meant to be repositories for the comparison and study of these specimens. The excellence of a collection derived from the quality and quantity of its individual holdings, which were judged both as examples of their type and with respect to the comprehensiveness of the whole, according to a philosophical doctrine of perfection.[23]

Museum collections thus contributed to the conceptual interpretation of scholarly data. By their visual array of exhibited objects, museums also gave actual currency to theoretical ideas. The personal exhibition gallery of Charles Willson Peale (1741-1827) expanded to include portraits of Revolutionary heroes (1782) and subsequently became the first American public museum, which embraced both cultural and natural history. In addition to these displays, Peale's museum exhibited experiments involving electricity and perpetual motion. To Peale, the museum was a visible "world in miniature," and in it he aimed to promulgate Linnaeus's system of classification. By seeking individual specimens, perfect of their kind, to serve as standards and exhibiting them according to a stratified spatial plan, Peale's museum helped naturalize the binary and hierarchical taxonomic system that Linnaeus had devised to represent objective reality. Moreover, the visual juxtaposition of objects relative to one another and to the viewer conveyed moral lessons and political precepts that were all the more persuasive for being subliminally apprehended.[24]

The emblematic inutility attributed to artworks in art museums was never a distinguishing feature of the objects kept in natural history museums. Among the pleasures that science museums have always purveyed is that of acquiring knowledge, and the knowledge promised is not merely of the specimens displayed but, through them, of the entire science of which they are a detail. The Smithsonian Institution's early curator, George Brown Goode, went so far as to exalt the referenced idea over the depicted object, declaring the museum "a collection of instructive labels, each illustrated by a well-selected specimen."[25]

Once collected, whether for the love of learning or of beauty, an object is necessarily aestheticized. Removed from its real-world environment, albeit for the sake of advancing knowledge of the world, it becomes an object for "disinterested" aesthetic attention. Individual specimens such as butterflies or crystals may well be admired quite simply for the beauty they possess in their natural state, but in the museum, these objects acquire an artificial value and effectively lose some of their original attributes. Detached from their place in the physical world, they inevitably undergo supraphysical alterations. They are enclosed in a framework of new meanings, associated with other museum objects, whose relation to the natural world, like their own, has become contingent and conjectural. Whatever its previous life has been, when an object enters a museum collection, it must be born anew.[26] Its rebirth is as a cultural object, tied to the human enterprise of science.

Science Centers

Science museums do not all give birth in the same manner, however, and not all of them give pride of place to collection in the conventional sense. Some museums employ objects in order to demonstrate their typical use or to display a physical principle or process found in nature. A type of museum known as a "science center" is similar to natural history museums in being chiefly didactic, but unlike those older museums, science centers teach through objects, rather than about them. Objects function chiefly as instruments or props rather than as collectibles. The objects kept in science centers may have been extracted from the world or copied from it, but they may also be artifacts specially designed, converted, or constructed for the museum's own purposes. The preservation and protection of these artifacts, however come by and whatever their price, are incidental to the science center's real mission, and so these institutions are devoted less to curation and collection management than to functional maintenance.[27]

Science centers are relative newcomers to the museum field, and their origins and history are not clearly marked. Victor Danilov, former director of the Chicago Museum of Science and Industry and a chronicler of the science museum movement, traces the emergence of science centers as a late evolutionary expression of museums of science and technology.[28] Fundamentally idea driven, they are preeminently contemporary and conceptual. Science centers are plainly knowledge rather than object centered, but the knowledge they foster is often experientially achieved through the manipulation of objects. Pieces of the world are brought into the museum not to be studied in isolation but to stimulate worldlike experiences directly in their visitors. Science centers have become extraordinarily popular in North America and also in developing countries, where they are seen to fill a need to prepare the public for modernization and industrialization. Very much a part of the democratizing museum movement, they appeal to new audiences that do not have the linguistic or historical expectations of earlier museum-going cultures. Science centers work by enlisting the participation of visitors to complete a museum experience, rather than by presenting "stand-alone" information whose content is independent of its reception. Science centers typically do not celebrate what eminent scientists have done but rather invoke the universal processes of science. Unlike historical museums, they do not illustrate the history of science or its results, and they rarely propagandize technology and its benefits. Instead of glorifying information, science centers strive to awaken curiosity and to inculcate a spirit of scientific inquiry in their visitors. Their exhibits are designed to provoke and gratify inquisitiveness rather than to instill awe. Prominent in the vocabulary of science-center enthusiasts are words such as "experience," "discovery," "participatory," "hands-on" and "interactive," which convey the idea that a dialogue takes place between an active museumgoer and the museum exhibit. The visitor is often required to interact both physically and mentally with an exhibit in order to complete its performance and render it meaningful.

This dialogic approach incorporates an activity-based pedagogic theory that has spread throughout the museum and educational communities. Learning, in this view, is acquired experientially, not passively. The role of the teacher or museum is to provide stimuli that will induce spontaneous interest and initiate curiosity. Museums are responsible for producing intelligently designed exhibits that provoke and reward inquiry, but the burden of learning falls squarely on the visitor, who is represented not as a receptacle to be filled but as an inquiring mind. The emphasis on collaboration between teacher and learner stems from a popularized, nonauthoritarian vision of the museum and of learning, as well as from a contemporary view of science.

Few scientists today make discoveries as did their forbears, by voyaging about the world with a spyglass. Many scientists do no physical collecting at all, but work with mathematical models, simulations, and abstract principles from which existents (as well as truths) are inferred. They work in teams, relying on verifiable reports from one another, and their exchanges more commonly transmit ideas and methodologies than actual physical objects. The evidence they gather is usually not available to ordinary perception and must be understood in terms of systemically defined, nonempirical concepts. The teaching of science, therefore, rarely begins with directly showing people physical things. Instead they are introduced to a way of thinking, and an attitude, that attend to the world in a particular interrogative manner.[29]

Science centers strive to elicit such thoughts and attitudes in their visitors by reproducing conditions and apparatus similar to those that incited such thoughts in others. They display and allow the public to use instruments used by scientists to make observations, to assay substances, to test hypotheses, and sometimes to draw analogies. These working objects are not "museum pieces" in the conventional sense. They are often pricey, but never priceless. They can be obtained from laboratories, industries, government agencies, research centers, and schools and may be copied, modified, or reconstructed to meet museum needs. Whether natural objects such as phosphorescent minerals or artifactual devices as familiar as telephones, they function in the science center more or less transparently, as vehicles of thought that aid visitors to think and learn to solve problems for themselves.

Exhibit fabricators in science centers rarely regard themselves as traditional curators or scholars, and many have little previous museum experience. Few of them have the artist's idiosyncratic sensibility. The exhibits they make are often ingenious and beautiful inventions yet may be materially and conceptually improved by other people without violation of artistic integrity. Unlike works of art, science center exhibits are neither unique nor irreplaceable.[30] At the same time, they are not specimens that must be preserved in multiples. Their function in the museum is essentially vehicular—that is, as conveyances of the visitor's thinking. And for that purpose, their own identity must be modestly transparent. Science center exhibits are to be used, not venerated. Their value is independent of the cost of their production, and like that of works of art, derives from the experience they produce.

Like artworks, science center exhibits are a source of aesthetic gratification. The sensuous pleasure they afford is enhanced by the intellectual delight of understanding them and prolonged by imaginative use. Connoisseurs of technological artifacts and machines insist that their beauty is not reducible to either utility or rational intelligibility, although these are among their chief attractions—celebrated occasionally even by museums of art.[31] Science centers also appeal to a spirit of spontaneous playfulness. Much like sophisticated amusement parks, they are places to come and have fun; their encouragement of collaborative exploration attracts people who might feel like "barbarians" in more traditional art and natural history museums. Yet science centers have a serious purpose. Indeed, more than most other museums, they address cognition directly—the process of knowing rather than the object known. Exhibited objects, though indispensable to them, are secondary to the exhibit ideas that determine their selection. These ideas are the active soul of the museum.

Museums of Industry and Technology

Science, however, is no more reducible to methods and attitudes—to abstract thought and hands-on manipulation—than it is to taxonomic collection or to "facts." Its history and social impact are ingredients of the workings of science and have an influence on its content. These aspects of science are explored in museums of technology and industry, which frequently have a limited focus, celebratory of a regional industry or manufacture of local renown. For this reason they also enjoy civic and commercial support. They may be directly linked with a production site and are often promoted by chambers of commerce as a touristic attraction. Unlike science centers and more like natural history museums, these museums are collection driven. They feature generic historic and contemporary apparatus and early models of machines illustrative of technological progress. They may or may not memorialize the individual persons who played a part in the development of an industry or process. Like art museums, museums of technology also celebrate uniquely important items, such as the first of a kind of thing—the Ford Model-T or a primitive computer— or a transformative moment that marks a historic sequence of events.[32]

The history of an industry can be told with a mixture of artifacts, models, diagrams, texts, film and video, and personal demonstrations, not excluding some of the participatory procedures now favored in science centers. Because these tend to include reflection on the social and economic conditions that surround a particular technology and, increasingly, on the environmental consequences of that technology's application, museums of technology and industry are coming to resemble general historical and archaeological museums, which use material studies as a basis for the interpretation of human history. It is no coincidence that the Smithsonian Institution's Museum of History and Technology, which opened in 1964, was merged in 1980 into the National Museum of American History. Though retaining its interest in the industrial growth of America, the expanded museum shifted attention away from engineering and craftsmanship alone, to focus as well on their sociocultural and human consequences.[33]

Some museums rely on corporations for support and maintenance of exhibits that are designed to demonstrate the particular industrial structures and techniques that pertain to their products. Since these embody the application of scientific knowledge and engineering skills to a specific purpose, the exhibitions have the potential to be highly educational as well as historically illuminating. At the same time, they risk becoming predominantly promotional of the "need for" and the "success of" the product sold by the sponsoring corporation. Unless carefully monitored, such museums can overstep their not-for-profit mission and become mostly market driven. Approaching the status of trade fairs or commercial theme parks, they are liable to compromise the integrity of their educational message.

Although corporate sponsorship of museums is increasingly necessary for economic reasons, it poses cognitive as well as ethical problems. It reveals the fluidity of the basic concept of the museum, however, and poses the broader question of whether education can ever be segregated from practical interests. Technology and the commercial agents of its growth have been major players throughout the history of America.[34] Their products are the treasure of contemporary vernacular society. The documentation of this triumph is surely comparable to that of the European ecclesiastical and dynastic successions that are narrated in the format of traditional art and history museums. Indeed, America is as much indebted to its industrial titans as museum benefactors—Rockefeller, Frick, and Carnegie, to name a few—as Europe is to its nobility.

History Museums

History museums, including local historic sites, make up more than half of American museums.[35] Their presentation and interpretation of objects play a large part in shaping our perception of ordinary living conditions as well as important events of the past. Remarkably, although historic reconstructions such as Colonial Williamsburg, Old Sturbridge Village, and Plimouth Plantation are seen by many more visitors than make up the readership of scholarly publications pertaining to the eras covered by these installations, the written works are more likely than the exhibitions to be subjected to serious analytic scrutiny.[36] Historical scholarship has, all the same, been touched by museum practice, notably in the area of the "new social history," whose evidence is drawn more from material artifacts left behind by the people who lived the history than from chronicles and literary remains.[37]

Most historic houses and museums are located near, and include items found at or original to, the place and period they represent. These museums generally maintain collections of objects valued for the record of the past inscribed in them rather than for their intrinsic aesthetic or material worth. Here too, some objects are implements typical of their time and place, others work synecdochically to evoke a range of sentiment and memory, and still others have unique and specific associations with historic personages. Perhaps beyond all other museums, history museums inhabit the ambiguous middle ground between objectivity and subjectivity where cognition and feeling, fact and value, intermingle. The material of history, now reduced to inarticulate "stuff," once was meaningful to those who partook of it. History museums profess to revive and restore that meaning.

Few people still believe that physical objects "speak for themselves," but neither are they mute. They signify within narrative systems.[38] In history museums, someone uses objects to tell a story to someone else that purports to correctly describe or give information about an absent person or group. Objects, like language, serve as principal media for the formation, expression, and confirmation of human relationships, and so museums that preserve objects are mines of knowledge about the workings of human societies. Historians and museum scholars, working at semiotic meta-levels, discover narrative veins within their collections and extract their meaning for visitors by applying epistemically effective exhibition strategies to them. Museums thus bear multiple responsibility for their collection and reassemblage of items that represent intended stories. Inevitably, therefore, history museums are implicated in the "politics of representation." Their mission can neither be simply connoisseurship—the appreciation of unique aesthetic quality—nor, in the manner attributed to natural history museums, can it be chiefly taxonomic. All stories and strategies announce design. They are at once its product and the means of its realization.

History museums strive to "recreate" the past in an idiom accessible to the present; but accessibility itself is a matter of interpretation. Today it is understood affectively and empathically, as well as cognitively and physically, and is meant to extend democratically to all segments of the public. But museums cannot reach all publics in the same manner. There is no guarantee that a message sent is identical with the message delivered, and even the most rigorous attempts to control the public's experience are likely to fall differently on different eyes and ears, since a diversity of past historical experiences compounds the diversity of the present.

Responding to the same pressures as all other museums, history museums have grown more experiential and more "interactive." Although they still deal mostly in material objects and have expanded the range of things they collect, many history museums are now less invested in collectibles as such than in their interpretive presentation. But what is the experience they hope to elicit? There is no single answer to that question. As texts, objects are notoriously polyvalent and less rigidly fixed than language within semiotic systems. Moreover, unlike language, things require force to be excised from one or another functional or natural environment where a particular significance is to be made evident. They are not arbitrarily constructed de novo out of neutral shapes or sounds but have an antecedent material life in a material world with prior meaningful histories.

The determination of which among several possible insertions of objects into a narrative perspective shall predominate in a given museum presentation is a complex judgment, arising out of political, economic, aesthetic, and practical considerations. This is an arena of scholarly disputation, and critics of history museums are typically harsher in their judgment of misassigned meanings (and meaningful omissions) than of the quantity and quality of a museum's physical contents.[39] What museums tell and what they leave out are functions of accumulated human intentions, and not wholly expressible in terms of the extensiveness or material quality of their collections. It is, for example, only to be expected that a slave shack or worker cottage be scantily furnished and that its appurtenances be well worn and shabby, but that judgment does not affect their historical or museum worthiness.

One increasingly popular way to meet the challenges of recontextualization, while doing homage to authenticity, is to concentrate on constructing an experience whose genuineness does not depend on that of the displayed object. Thus theatrical stagings of "recreated" moments of history are becoming more common, and mediation sometimes takes the place of traditional physical conservationist priorities. Objects, whether carefully preserved originals or accurate replicas, are used as means to an end, rather than as ends to be contemplated for their own sake. Their value, like that of exhibits in science centers, is thus contingent—inclusive of material components, complexity, rarity, craftsmanship, and cost—but based above all on their status within a system of meanings.[40]

Meaning status is not exclusive. Identifiable objects can persist, uneasily and multiply, in a cluster of coexistent meaning systems. An item used by a specialist as evidence for scholarly historical research may be a commemorative object to a participant in (or survivor of) a historic event, or it can hold chiefly aesthetic or entertainment interest for a detached onlooker.[41] The meaning of objects oscillates wildly from user to observer and between distinct communities, regardless of the museum's endeavors to exert a standardizing control. The controversies provoked by such polyvocality must be approached from the vantages of all the communities that museums serve and represent. Obviously, this ambiguity of objects is a problem for museums faced with the task of constructing exhibitions with multivalent appeal. Elevated on the one hand to the status of "things that tell a story," rather than as secondary reinforcement of verbal documents, the objects are demoted on the other hand from "realia" to "media," a degradation from intrinsic to instrumental value. No longer ends in themselves to be appreciated aesthetically, even works of art are now semiotically transformed.

When they are displayed in historical context, they become social documents—things that tell a story—and the museums that display them are at
pains to make the most of their referential agility.[42]

Though never absent from the museum world, didacticism is now more
central to it than ever. Museums of all kinds share with other educational
institutions a preoccupation with teaching the people who use them. Before the days of marketing and visitor surveys, museums paid slight attention to demographics. They addressed the potential museum audience
essentially as similar vessels—some more receptive than others to their ed-
ifying message. In reaching out to new users, museums have crossed both
social and disciplinary lines. The vessels they approach have become less
alike. Imbued with popular culture and informed by academic learning
theory, museums might discover a paradigm of educational endeavor even
closer at hand. A sterling model can be found in their own institutional
history in those museums designed to acculturate preliterate and semiotically adaptable children.

Children's Museums

Thanks to their concentration on material studies, most museums are comparatively well positioned to address preliterate and multilingual audiences. Although this was not previously their paramount objective, they
have the means to generate simultaneous, many-leveled experiences attuned to a multiplicity of intellectual styles and capacities, not all of which
are linear or conceptual. Museums gave little thought to children and their
needs as long as collection and scholarly research were their chief concern,
but once they turned to the visitor experience, the developing mind of the
child became a matter of great interest to them.

Children's museums have been around for a century. Sometimes they
possess collections, and they do display objects, but they are not historically or primarily charged with the care and preservation of collections.
Since their inception, their aim has been to evoke certain types of experience within their young audiences.[43] Children's museums, like so many di-
minutive projects, were intended by their sponsors as playful rehearsal
space to introduce children into the culture for which they were destined.
The first American children's museum, founded in Brooklyn by mostly
Jewish, upper-middle-class residents, was meant to pass on to the next
generation the Eurocentric values of their community. The museum's benign plan was to shape the children and equip them with skills to meet

adult expectations. Like miniature kitchens for girls and toy machinery for boys, children's museums were to prepare young people for the occupations of middle-class life. They would expose children to mythologized and expurgated adult adventure, like fairy tales in the round. However much other museums might ponder their primary mission, children's museums were never in doubt that theirs was to teach.[44]

They have not deviated from that initial objective but, like other museums, have adjusted their appeal to an audience of "doers" instead of "viewers." The communities they serve have changed, however, and children's museums have needed to adapt to new social and demographic features of their surroundings. To accommodate the interests of new waves of community residents, many without a tradition of adult museum attendance or with detached spectatorship, children's museums have collaborated with public-school curriculum reform movements and sometimes with neighborhood action groups. They have joined with these other agencies to champion new methods of learning by doing and to teach basic social rules and survival skills. As before, they use things as teaching materials, but in a new way, encouraging visitors to become active learners prepared to advance beyond the cultural restrictions of their parents' generation.

Like science centers, children's museums retain the conventional museum's affection for the material qualities of objects; this emphasis distinguishes museums from schools, where language is central. But both schools and museums have come increasingly to resemble activity centers; some, indeed, are initiated for that purpose by educationally inspired parents and neighborhood collectives. Children's museums have served transitional communities, helping antagonistic subgroups to understand one another's cultures.[45] Over the protest of some staff members, museums have even taken on some of the functions of day-care centers, a role for which not all are well equipped. Some take part, along with other service agencies, in publicly funded after-school programs designed to help children make the transition into adulthood.[46]

User orientation—the explicit adaptation of museum exhibitions and programs to the capacities and needs of young audiences—was a radical departure from the curator's-eye-view that formerly motivated museum collections. But children's museums are building the next generation of museumgoers, and their visitors, having reached adulthood, will not bring the passively reverential attitude of their parents to museums. They will approach objects pragmatically, as props meant to stimulate experience, whose function is to entertain and edify, and whose ultimate identity is subjectively and contextually determined.

As all museums face changes in the communities they serve, the techniques developed by children's museums to attract and hold audiences are everywhere coming into widespread use. Museums that perpetuate "official history" can no longer rely on the stability or common interest or complicity of the public, and they must be prepared for vociferous resistance. Traditional boundaries between insiders and outsiders, and between teachers and taught, have become blurred. Those who learn are affirming the right to their own subjectivity and are forcing those who guide them to acknowledge their part in the making and unmaking of reality. Grown self-reflective and self-referential, museums must look at themselves, not only as teachers, but as objects—seen through the eyes of another.

Museum Taxonomy

This exploration of museum types does not pretend to be comprehensive. I have not discussed all those institutions to which the generic term is applied but have sought to articulate a logic of museum kinds. Expecting to find certain concepts common to museums, I found instead a great deal of volatility, and, above all, the replacement of genuine objects by real experiences. Different kinds of museums have emerged successively, and they are still proliferating—now at a slightly diminished rate—even as the existing institutions are redefining themselves in the terms of those that are replacing them. They are purveying new kinds of experience in light of current museological theory and cultural practice.[47]

The phenomenal interest shown in museums today is itself worthy of examination. It betokens an awareness that museums are part of a sociocultural system that creates and disseminates value. It recognizes that museums also confer identity. The physical objects that fill museums can be weighed and measured and labeled as so much matter, but what they are depends on the mutual reification of subjects and objects according to a system which the museum propagates. No more than that of a word can the meaning of an object be self-evident. Alternatives are always possible, but, as with words, there are regular, structural relations of objects coded into distinct cultures. Museums are prescriptively engaged in fixing these encodements, and how they do it determines their type.

To pose the question, What are museums and what do they do? is to inquire about the place of an institution within a signifying system that mediates objective reality. It is to ask what museums' special relationship to objects is, and how they integrate the careers of things with the lives of people. Some theorists believe that the objects that humans produce and gather have a life of their own, reproducing themselves and evolving interdependently with biological species. The psychologist Mihalyi Csikszentmihalyi maintains that things are both products of human intentionality and determinants of it, and holds that we are as much their creation as their creators.[48] This plasticity of objects that enables them to be both common and unique, typical and singular, product and producer, lies at the root of the museum romance with objecthood. The different types of museums that have come into being through successions of historical accidents have capitalized on this remarkable capacity of objects to lead many lives. To understand this phenomenon, however, we must not look at objecthood alone, but also at the human communities that institutionalize and preserve it.

3. Museums and Communities

Experience is a private affair. However produced by objects or ideas, experiences take place in and "belong to" the creatures that undergo them. Although human beings endure their experiences individually, they are not immune to the experiences of others and are believed to partake of shared and common experiences. It seems clear that one's involvement with various groups of people has an impact on the quality, and even the occurrence, of particular experiences. Institutions that guide people's thoughts and actions collectively therefore also affect the individual experiences of the persons they include. In short, although experience is a personal and subjective event, it is inscribed by social conventions and forces and expressed in communally meaningful forms. Like other institutions, museums have a part in the articulation and dissemination of those conventions. Museums mediate among and between social groups by offering tangible means for the production and delivery of experiences according to standardized patterns and practices. Responsibility for standardizing these patterns and practices does not rest with museums alone, however, but reflects their place within a civic order that varies and changes direction over time. The current dynamic is toward greater integration in a world of many communities, but also toward greater acknowledgment of their differences.

We have seen that collections of objects are congregations of meanings abstracted from intense human interactions. Although "every collection is someone's dispersal," the activity of collecting turns the museum's gaze inward to research, management, and the security of its treasure.[1] Now and again, however, museums are obliged by the nature of their collections to face outward and to renegotiate agreements with newly distinguished partisans.

Who are these partisans of the "museum community" and what is owed them? Although museums have served a selected public for six hundred years or longer, their public role has expanded over the last few decades. The number of museum visitors in the United States doubled in the twenty years between 1965 and 1985. Museum outings are now a major family recreation, often inspired by one member's introduction through a school or community group field trip. But visitors make up only a segment of the museum community. Other stakeholders in museums are the people who build and work in them, their boards of trustees, donors, and benefactors, the scholars and academics who use them for research, the producers, societies, and cultures whose creations are preserved there, and those persons, past and present, whom they represent. Even those who lack representation have a virtual place there: for example, the 50 percent of Colonial Williamsburg's inhabitants who were enslaved and who were not depicted in the early reconstruction of that village. Are current abutters and neighborhood nonvisitors part of the museum community, or does their voluntary absence exclude them?[2] What about those who stay away because they are physically or mentally unable to enjoy museums, or who feel intimidated by them? Is there a generic museum community, or do different museums have distinct communities depending on their type and location? Does the community include past generations and persons yet unborn? Are there gradations of responsibility that the museum owes to any or all of these, and are there reciprocal obligations owed by community members to the museum? If so, how are these ranked? Do museums have a choice in selecting "their" communities?

Any answer to these questions presumes to know what a museum is and what it ought to be. Also implicit is a concept of what a community is and what it means to be part of one. Contemporary usage tends to associate *community* with warmth and intimacy and therefore to regard membership in a positive light.[3] One logical implication of *community,* however, is that something or someone lies outside of it. Pious global claims notwithstanding, the idea of a universal community is nonsensical. That which binds the members of a community to one another is something they share in common that differentiates and separates them from something other than themselves. It does not follow that the identifying feature is good or bad—a band of thieves can be a community—but it does follow that the notion of community is inherently "othering." There is that which belongs and that which does not belong, and consequently relations among the members of the community differ significantly from relations between those members and whatever remains outside.

Although relations between "insiders" and "outsiders" are not invariably inimical, a tendency exists for the one to view the other with what Julia Kristeva has called *abjection,* a feeling composed simultaneously of revulsion and fascination.[4] The othering relation is constructed by the subject insider's assuming an identity that marks the object outsider as a strange and exotic other. Museums contribute to such othering endeavors as nation building and the welding of cultural commonalities. By profession, they collect, study, present, display, exhibit, and explain *objects,* thereby aligning themselves with a community of self-identified subjects. The experience of these subjects is inherently privileged, assuming cognitive priority even where what is collected is also experiential, pertaining to the experience of a designated other or outside group. As museums reach out to those who once were outsiders, welcoming them as fellows into the embrace of their cognitive camaraderie, they intend to expand the ranks of insider subjectivity; but this is not easily accomplished. The insider experience is doubly alien to former outsiders, in that the distinction marking this status exists only relative to the insider community, whose categories of meaning and rank do not apply elsewhere. So—if outsiders are to become insiders, they must adopt as their own the perception of themselves as reconstructed outsiders, a paradoxical option on both cognitive and ethical grounds. To remain an outsider is to be insensible of that condition, and to become an insider is to repudiate it—and so to disavow one's prior identity. Affirming "outsiderhood" positively is not an option. Meanwhile, from the museum's perspective, expanding its boundaries to include outsiders must challenge those parameters that made it a community of insiders in the first place.

The editors of the book *Museums and Communities* admit to abandoning a projected title that contained a proprietary reference, as if museums owned and managed "their" communities much as they organize "their" collections.[5] As these editors point out, museums intersect with a number of communities—many of which are alive and reactive—and do not *own* any of them. Even "their" employees are free contractual agents. Yet the problems and politics of possession converge on the museum's community relationships as much as on its collection and exhibition philosophies.

We can examine the museum in light of the several communities that constitute its identity, but just as the language of "inside" and "outside" is conceptually problematic, so does the concept of *ownership* obfuscate the relation between museums and communities. Although it risks circularity, one approach that seems plausible is simply to consider the groups of people that are significantly affiliated with the museum.[6] One among these is the staff, including the director and those persons who do the daily work of operating the museum. Arguably the most influential force that shapes the museum's character, the staff is largely invisible to the museum-going public and to critics and commentators who discuss museum contents. But a new awareness is emerging; for, correlative with a transformed concept of what the museum is and does, the expectation of who does it and by what means has been altered. The new generation of museum personnel differs from its predecessors in cultural as well as professional formation.[7]

The Profession

The professionalization of museum work has alerted the public to museums' social role and status, but it conflicts in some respects with the endorsement of pluralism as a social end. At the same time that museum training is becoming more regularized and staff hiring more routinely based on certification, museums are turning to nonprofessional, noncertified, indigenous sources who are "native speakers" to authenticate their exhibitions. This reliance by museums on "community" sources is not an affirmation of deference to superior knowledge but purports to respect that community's right of self-representation. In other words, the museum means to include both subject and object—representor and represented—in its cognitive enterprise. The experiential wisdom of the latter supports their claim to expertise but does not outweigh the certified skills of the professionally trained representors, in whose eyes experiential subjectivity enlivens and enriches an exhibition and makes it memorable but does not illuminate it cognitively. Thus including both parties in the museum community may strike a blow for democracy but often provokes a conflict of methodological priorities.

The trend toward professionalism has produced a community of persons who possess specialized knowledge and technical abilities, acquired during a period of study or an apprenticeship that is normally overseen by members of the profession.[8] No doubt this movement has resulted in many improvements, such as more efficient management of museums; better physical facilities for the preservation and display of objects; more effective systems for retrieval and sharing of information; greater amenities for scholars and the public; closer attention to certain ethical aspects of collection and deaccessioning; and general codes of conduct. By way of regular meetings, journals, workshops, and electronic avenues of communication, this professionalism has also shaped a sense of identity and personal commitment to their work among museum workers. The satisfactions of belonging to a cohort, generally in a pleasant environment, and the feeling that one is engaged in valuable work with a social purpose, are seductive rewards. They are often a counterweight to the rather low pay that all but the highest-ranking museum employees receive.

Shared interests, a common language, and mutual pleasures are community-building features of many professional organizations. They are a legitimate foundation of friendships, and they cement communication within a group. They also strengthen the group's collective position in the world, providing a ready base for advocacy and the promotion of the group's goals. Professional ties intensify the self-valorization of the group, so that members tend to protect each other and to be unable to hear criticism that emanates from outside the group. Elaborate self-imposed procedures sometimes camouflage the intolerance of external criticism, under the pretense that only insiders have the specialized qualifications required for apprehending infractions. Opponents of the trend toward professionalization within museums have sometimes argued that, although maintaining standards is important, there are no specialized skills unique to museum work that set it apart as a profession from other skilled activities.[9]

Such controversy notwithstanding, a professional structure is now in place with national and international representation, numbering thousands of institutions and individuals who communicate regularly among themselves through publications and programs, and it has resulted in a de facto profession. Its declared mission is public service, and its advocates in government and the nonprofit sector struggle to make achievement of that mission possible.

From the public's point of view, however, professionalism tends to augment the museum's insulation from those other communities that constitute the social order. Museums continue to be seen as places of social and intellectual privilege. This perception may stem from a misplaced projection of the status of wealthy donors and trustees onto less-affluent wage earners, those who work in and those who visit the museum. Ironically, public ambivalence toward elitist snobbery and the cult of expertise inhibits the achievement of democracy and hinders the museum from realizing its avowed goal to expand conceptual boundaries that would equalize the status of knower and known, collector and collected.

The Collected in the Collection

As collectors of things of cultural interest, museums are pivotally positioned to disseminate cultural values, a delicate balancing act in a multicultural space. Since they are not neutral "data bases," free of cultural
burdens, museums inevitably impart their own interpretive assessment to
the objects collected and to the act of collecting. Collectors are deeply invested in and lend a personal quality to their collections, just as exhibitors
cannot but be present in the exhibitions they mount.[10] Obversely, the collected, having been appropriated, infects the character of the collector.
Collector and collected are thus reciprocally constituted but do not necessarily enjoy equal status.[11]

Where collections are made up of remnants of living cultures expressed
by actual people, they who are "collected" are now demanding a voice in
their own representation.[12] As museums reach out to include more communities, they are finding resistance among the living "collected," who
refuse absorption on any but their own terms. Museums are encountering
demands that are unusual not only in light of their practical inconvenience, but also in the self-reflective pressure they impose. Whose sense of
temporal continuity should prevail, for example, when an object is
deemed by its tribal possessors to be animated by a spirit dating back a
thousand years, but contemporary carbon dating identifies its manufacture within the present century?[13] The vantage point of the collected ignores distinctions familiar to the collector and replaces them with
observations that, conversely, seem distinctly odd. Museums that valorize
these observations meet themselves in an act of reverse objectification.[14]
Paradoxically, then, the move toward more inclusive community increases the pressures of self-alienation.[15] Outreach thus tends to call attention to the manner in which otherness is a condition of community.

Prompted by such reversals, museums are reconsidering many complex
decisions that once seemed simple. The very introduction of an object into
a museum is not universally seen as a celebration of it. Could it be an im-
pertinence or, worse yet, an insult? The contemplative gaze prescribed for
appreciation of the fine art of the West appears as an act of violence when
directed at objects not designed for the same purpose. The classifying gaze
that seeks those similarities in difference and differences in similarity, so
illuminating to Western science, may likewise be viewed as aggressive.
The eye that appropriates can intrude as much as the hand that steals.
Given these challenges to the conceptual foundation of the museum, its
subordinate typologies are also shaken, and in any case, museums are

abandoning them in practice. As they do so, they relinquish much of the taxonomic language that formerly demarcated kinds of museums and that also was used to rank historic cultures and entire civilizations.[16]

The taxonomic instability now evident in museums is undoubtedly traceable to a number of causes, but one factor must surely be the newly validated judgment of those who were once present in museums only as the silent "collected." Are there any benefits to those newly given vocal status within that community? Why should they choose to accept an invitation that enlists their complicity with a system that heretofore denigrated their group memory and experiential knowledge, in favor of a suspect analytic objectivity? There are, of course, obvious political and economic rewards that justify conciliation, but the cultural and epistemological benefits are less evident. The "collected," in whose place the museum has traditionally spoken, face the dilemma that by speaking they now assume responsibility for the objectified identity that they are alleged to represent. And should they refuse to speak, they give tacit consent to the passivity of their represented condition and acquiesce to its enforced silence.

There is no guarantee that they will be heard, for whoever joins the museum's colloquy is compelled to adopt its conversational form. Spokespersons for the mute objects in the museum must learn the language of the collectors and conform to the standards that engendered the museum in order to be audible in that community—a community whose members do not easily share or give up the authority of their own expertise. Indeed, "native interpreters" and "resource people" are "inexpert" when it comes to interpreting "museum objects," for their expertise, unlike that of the museum professionals, pertains to an earlier incarnation of the objects that have journeyed from a known world into a strange new environment.[17] Only those inducted into the museum profession actually possess the expertise to deal with "museum objects."

When outsiders to the museum tradition take the interpretive initiative and speak in their own subjective voice, they recall a prior life that the museum objects no longer possess. As "native speakers," they remain outside the plane of museum discourse, addressing unasked questions and unremembered memories that are as obscure to conventional museum audiences as to professional museum staff. Enlargement of the "museum community" to include these formerly excluded people is thus possible only through a transformative process of mutual reeducation, whose benefits must also be equitably redistributed and whose ultimate effect is self-erasure.

Visitors and Other Museum Users

At their origin, museums were not motivated to attract public patronage. Collectors collected for themselves, and they opened their doors in hospitality only to the fraternity of fellow collectors. The public-spirited philanthropists of the nineteenth century did aspire to broaden their audience, but not for the sake of advancing diversity. Their paternalistic goal was to uplift and enlighten and thereby to homogenize a society whose diversity they abhorred. They hoped to instill the love of beauty and truth in a benighted populace. Their ideal of cultural expansion, like their faith in manifest destiny, was not to proliferate difference but to melt it, to absorb the great mass of humanity into a single, harmonious, uniformly unblemished whole.

The contemporary appeal to nontraditional audiences comes out of a different and somewhat more democratic worldview. It is a positive call for polyphony. The 1984 report by the American Association of Museums, *Museums for a New Century,* commends the proliferation of voices and cultural pluralism of American society as primary forces of social change, which it applauds. The authors welcome a spirit of "global community" that respects ethnic and cultural differences, and they write with approval of participatory, nonhierarchical modes of decision making that foster such a spirit. They hail this departure from museums' past practice while acknowledging the difficulty of reconciling it with the growing professionalism of the museum field—a trend that they nonetheless endorse with equal enthusiasm.[18]

The drive for pluralism and diversity that marks recent thinking sought at first only to bring more people of different races, genders, ethnic origins, classes, generations, physical competencies, and cultural and sexual lifestyles into the museum as visitors and as workers. Gradually, however, the museum world discovered that in order to become physically and psychologically accessible to more kinds of people, museums would need to make deep changes in their content and message. The magisterial aim did not disappear suddenly or altogether, but many protests later, and after long and painful consultations, significant accommodation to diversity did take place at nearly all levels of museum operation—and new visitors did begin to arrive. Today, however, museums face a backlash under the banner of an assault on "political correctness." The public, long accustomed to the voice of objective authority proclaiming standards of unequivocal quality, is understandably puzzled by what appears to be the museums' sudden reticence and uncertainty. Still in the habit of revering museums as impartial dispensers of impeccable taste and true information, people are perplexed by the new look that museums have assumed as nondirective centers of inquiry. This apparent submission to a challenge posed by outsiders to the museum world seems to its detractors like a craven bending to purely political pressures.

To its critics, multiperspectivalism is not a genuine exploration of diversity but a concession to bias. As they perceive it, the museum that yields to outside pressure betrays its historic duty to bring expertise to its traditional work. This looks like a failure of commitment and intellectual integrity, which command disinterested impartiality. By giving in to special interest groups, the critics say, the museum abandons its fundamental mandate to diffuse knowledge. Let us be clear that the opponents of pluralism do not object to the collection and exhibition of artifacts from diverse cultures. That appropriation falls within the scope of "licensed curiosity," whose merited reward is "the extirpation of error and the diffusion of truth."[19] But cross-cultural outreach, as they typically understand it, must be tempered with faith in human universals and absolute values. Other cultures must be shown to be only circumstantial adaptations that bespeak a common unity. The objection is therefore not that diversity is depicted, but that all world hypotheses are represented as equally credible.

Those who advocate diversity and outreach do find the alternatives credible. They are intent that the museum not merely replicate its own reflection, but that it expand community by actually becoming diverse.[20] To accomplish that end, museums have begun to approach communities in new ways, asking them to engage more actively in the production as well as the reception of museum exhibitions. More broadly, museums are responding to economic and demographic challenges. Turning to the living cultures that have transformed their immediate neighborhoods, some museums are inviting local residents to talk about themselves. They have learned that this means more than asking and recording answers to survey questions. They are finding that museum staffs and community respondents share neither the same interrogative premises nor the same sense of history, nor do they hold symmetrical views of one another's speech and silences. So, while some communities remain mutely distant, others, recognizing the opportunity to tell their own story and rectify some historic misapprehensions, have responded to the request for dialogue by turning it to creative advantage.

Rowena Stewart, director of the Motown Historical Museum in Detroit, points out: "Traditional museums [had] helped to convince most Americans that white Anglo-Saxon Protestants made up this country, when in actuality the nation was made up of slaves, free men and women, indentured people of all races, and men and women of various ethnic groups."[21] If traditional museums were able to visually reinforce the concept of a preeminently white America, why not subvert their methods to one's own empowerment? Adapting European technology to the oral tradition of Africa, black museum founders pronounced themselves "keepers of the record"—a different record, attuned to the African American struggle that had been collected in music and stories and festivals since long before the Civil War. These new founders worked for the placement of that record in institutions that would be truly responsive to a broader public, one that included themselves.

Emboldened to speak in their own voices, small museums committed to documenting specific heritages emerged in many communities where inhabitants had previously figured only as exotic minorities or as subordinate "others" in traditional, encyclopedic museums. Disclaiming universality, these new museums enjoined ordinary community members to take a responsible part in the validation of their own culture and experience by assembling exhibitions and collections that were meaningful to themselves. "Museum object" thus acquired a radically new denotation, though retaining its familiar sense connoting emotive value and cultural significance.

An example of an exhibition that would not have been mounted, let alone appreciated, in a traditional museum was John Kinard's 1969-70 show at the Smithsonian Institution's Anacostia Museum, which is located in a predominantly black neighborhood in Washington, D.C. "The Rat: Man's Invited Affliction" depicted in horrendous detail the life cycle and urban ecology of rats. It was extraordinarily well received by Washington's black community, since it confronted a problem well known to poor city dwellers and helped them deal with an all-too-common experience. The museum exhibit actually introduced elements of the community to one another and brought them together in common struggle.[22] Rather than presenting the community in terms of an abstracted image of exotic "otherness" for inspection by others, it showed the community to itself in terms of its own problems and possible choices.[23] The exhibition demonstrated to the community that history was not somebody else's story to which they were but a miserable appendage.

Metaphors abound to approximate new ways of assimilating neighborhoods to museums and museums to neighborhoods. "Dialogue," "consensualism," "partnership" and "meeting ground" have all been invoked to conjure images that depart from the linear and hierarchical structure of the old, collection-driven museum, which stands aloof from the neighborhood in which it happens to be situated. The endeavor to express oneself through the medium of museum exhibition is, however, a compromise for anyone not reared in the folklore of that objectifying mentality. It requires moving beyond the memory of cigar-store Indians, pig-tailed Chinese coolies, Aunt Jemima cookie jars, and myriad other degrading representations that have prevented museums from actually being meeting grounds for diverse populations. None of the currently operative metaphors preserves a reference to the traditional museum's collection orientation. All of them subordinate the exhibition of objects to a relational focus on building community and on shared experience.

Writing about New York's Chinatown in the 1980s, and the formation in 1990 of the Chinatown History Museum, which he directs, John Kuo Wei Tchen points out that this supposedly monolithic community is composed of people whose "Chineseness" is formed by many layers of dispersed influence: "While a person may be an 'overseas' Chinese and live in Chinatown, he or she is also a Lower East Sider and a New Yorker, and may also have lived in other parts of the United States and other countries."[24] The Chinatown History Museum set out to share authorship and interpretive responsibility for exhibitions with this complex community, using the institution to reconcile intensely private views of history with scholarly research about large-scale socioeconomic and cultural theorizing about "how and why life has become the way it is." In doing this, the museum hoped to appeal not only to local residents, who for once could see their own lives represented recognizably, but also to tourists, historians, scholars, other immigrants, New Yorkers, and mainstream museum visitors, who might gain a better sense of what history means by seeing it realized in personal experience.

Scholars are inclined to freeze history to fit textbook standards. Long-term museum exhibitions also tend to present the world in fixed slices, whose massive, long-lasting representations overwhelm the small-scale adaptive and assimilationist practices of living cultures. But most communities today are short-term, "border" cultures with mixed and borrowed habits. Their members eat bagels with tuna and mayonnaise and put Chinese herbs on their pizza. Under their saris and kimonos, they wear tennis shoes made in Mexico, and they buy Native American Barbie dolls for their children. Rather than dismiss such images as commercial kitsch or as "tending toward" universal truths, we might reflect that all societies, given the opportunity, have traded with outsiders, sometimes exploitatively, but often happily and to their mutual advantage.

To wish it otherwise is to yield to the dominant conservatism that clings to familiar inequalities—the dependencies of childhood, gender, and colonial status, as well as those of race and class. Museums might alleviate the impotence caused by ignorance by making the world's cultures more benevolently accessible to one another.

Research and Scholarship

The ambition to open and demystify the knowledge community does not detract from the place that scholars occupy in the museum either as independent researchers, resources, or as collectors. From the preservative vantage, scholars' contribution to museums is on a plane with that of collectors and, in effect, coordinates with it, since undocumented items are of little value to museums, and collectors thus often need the expertise and evaluative services of scholars. As reservoirs of information, scholars are also indispensable to museum educators, who rely on them to teach docents, who in turn pass their knowledge on to the visiting public. The place of scholarship in museums that are collection driven is not in doubt; as museums shift their ground to more generalized enquiry and the production of experience, however, the role of scholars also needs to be reassessed and clarified.

The value of scholarship to the world has always been controversial. Where learning is prized as a rarity, those who possess it have been held in high regard, but where it is treated as a utilitarian skill, like reading or driving a car, it ceases to inspire awe. Among the effects of the "democratization" of museums, as of all educational institutions, has been a decline in the respect paid to specialized scholarship and a corresponding elevation of experiential knowledge held to be accessible to everyone. Although learning is by no means available to all who seek it, it is no longer associated with social privilege or the presumption of intellectual superiority. People now generally believe that the pursuit of knowledge, like that of life, liberty, and happiness, is a right more or less universally guaranteed by nature. It does not follow that everyone who seeks it will achieve knowledge, but at least they are entitled to access; and so, the reasoning goes, no one should be denied the resources that have traditionally been available only to scholars. Setting aside the practical impossibility of realizing this goal, despite the prospect of huge advances in technology, scholarship appears in a new light. Like water and air, it has become commodified.

What would a display of scholarship "in action" look like? Would it resemble Rodin's sculpture, *The Thinker?* By what representations shall the public be invited to share in the quintessentially secluded enterprise of reflective thought? Can museums find a way of posing scholarly work in a manner consonant with their own social mission and also consistent with the slow and rigorous pace of scholarship? Some museums are beginning to work collaboratively with members of the academic community to achieve that end. They are employing working scholars as "living exhibitions" to display the process of "doing research," much as historical museums demonstrate the technique of actual craftspersons. Striving to dispel the notion that scholarship is for purely individual gratification, museums teamed with academics are working to conjoin private intellectual pursuit with publicly shareable experience. Unexpectedly, it may turn out that scholars—especially scientists, thanks to their long familiarity with collaborative investigation, peer review, and uncompromising mutual criticism—will be instrumental in helping museums reach their goal of doing "public service."

These museum representations of scholars at work or scientists doing research are still uncommon. It is more usual to present the results or products of such work. However, to display work in process tends to humanize it and reveal its experiential core. It is not easy to dramatize thinking or to illustrate its collaborative quality. How does one give visible form to the excitement of an intellectual process? We know the contagion of these procedures from the fact that they engender working communities; indeed, they pass regularly from scholar to scholar and from master to apprentice. Just as museums seek to inspire hypothetically shareable sentiment and sensibility—a common responsive experience—they might succeed, with the help of scholars, in designing ways to activate a collaborative cognitive capacity, potentially present in everyone.[25]

Methods of research and experimentation vary from field to field and are typically mystified. Noninitiates are expected to accept the conclusions of scholarship on authority, a passive behavior that contradicts the very essence of scholarly research and that scholars ordinarily treat with suspicion and scorn. Museums could therefore do a great service to both scholarship and the public if they undertook seriously to display the dialogical nature of research, revealing its conflicts and resolutions and its limitations. To distinguish scholarship from intuitive brilliance and the flash of genius, one must appreciate, at least in principle, how research differs from casual opinion and uncritical judgment. Through participatory exhibitry, museums can cultivate respect for intelligent problem posing, well-designed thought experiments, skillful use of many types of investigative apparatus, practiced ability to estimate and infer from limited detail, and the capacity to pose critical questions that illustrate how evidence is sifted and evaluated—all conditions of credible scholarship.

Scholarly practice is normally learned and taught in a context of community. It exists and is validated in the public domain. Its process, and not just its accomplishments, could be exhibited by museums working in collaboration with productive scholars. Together, they might forge a genuine bond of mutual respect and community, arising out of the experience of their combined intellectual labor.

A Community of Communities

However defined, the "museum community" is a multitermed relationship. Those who build and work in museums are not only paid employees, but also the institution's most constant users and critics. They esteem museum work as a social benefit and include themselves among its beneficiaries. The community addressed by the museum spans the past and the future. It comprises the living and the dead. Whoever visits or is represented there contributes a presence to the museum's identity, but even those who are absent are also consequential. It is illogical to contemplate a universal community of any kind, but not unreasonable to hope that broadened museum outreach can help existing communities come to a better understanding of themselves and one another.

The historic mission of enculturation that gave birth to the modern museum is currently under siege, and with it the alienating epistemology of objectification. We can observe, with some irony, the museum's own submission to the weapon of scrutiny that it wielded so successfully for several centuries. The objectifying gaze is no less painful to endure when turned upon itself. Perhaps this is a time for community building among museums, and between museums and other institutions. New partnerships are rapidly evolving to reallocate cultural resources and skills. Affirming their part in the emerging civic constellation, museums are becoming a destination, a site in the city marked by an asterisk on the map. Yet despite their new popularity, their identity remains blurred and their destiny obscure.

This is not the place to examine practical procedures of governance and administration, much less to prescribe them. It is clear that as museums compete more aggressively with for-profit leisure and touristic attractions, they are also adopting their style and substance. Likewise, as they gain support from and introduce the managerial efficiencies of the corporate world, they incline to resemble those business structures as well. Preserving their integrity as a community of communities while subsisting in the "real world" is therefore a precious charge. To meet it, we must turn again to the central question of what a museum is and try to understand its mediating role between object and reality.

4.   Transcending the Object

Museum spaces are "full of verbiage," says one critic, who goes on to complain that the act of museumifying takes an object out of use and immobilizes it in a secluded, atticlike environment among nothing but more "incessantly babbling" objects, another space made up of pieces.[1] Graveyards and department stores represent the extremes of entombment and exchange that are a common fate of things, and museums are often compared to both. The ultimate materialistic enterprise, museums seem to replace persons with objects, extracting their life and thought, and to presume, by these means, to immortalize the spirit of civilizations past.

The Being of Objects

To understand the alchemical process by which museums transform the dross of matter into the refined substance of history, knowledge, and art, we must first consider what it is to be an object, and next, what a complex series of artifices is made when objects enter the museum. Withdrawn from the molecular realm of matter and energy and deposited into a world of subjective intention, objects are formed through acts of attention. Some things pass on to further states of fictionalization in museums; others do not. Museum objects presuppose a prior state of objects, whose identity they engulf and reproduce but do not exactly perpetuate. Whether or not objects have a nature or exist in nature, they have multiple lives. They exist conceptually in the plane of mental phenomena and concretely within articulated systems of objects.[2] All objects are thus, in a manner of speaking, artifacts, cross-fertilizations of encounter and interest, and whether of natural or human making, they are destined to dual citizenship.

Materiality is not essential to objecthood. Neither is perception a sufficient condition of objective being; to exist as object is to be represented before an actual or potential consciousness.[3] Semioticians treat objects, along with words and images, as 'units of meaning' or 'sign functions', whose existence is not only inherently relational but also experiencable only as a social event.[4] Existentially and as subsistent mental entities, objects inhabit systemic frameworks that relate them both to subjects that construct meaning and to other objects that are part of meaning systems.[5] Frameworks imply framers, to which a system and its elements refer. Most of us are not the original framers of the systems we use, a responsibility that would isolate us from one another and defeat the purpose of communication. We simply inherit systemic legacies without giving much thought to their source or potential consequences. Creative people sometimes devise new systems that link with existing systems, diverting their course to produce heretofore unthought-of configurations. Objects are thus functional granules that interrupt, but do not destroy, the continuity of experience.

Contemporary readers are bemused by the fantastic list of "ancient categories" ascribed to "a certain Chinese encyclopedia," which classifies animals as:

> "(1) those belonging to the emperor, (2) embalmed, (3) tame, (4) sucking pigs, (5) sirens, (6) fabulous, (7) stray dogs, (8) included in the present classification, (9) frenzied, (10) innumerable, (11) drawn with a very fine camelhair brush, (12) et cetera, (13) having just broken the water pitcher, (14) that from a long way off look like flies."

Pondering the design of the framework that could possibly have objectified these disconnected items, Michel Foucault notes that our very wonder at this odd taxonomy underscores the limitation of our own system of thought.[6] What interpretations, then, are not possible to imagine? Common to Borges's weird concoction and those more ordinary linkages pronounced 'rational' is what Foucault calls a "tabula," which "enables thought to operate upon the entities of our world, to put them in order, to divide them into classes, to group them according to names that designate their similarities and their differences—the table upon which, since the beginning of time, language has intersected space." Just such a grid or "hidden network" governs the order in which things are normally experienced as real. "The fundamental codes of a culture—those governing its language, its schemas of perception, its exchanges, its techniques, its values, the hierarchy of its practices—establish for every man, from the very first, the empirical orders with which he will be dealing and within which he will be at home."[7] Once recognized—laid out, so to speak, upon the operating table where they may be dissected—these codes are revealed in their 'nonnatural' arbitrariness, and they become somewhat invalidated by that exposure. Having been proclaimed to the world, they are deprived of inevitability and laid open to question, perhaps in light of another system that would order the world differently.

Foucault explores the modalities of order that have shaped the basis of knowledge, the archaeological foundations of its possibility, finding there a seismic disruption when man (meaning a few prominent members of human society) abandoned the idea of a universe that is given once and for all and pronounced himself to be the author and arbiter of his own existence. Self-creation, however, entails the radical demarcation of self from other, and so their mutual alienation and objectification. One need not buy into every tenet of Foucault's philosophy to recognize that all cultures define themselves relative to others, whose strangeness they enforce through every institution under their command. Thus language, science, religious ritual, family, and economic practice conspire to perpetuate the socially othering system that preserves a guarded selfhood and sustains the unstable ground that supports it.

Objects, perceived as not-self—the cup I hold, the dog I stroke, the sounds I hear, the book I imagine, the audience I address—are approached with a peculiar intention. They are outside one's control yet subject to possible dominion. They can be seized, petted, known, loved, swallowed, destroyed, imagined, and thereby appropriated (made one's own.) Taken as possessions, objects (including persons) aggrandize the self, but only so long as their identity remains virtually distinct from that of the possessor. Objectivity dwells in that precariously suspenseful relation between self and not-self.

We commonly understand objects according to an economic model—in terms of their production, exchange, and consumption—but this confuses their commodification, which is but one way of having a meaning, with their identity. Identity emerges in the fixation of social selfhood, but objects are not thereby fixed absolutely or forever. Like persons, objects have a social life. They come to be what they are in relation to others things and can be transformed by their experiences. There may even be a normal sequence of phases in the life span of some objects, somewhat like a "career," and these careers interact dialectically with the careers of persons and groups.[8]

From the perspective of a society, continuity and endurance are promoted by naming the things that matter to it, providing for their preservation, indoctrinating members with knowledge of their value and use, and creating occasions for their presentation in everyday or ceremonial life.[9] These ends are accomplished through innumerable participatory rituals and institutions, including the multifarious disposition of objects—through gift giving, recreational activity, aggression, commercial exchange, religious observance, self-adornment, medicinal practice, artistic display, and socially sanctioned rules of entitlement. Self-knowledge on the part of group members coalesces with and absorbs these behaviors yet does not entirely preclude a distanced appreciation of comparable foreign practices. Self-knowledge can be tested by circumscribed exposure to unfamiliar objects belonging to other frameworks of being. Liberal societies fortify the selfhood of their members by constructing a preferred framework and refreshing it now and then with controlled glimpses of otherness. Conservative education, by contrast, protects its framework through demonizing otherness and forbidding exposure to it.

Selfhood and objecthood are thus dynamically held in unstable equilibrium. They are mutually dependent, yet each exists potentially at the other's expense. The survival of self demands stability, which is gained by the gradual assimilation of otherness and the punctuated continuity of sameness. Objects are the residue of self—its congealed meaning—and their persistence in space and time is testimony to the reality of selfhood. This is what makes them so interesting. Collectively, and from generation to generation, societies construct selves correlatively with their construction and acquisition of objects, thereby creating a reality in which people and objects are mutually constituted.

Museum Objects

If people and objects ground one another's primary significance in the real world, in the rarefied world of the museum, objects have a second order status. Their substantiality is sublimed and sacrificed to the order of meaning alone. Although famous for their collections of objects, and now closely scrutinized by students of "material culture," museums are notably concerned with the propagation of meaning. The objects they house have no less mass nor girth than in their premuseum state—an important consideration to those charged with packing and shipping them—but to the curators who acquire and dispose of them, the transfigured identity of the objects inducted into museums has only a residual relation to their physical bulk. In the transition from object to museum object, things gain and lose dimensions of use and exchange value as well as other dimensions of meaning. Qualitatively, and without visible change, things are divested of those very properties that made them eligible for selection by the museum. What was one of many becomes unique; what was functional becomes idle; what was private becomes public. Yet the present condition incorporates the prior state and depends on it for its own meaning.

As keepers of collections of objects, museums are obviously not the first to bestow meaning on the objects they collect. At least one layer of interpretive interventions separates them from that moment of ontological arbitration. Nevertheless, museums play an important part in the validation of object status and an equally large role in the withholding of that status through exclusion or misrepresentation. Museums share responsibility for the maintenance of object systems, whose presence stabilizes social existence and the reconstruction of the past.

To be a museum object is to have prima facie value independently of the material properties an object may possess and partially independently of the object's status in an earlier incarnation. However its material worth is calculated, an object's museum value derives from different norms. Humble commodity status does not limit an object's prospects for an exalted museum career. A shredded birch-bark basket or a tattered woolen cloak can be as highly esteemed a museum possession as a jeweled goblet. Materiality, though a prominent quality of museum objects, is not even a necessary condition. Since the things that museums ultimately preserve and present are nonmaterial, the physicality of the objects used to represent them is secondary to their function as signs or symbols.

The preoccupation of most museums with the pragmatics of managing matter is therefore misleading, not unlike the pragmatics of parental care, which is similarly taken up with an endless struggle against unwanted substances in undesirable places. In both instances, the distractions disguise the real merits and satisfactions that the institution affords. Museums are actually warehouses of material things only superficially. At bottom they have always been reservoirs of meaning. Paradoxically, however, the objects that museums collect, pried loose from the contexts that first consecrated their meaning, shed their old meanings when collected and acquire

new ones. Notwithstanding expert authentication and recognition by connoisseurs, museum objects retain only the penumbra of the objects they
supersede. Their substantial soul is sublimed.

From whatever historical starting point one traces the museum's inception—the Pythagorean temple of the muses, the library at Alexandria, or
the Renaissance cabinet of curiosities—the investment in meaning is ever
paramount. Random as their order may seem to eyes and minds more accustomed to flow charts and time lines than to Borgesian fantasies, medieval and Renaissance collectors assembled their cabinets with selective
care. The long-surviving treasury of the Holy Roman Empire, preserved
by the Austro-Hungarian Habsburg family from the thirteenth century
until its dissolution at the end of the First World War, began with a hoard
of personal wealth that came to be symbolic of sovereignty. Property, especially that taken by force from others, is evidence of the power of its
owner and represents accrued magnificence.[10] But symbolic wealth is not
its only raison d'être. Collections of material treasure also convey ideological lessons. Cataloged in terms of an ideal of organization, Renaissance
cabinets of curiosities were described by Francis Bacon as a *theatrum
mundi,* a microcosm of the world, such that: "You may have in small
compass a model of the universal nature made private."[11]

Initially, the juxtapositions found in nature were conceived as mirroring
the conjunctions decreed by God's will, but gradually, under the secular
spell of the Renaissance, the order of nature became a source of fascination
in its own right. Human ingenuity, by "careful and deliberate assemblage of
signifying objects," could replicate God's creation. Some collectors sought
even to improve upon God's occasional lapses by devising rationally defensible ordering schemes, which reveal a protoscientific interest that prefigures
the use of collections for teaching and research.[12]

Collections might or might not differentiate between natural and manufactured objects. That distinction, which seems self-evident today, is less
obvious when human production is understood simply as one among
many of nature's processes—worthy of note chiefly as a representation of
part to whole. If meaning is inherent to nature, a collection of signifying
objects is inevitably a metaphor of the whole, whose interpretation can be
bent according to distinct criteria. An item withdrawn from one collection
and introduced into a second will thereby assume new meaning and will
at once alter the signification of both the collection that is diminished by
the item's absence and the one augmented by its presence. Over time and
through successive generations of preservers, collections and the objects
they comprise thus pass through multiple prismatic meaning shifts.

Changes in museological practice reflect both philosophical and pragmatic cultural environments. Objects that once were revered as evidence of power, personal wealth, or divine reason, or merely as curious artifacts, could come to inspire appreciation as creations of artistic genius. But such recognition must await an understanding of human creativity and aesthetic judgment that was not current in Europe before the seventeenth century. An independent science of aesthetics that attended to Beauty as a perceived quality was proposed in the eighteenth century by the German philosopher Alexander Baumgarten.[13] Art history and criticism emerged around the same time, elevating artists over artisans, and giving legitimacy to the concept "work of art."[14] Royal collections, which had long included paintings, engravings, and sculpture, now honored these by keeping them in galleries separate from those in which medals, coins, and decorative crafts were stored. Art, retrospectively appreciated, was taken as the work of inspired members of a brotherhood, and its enjoyment testified to the taste of a privileged class. By the late eighteenth century the huge Habsburg collection had been subdivided under separate curatorships. Science, art, and artisanship were now detached from one another, and the collections dedicated to each were organized and maintained according to distinct museological principles.[15]

By the end of the eighteenth century, when museums were opened to the public, the objects in their collections again underwent didactic meaning shifts. New moral and practical lessons were to be imparted by them, along with generic *Kulturbildung* (literally, "construction of culture") and civic pride. The palace of the Louvre, transformed in 1793 by Napoleon into the "Palace for the People," was stocked not only with the spoils of conquest, but also with the symbols of a new order. Carol Duncan describes how the objects that formerly glorified princes "had to acquire yet another layer of meaning, a layer that could obliterate, contradict, or radically distort previous meanings and uses."[16] In the brilliantly designed museum context, objects that had been displays of material wealth and social status were magically converted into tributes to spiritual glory. The new science of art history, put to this eulogistic end, still does its work in the iconographic trappings of the major art museums today, interweaving a mythology of national character with that of artistic genius.

Art museums may speak most unreservedly to the aesthetic imagination, but all kinds of museums participate in the transubstantiation of objects, exchanging the energy stored in one dimension for newly contrived expression in another. Museums thus are depots of sorts, though not simply repositories of static relics. They are dynamic transformers in which energy is converted, redistributed, and rereleased.

The Fictitious Object

Modernism and the new art museums of the nineteenth and twentieth centuries added a level of meaning to objects that intersects with that inherited from the grand historical tradition and gradually displaces it. Formalism purports to excise the object from all contexts except that of a universal aesthetic, thereby breaking down some of the carefully constructed associations of the preceding centuries. Oddly reminiscent of the eternalism of the Middle Ages, modernist museum theory locates transcendent value in the collected object. In particular, objects identified as works of art are conceived to lead a life of their own, beyond time and in a fictitious space outside the world of everyday affairs.

Unlike the objects brought together in medieval collections, however, those assembled in modern museums represent a secular eternity—an everlasting emptiness. Instead of depicting a dazzling multitude of particulars produced in the "shuffle of things" under the ever-watchful eye of an emanating God, the modern art museum invites its visitors to escape entirely from the glut of history.[17] It summons them to partake of transcendence, initially for the sake of contemplating a realm of universal Law and Beauty, whose messengers are "pure" objects. Subsequently, the messenger becomes the focal interest; the pure object takes over its environment and even absorbs the spectator into itself. Brian O'Doherty describes the ritual space wherein "perceptual fields of force" combine to perform their act of transubstantiation:

> A gallery is constructed along laws as rigorous as those for building a medieval church. The outside world must not come in, so windows are usually sealed off. Walls are painted white. The ceiling becomes the source of light. The wooden floor is polished so that you click along clinically, or carpeted so that you pad soundlessly, resting the feet while the eyes have at the wall. The art is free . . . "to take on its own life."[18]

With the advent of the artwork as an entity with "its own life," works of art are destined by the artists who produce them to fulfill that life isolated in galleries and museums. Other things that began their life mundanely, as objects performing ordinary functions—bottle racks or desks or candle snuffers—can also be elevated to the status of artworks through selection by an artist or curator for inclusion in the museum. The modern art museum, departing from the taxonomic compartmentalizations of its nineteenth-century ancestor, aestheticizes every object placed within its walls, so that eventually the fire extinguishers and exit signs (not to mention driftwood and bric-a-brac) take on the aura of artworks. The object reverts to its prior status when taken outside the museum; or, if it be placed in a museum of history or ethnography, it acquires a new cultural significance distinct from the meaning bestowed either by the art museum or that which preceded its museum exposure.

As a museum object, however, or an object created for the museum, a thing inhabits fictional space, defined by its own laws. These laws, although pointedly reactionary with respect to the everyday laws of "real things"—there are no laws of falling bodies here—conceal their parasitic allusiveness behind the facade of autonomy. Modern works of art possess integrity, self-sufficiency, and a formal purity uniquely associated with their fictitious objecthood. They belong to an art world. Complete within itself, that world is nevertheless a site of contentious dispute. Wars within the art world have real world economic repercussions, but inside the protected space of the museum, the clash and clamor of aesthetic strife is strictly mythological.[19]

Real-world transactions have fictionalized counterparts in the art world, but these worlds are not isomorphic. They are not linked by the mirroring or tropic relations that bound the medieval cabinet to the physical world, itself linked at one mimetic remove from the divine. The modern art world is a projection, but only of abstracted portions of the real world. It is neither mirror nor emblem; nor is it a promise of intelligible perfection. Projected from single points of earthly consciousness, its illumination does not converge worshipfully to a center. Art produced for art-world consumption edits, distorts, and dialecticizes, or renders for disputation, objects taken from the real world. What onlookers from the public see or hear is just a message—not an illumination. Self-contained and self-sufficient, its only end is to gratify, and the pleasure it provides is gratuitous. Art is for art's sake alone.

Things acquire an obscure deathlessness as they pass between the permeable borders—from real world, to art world, to fiction-producing museum world. Fire or vandalism could annihilate their corporeal presence, but more subversive destruction is wrought by critical opinion and adverse judgment that leaves their physical being, but not their fictional identity, intact. The judge or critic, who might be you or I, is correspondingly a fictitious being, an artifact of the art world. Brian O'Doherty describes the critic as "eager to carry the weight of meaning but not always up to it." Spectators strive to reduce themselves to the scale of the art world, but most are not equal to the intellectual burden of becoming a disembodied Eye (the organ required to relate to the museum object but not much good for anything else). Upon entering the museum, the ideal spectator must set aside the concerns of everyday life to commune with the transhistorical art world. Concentration on that task must be absolute, and the ideal museum must be purged of all distractions, to intensify that other-worldly state of exaltation. No extraneous furniture should bar the fictional spectator's view, and homey activities like eating or laughing are frowned upon by fellow visitors and uniformed guards.[20]

If spectators are unable to endure the anechoic environment of the art world and find themselves hungering for the familiar noise and bustle of the real world, no more could artists survive for long without the real world's intercourse that supports them. The fictitious art world is a temporary surrogate, fueled by continuous traffic emanating from the real world. Art world immortality is ironically short-lived unless revitalized by new meanings imported from the real life below. Thus museum objects lose their luster if they are left to spin out their extraterrestrial lives unrenewed. Museums are full of things languishing in a state of moribund exaltation, unredeemed until and unless a hand or eye from the real world touches them with the enchantment of new meaning.

Periodic reclamations do happen. A new museological interlude began sometime in the 1960s, and the disembodied Eye was dismissed for its passivity. A surge of energy, sparked by political activity in the real world, inspired intellectual reappraisals that shook the art world. For a moment, the streets of both worlds belonged to the people. Tumbled from the height of benign irrelevancy, the art world retrenched. Its destiny merged with that of the real world to such a degree that some of its occupants became real-world personalities. Led by Andy Warhol, certain artists made artworks of themselves, and works of art collapsed again into the ephemera of everyday life. These reborn art objects mocked the legitimacy of an aesthetic that had opposed itself to the vitality of the mundane.[21]

Museums confronted that revalorization of the vernacular in a variety of ways. Some faced the awful recognition that their collections lacked historical breadth and depth. Those most embarrassed were art and history museums that had intentionally restricted their collection to the refined taste of a privileged class. But even those that had featured the typical or its exotic counterparts, mostly history and anthropology museums, had neglected the flow of the ordinary. Few authoritative records remained, moreover, to speak on behalf of those vernacular objects that had somehow made their way into collections and now lay moldering in musty basements. Their meaning had to be reconstructed through the distorting lens of scholarship, itself hampered by the limited evidence available.

Scholars had to learn to make inferences from new kinds of evidence for which semiological rules had not been written. And those most literate in their interpretation, the primary users, lacked the authority to provide it. They might, moreover, be mistrustful toward snoopy strangers from whom only derision and misunderstanding could reasonably be expected.

The Interpreted Object

Museums therefore looked to broaden their pool of interpreters, diluting scholarship and skilled professionalism with personal anecdote and informal storytelling. They relaxed their dependency on "authentic" objects and turned instead to reconstructions based on oral histories and experiential recollection. These approaches could be combined, bringing memory and research together, by telling narrative tales and then locating or fabricating objects to illustrate them. Instead of being ends in themselves, objects were, again, linked to a tale.

Defending a story-centered exhibition strategy, Spencer Crews and James Sims, curators of the Smithsonian Institution's exhibition "From Field to Factory," declared that authenticity is located not in objects but in the historical concepts they represent. To illustrate the migration of African Americans from the South to the North in the period between 1915 and 1940, the curators used artifacts that were historically correct and typical of objects that would have been used at the time, but not all of these objects had a verifiable connection to actual persons. Crews and Sims held that objects' provenance—who owned, occupied, wore, or used them—declines in importance relative to their corroborative power. Particularly, with the advent of mass production and consumption, identical items sold from catalogs throughout the country are more interesting to visitors as representative of cultural trends and traditions than for their specific history. Their truth is embodied in the general rather than in idiopathic instances.[22]

"From Field to Factory" was designed to confront the visitor with historic reality in a new way: "The visitor can move between reasons for leaving the South and reasons for staying; issues of violence and segregation can be approached with whatever degree of engagement the individual viewer wishes. But everyone must go north, and walking into the segregated Ashland train station, everyone must make a choice that puts him or her into one of two categories, either 'white' or 'colored,' thus encountering racism concretely. At the doors of the Ashland station, the condition of legal segregation is authentic. The object is a reproduction, somewhat diagrammatic in form but not metaphorical. Imaginative truth is experienced, for the aware audience collaborator, as present truth."[23]

This exhibit was contrived as an event to draw the audience in as "co-creators of social meaning." The measure of the exhibit's success is experiential—visitors' evocation of imaginative truth as present truth. Authenticity, according to this model, is defined as success at "touching the life of the visitor," and this is accomplished as much by the spectacle, or poetics of representation, as by more customary confirmatory procedures.

The formal study of material culture, the syntax and semantics of objects, was first undertaken empirically, by anthropologists and archaeologists. Sociologists, forensic scientists, and social historians who investigated human artifacts tried to reconstruct what people do with things and for what reasons. Believing that things could "speak for themselves" directly and unambiguously, positivists of an earlier time held that to come between a thing and a perceiver with an interpretation was not only unnecessary but mendacious. Students of material culture now take the opposite view, holding that all systemic intervention by humans into nature—whether planting orchards, damming rivers, cooking, dancing, or collecting—is to be considered a form of human artifact production. All such arrangements are affairs of imagination and so are inevitably interpretive. Like recorded language, which itself is a conceptual artifact, objects are primary sources of information about organized human behavior, and museums are prime centers in which objects are stored and live out their multiple lives.

What is common to museum objects throughout centuries of collection and exhibition, then, is not their material history, but the mutations of interpretive fashion. A certain theatricality makes an interpretation plausible but cannot alone command credibility. How do ideas gain currency, especially those that go against a conventional grain? Persuasive presentation—diction, music, and spectacle—has always been valued next only to sound research. Typically, curatorial expertise has involved judicious selection, taste, artful arrangement, and clever illumination of objects. But now, more than ever, salesmanship counts, and museums are heavily invested in performative strategizing. Many an institution has consequently been plunged into a dither of market research. In courting larger constituencies, museums have become not just dialogical but polylogical. Having invited multiple expression, they are host to a multitude of expressive styles and are unable to discriminate among the imaginative truths they make present.

Many voices create a noisy babble. Sometimes they harmonize, but museums cannot take that for granted. The new sounds vibrate with movements in the political sphere. The call for self-determination came to museums in the 1960s, as it did to other institutions, and led to an uneasy coexistence of professional experts with "native interpreters." The sharp voice of the former was, in its own way, almost as discordant in what had traditionally been a haven of connoisseurship as were the rebellious notes of those previously excluded. In the museum as elsewhere, amid the clash of claims to legitimacy, identity politics took the place of centralized order.

The Politics of Objecthood

Whether intentionally or not, museums became centers of cultural resistance. Their invitation to self-expression coincided with other liberatory movements in literature and the arts. A theory of criticism, formally introduced in the 1970s and designed to illuminate the interaction of reader and text, began to gain political currency in wider domains, including the museum world. "Reader response theory" advances the idea that the actively receptive voice of the reader joins with that of the author in the constitution of textual meaning. Expressed in the language of things, the theory affirms that object is to interpreter as text is to reader. As texts without readers are empty, so museum objects are bare receptacles without the agency of museum visitors.

Like a literary text, an object represents a potential effect that is realized only in an act of apprehension equivalent to the act of reading. That act may concur with, but can also resist, the author's act of writing or the judgment of a curator.[24] Meaning is not "put into" a text or object to be "taken away" by someone who "finds" it there, but comes into being through intersubjective participatory experiences. Taking reception seriously shifts the balance of authority away from the author. It pluralizes and politicizes the range of possible meanings. In the museum, the voice of the curator blends with and possibly competes with the voices of other performers. No longer is there a single treasure to be found under the guidance of an expert; rather, a multitude of performative encounters occur that have constituted the object, perhaps over many centuries. In these encounters are met the original makers, users, artists, historians, critics, scientists, chroniclers, collectors, museum staff, and current visitors.

All participants bring certain dispositions to the encounter and find more or less gratification of their expectations. No one of them has a greater claim than others to possession of the "true" meaning of the object, and so its catalog description devolves from compromises that may reflect some inequities. We might imagine the bewilderment of the stereotypical middle-aged white male visitor to a history museum, faced with a jointed metal prong attached to a wooden handle. His female companion, though never before having encountered such an object, might confidently pronounce it a "curling iron." For her, instruments of beautification, of whatever antiquity, are as central a part of the social environment and as easily recognizable as weapons and locomotive devices are likely to be of his. Once informed, he can explore the genealogy of the object. His research, however will be empirical and utilitarian, whereas hers is empathic and kinesthetic. His understanding will advert to manufacture and technical operation, whereas hers will approximate that of the user. Both experiences will, of course, be variations on those of curators, conservators, exhibit designers, docents, donors, and museum trustees, all of whom are party to the presentation.

To deny unique propriety to any one interpretation, however, is not to declare the equivalence of all. Some readings cancel others, and not all readings can coexist compatibly. Interpretive incongruities provoke political discords that a loosened museum hierarchy has been unable to resolve. Perhaps no singular normative scheme is adequate to do so. Possibly the richest and most satisfying museum experiences will be those that take place at confounding intersections where dissonance is sharpest. Objectivity is not negated by such clashes, neither is it undermined by the absence of definitive criteria for the making of judgments. What is revealed at such junctures is the constructive role of intersubjectivity, which is not at all the same thing as agreement. Meaning does not emerge from the sheer presence of multiple voices, much less from their enforced unison, but from careful cultivation of the habit of discerning and learning from their difference.

I suggest that objecthood, like textual meaning, results from multileveled acts of attention by individuals, social groups, and institutions. Socially objectified things are imbued with meaning, layer upon layer, within sanctioned structures of reference. As collectors with normative power, museums have the option of attending to only the most prominent meaning strata of objects or of exploring the deeper layers of complexity. Traditional museums chose the first option; contemporary museums, driven by political pressures from below and by coincident conceptual innovations, are dealing with the disrupted meanings projected from margins of dissent and opposition. Thus, it is not the focus on meaning as such that distinguishes today's museums from museums of the past, but rather their sensibility of the obliquely meaningful. Neither is the transformativity of meaning altogether a new idea. Museum collections throughout history have endured meaning shifts, usually serially but sometimes synchronously, without notable alteration of their physical content.

Museums still collect objects and still take pride in the size and quality of their collections. They continue to preserve and study objects, but their chief occupation is neither to discover nor to keep them. It is to foster the intersubjective constructions that objects elicit. No longer content to be styled as graveyards or department stores, museums now are cast as impresarios of meaning performances. They have become manufacturers of experience.

From Object to Experience

What is the meaning of the Holocaust or the moon landing or the Japanese internment camps? Some of the most sensational museums and museum exhibitions today evoke an "experience" of those events with the help of a few artifacts. These exhibitions are not about the objects they include, but they use historic items such as freight trains, rocks pried loose from the surface of the moon, soldiers' canteens, gas canisters, and children's toys in the service of a story, which is elicited rather than told. Objects can work as evidence for a thesis or recall by their presence that an event took place. As causal markers they trace how something happened, but the same objects can also speak in one or more voices to bring an event to mind with a particular emotive cast. Commemorative exhibits are conceived less to impart information about events than to stimulate a corresponding feeling or experience in museum visitors. Many visitors to the U.S. Holocaust Memorial Museum in Washington, D.C., for example, report feeling a sense of dread and oppression from the moment they enter the building and are herded into the elevator and down narrowing corridors from which there seems to be no escape. This sensation is the effect deliberately crafted by the museum's designer, Ralph Appelbaum, who wrote: "It is the act of controlling a few hours of someone's time and setting them up to receive a certain experience."[25] The exhibition constructs an environment using physical props, often including suggestive music and theatrical staging, to excite an experience in visitors that is both subjective and shared.

The experience animates the museum objects ambiguously. In a sense the object is not really there. Many science center exhibits, for example, are scaffolds for experience that occurs only as visitors make it happen within themselves. Perceptual phenomena such as visual illusions and afterimages obviously could not occur without the congruent presence of the visitors' optical physiology and the activation of the devices contrived to produce the event. The museum object in such cases is not something that can be collected or stored, but the museum controls the conditions under which visitors can be expected to "have the experience."

The case of the science center may be radical in its severance of apparatus from completed experience and in the reliability with which the experience can be controlled.[26] However, the displacement of the museum's focal interest from object to subject, or rather to their conjunction in experience, reflects a trend among all museums. The shift also entails a profound reconceptualization of authenticity, for the museum's commitment is now to the authentic quality of the experience to which the object has become a means. The provenance of the object is then secondary to its subjective effect. This effect, and not the historically legitimated object, is the "real thing" that museums strive to achieve. Certain kinds of stimuli are known to produce experiences more effectively than others, and traditionally "real things" are not always or necessarily the most successful. Simulations can work very well. A public weaned on television and computer screens is unfazed by representations that are not in "real time" and will often enthusiastically accept "real" interactive spectacles imaged in virtual space.[27]

The advent of installations and conceptual art and the reconceptualization of all art that followed in their wake point to the systemic management of the experiences that constitute art. Art museums, together with other institutions of the art world, work to produce qualitatively predictable art experiences that might, in principle, take place anywhere. The institution houses the programmatic conditions under which artworks are to be realized, but the works of art experienced there are no more "contained" in the museum than readings, as distinct from texts, are "contained" between the covers of a book. Not its collected objects but its affirmative power to reify enables a museum to control and articulate the experiences that visitors undergo.[28] This power cannot be reduced to a single locus, let alone to a body of physical things. It derives from a complex history of conscious and unconscious social exchanges to which many performers have contributed.[29]

In the past, collections of objects were valued according to such discipline-specific standards as rarity, typicality, historical importance, beauty, or representative merit. As yet, no set of clear criteria has been defined to judge the quality of experiences. Their inherent privacy makes experiences less accessible to interpretation and evaluation than objects, which have an ostensible public face. Just what sort of experiences do museums aim to achieve— pleasure? edification? satisfaction of curiosity? enlightenment? awe and wonder? No doubt, all of these have a part in the "museum experience," but they do not initialize the experience uniquely or justify institutional investment in it.[30]

Exhibition teams composed of curators, exhibit designers, educators, and evaluators are striving to bring about certain types of experiences consonant with the chosen character of particular museums. Their objectives reflect other normative social expectations as well. They relate to theories of cognition and to beliefs about what motivates people. They comply with current presumptions regarding the obligation of museums to the public and to ideas about what the public is and should be. Notably, museums now advance themselves as public institutions with a primary responsibility to people and their values rather than to the value of objects. Thus an interest in phenomenology and affect has displaced the taxonomic and preservative impulse with which modern museums began.

Where confidence in epistemic homogeneity and the singularity of truth prevailed, traditional museums could assume general acceptance of their didactic authority. Contemporary museums have sacrificed that certainty to a pluralistic relativism, but they continue to have faith in some emotive uniformities. A sense of ownership that goes with personally undergoing an experience is taken to authenticate the reality of that experience; and museums, along with other institutions, are vetting the possibility of generalizing that subjective affirmation.[31] Private assent, reinforced by replication, is equated with public confirmation and is alleged to confer universality. Powerful and widely shared feeling now purports to establish reality more conclusively than does a formally executed proof or controlled investigation.

The techniques of collecting objects have therefore given way to the technologies of experience production. The impact of these experiences is undoubtedly genuine, but they are no less manufactured, and hence artifactual, than were the museum objects that they supersede. The emphasis is now on process and construction rather than on product. The public is encouraged to attend to procedures that were formerly kept in the background, much as food preparation was not exposed to dinner guests. Museum visitors are also invited to observe themselves and each other's interactions, framed within the excised portions of the world that the museum exposes. Thus, while the museum romance with the "real thing" has not subsided, and professions of fidelity to reality persist, the reality denoted is a subjective one that each museumgoer construes and must personally appropriate.[32]

The transcendence of objects and the exaltation of experience raise issues that museums have yet to address. Greater integrity of the experiential over the objective approach has not been demonstrated, but there seems to be a growing consensus that heartfelt experience is somehow more honest and universally more accessible than culturally weighted objects and meanings. Sheer intensity of experience, however, is not a guarantee of cognitive merit or moral excellence. Neither is such experience necessarily even memorable. There are no public protocols for the evaluation of experience, and few measures of its private quality. Nothing in the particularity of experiences corresponds to the familiar substantiality of material things—the quality that made them eminently collectible. Experiences are volatile and unruly. Only the crudest and most stereotypical of them are readily named or describable. These are also the most commodifiable, and some can be summoned more or less at will.[33] Those people who have the skill to conjure experience uniformly and deliberately could be dangerous demagogues, ambitious to control the lives of others. At least, their benign motives cannot be taken for granted. Museums should therefore be as wary of oversimplifying experiences as they formerly were of mistakenly acquiring fakes or of misinterpreting objects.

An abiding faith in a single human community drives many people to look forward to the orderly enjoyment of an experience that can be universal. Whether or not such an experience is attainable or desirable remains undetermined. Although the hope of achieving universal understanding should not be discouraged, it is not clear that propagating experiences in which everyone can participate is the way to fulfill that hope. Neither is it obvious that undergoing such experiences would bring us any closer to a shared reality than the exhibition of collected objects has already done.

5. Museum Experience and the "Real Thing"

"I think a picture is more like the real world when it's made out of the real world," said Robert Rauschenberg early in the 1950s.[1] Disparaging such literalism, a character in a story by Henry James, half a century earlier, confesses to a "preference for the represented subject over the real thing," which remains always and stolidly the same. The real thing, says James's fictional artist, resists being representative because its own indelible character excludes any other presence.[2] This very integrity, or stolid self-sameness, is the merit of the real things that museums persist in celebrating and that museum audiences profess to revere.

Visitors still expect to find the "real thing" in a museum, but they rarely reflect on what that entails. The neologism "museal" is applied to objects taken out of their lived environment and left, like goldfish out of water, to languish and die.[3] I have argued that objects are reborn in the museum and acquire a new "museum reality" as a result of their displacement. From the vantage of their new context, they are presumed to illuminate the primary reality from which they have been separated. They become data carriers, whose original opacity grows translucent in the specular light of prevailing interpretive theories.[4] With no perceivable change in their physical substance, things nevertheless undergo a semiological transubstantiation. But the familiar reality once associated with their sheer physical presence has certainly been compromised, and a new metaphysics of museum-being is necessary to explain them.

"Reality" has held an honorific meaning from the beginnings of Western philosophy. To the ancients it connoted that which is stable and unchanging and is properly contrasted to that which appears fleetingly in space and time. Since material things come and go, they were regarded with suspicion by early Greek philosophers and were treated, most famously by Plato, as mere imitations of a higher reality that transcends matter. Plato believed that physical objects are inherently unknowable since they are constantly subject to alteration. The perception of things could stimulate inquiry, however, and thereby lead to the understanding of abstract ideas or principles that are fully knowable. These could be faintly recognized, Plato thought, as the impressed reality resident in the objects that exemplify them. The knower must beware of seduction by objects, however, since they are charming mnemonic aids that could easily lead us astray. The notion that the true nature of things lies beyond them in a world of absolute, changeless reality is at the foundation of seventeenth-century science as well as philosophy. Scientists replaced the Platonic ideas with the mathematical order of natural law but held on to the conviction that common sense experience is deficient in reality, and that physical things should be approached with skepticism. Although modern science and philosophy are less mistrustful of the senses and accept the reality of material things, important legacies from Plato continue to influence contemporary thought. One is the high esteem in which reality is held. The real is equated with the true and the good, and preferred to the illusory, the false, and the wicked.

A second Platonic legacy is the belief that reality permits of degrees—some things have more reality than others. Combining the two classical premises, it follows that the less real is less desirable than the fully real, but it is not necessarily without value altogether. Sometimes an inferior but more available object proves to be a means to achieving a remote and superior end. Thus physical objects have their place in the grand order of things and can serve mediately to bring us closer to reality.[5] Collections of objects in museums can therefore be evaluated on a double scale that measures both the inherent reality of the included items and their conductive ability to approach absolute reality.

A third Platonic legacy that conditions modern epistemology is the belief that the real exists independently of human subjective experience. Regardless of anyone's knowledge of it, reality subsists unchangeably. Contemporary philosophers have deviated from this position to define objectivity in terms of potential or actual agreement among subjects, but many still link subjectivity with private fantasy and the unreal. Some philosophical skeptics question whether it is meaningful to affirm or deny the existence of anything that transcends the possibility of human experience. Modern science, however, regards the real as accessible by way of properly used mediating devices and conventionally agreed upon procedures. Proven methods, cautiously applied to identifiable data, with the aim of testing hypotheses, are held to illuminate reality, bearing in mind the caveat that the data and the methods are themselves open to challenge. Since even uncontested data could support several alternative representations of reality, it is possible to construe reality as neither simple nor permanent. Reality might be multiple and in flux. At the opposite pole from Platonic absolutism are theories that describe reality as humanly fabricated constructions, held together in cultural enclaves whose civil and political practice shore up interest-driven belief systems.

Museums are a product of the modern era and do not rest solidly on a Platonic foundation, but some of Plato's legacy lives on in qualified idealism and in the museum's professed dedication to the preservation of the "real thing." This heritage is complicated by a commitment made with equal ardor to the collection, preservation, and exhibition of material objects. Are museums caught in a contradiction? Whatever else their mission might encompass, museums have always addressed the senses and treasured the variety of things discovered in the material world, if only as an antechamber to a greater reality. Today, museums are central actors in the expanding field of material culture studies, and they are ambitiously collaborating with scholars in research and academic institutions in advancing this worldly mode of understanding.

Having suggested that contemporary museums feature objects as means to experience rather than as ends in themselves, we must consider the effect that such transferal of significance has on the objects' relation to reality. If the attribution of meaning to objects is already a concession to their subjective unreality and impermanence, then surely their subordination to "museum experience" must cast even greater suspicion on their reality.[6] Are museums at risk of abandoning objectivity altogether and hence becoming "out of touch" with reality?

Appearance and Real Things

The animus against sensory experience and "mere" appearances that infected Western thought has long poisoned aesthetic theory and denigrated the satisfactions that are at its core. Plato's disciples have yielded to the attractions of the realm of appearance, but they have never given up the

ideal of surpassing it. The things of this world are fragile, and their evanes-
cence testifies to their unreality. For centuries, the seductive transiency of
the beautiful moment has spurred the quest for the eternal, and many a
museum collection was begun as an *imitatio dei,* in a spirit of exaltation of
unearthly reality. To collect was equivalent to worship; to adore even the
fleeting shadow was to touch transcendent Being.

The reigning Western aesthetic doctrine since the Enlightenment admits with Plato that all art is semblance, but it strives to ennoble appearance as that which raises art above the "mere" reality of the mundane
world. According to the modernist aesthetic, the vocation of art is, precisely, to produce illusion, but an illusion that is more, not less, than the
banal "real thing." Lifted up by human imagination, illusion leaves behind that poor reality that can only be reproduced and imitated. In the
age that spawned the museum, human ingenuity created a new reality,
fully as authentic as the one it surpassed. Fine art, in particular, invented
a world of "seeming" that was autonomous and unbounded by the conditions of ordinary reality.[7]

The fine art museum, which emerged with romanticism, was expressly
committed to the celebration of those appearances that elevate viewers to
the realm beyond ordinary reality, and so, ironically, what is "real" as fine
art must be "unreal" in a more familiar sense. This romantic doctrine has
been severely tested by the art of recent decades, which deliberately fuses
appearance with the "merely" real. Museums are recurrently confounded
by the paradoxical task of toggling from "higher" reality to "mere" reality
and back again. When the conventions of illusionism are breached to escape
"mere" imitation, one is forced to confront appearances made real. The
effect is as much a reification of the aesthetic realm as an aestheticization of
reality. This annealment of appearance and reality is not confined to the
arts. Anything is expressible as appearance, and all types of museum collections are exploding semantically under the pressure. The museum enterprise, undertaken initially as a well-bred strategy meant to tame the material world by rationalizing it, turns out to be implicated in a program of
reality appropriation conducive to both mystification and violence.[8]

Were Plato alive to pass judgment on museums today, he might well
think his mistrust of appearances and their malleability well grounded. To
twentieth-century minds, intent upon excavating meaning, however, obses-
sive management of appearance aims not to obscure reality but to dominate
it.[9] Notwithstanding their preoccupation with appearances, museums have
not abandoned their devotion to the "real thing." "Mere objects" and
"mere appearances" actually exist nowhere, but museum objects, which

are both object and appearance, do exist, albeit their layered reality is a source of genuine puzzlement.

Authenticity and Real Things

Platonic metaphysics is the basis of another construal of the real, which contrasts it with the false or fraudulent. An imitation, however close, is inherently deviant from its original and thus is a falsification of it.[10] Determining a thing's authenticity often involves tracking it to its source and monitoring any interventions that might have modified it en route from that point to its present state.[11] Museums properly take great pains to ensure that the objects included in their collections be neither fakes nor forgeries. Both of these terms, which are sometimes used interchangeably, are referential. A fake resembles another object in appearance and may be mistaken for that object. Its primary value derives from that resemblance, but fakes can also come to be appreciated on their own account for other reasons—economy, efficiency, moral independence, or even, of late, for their ostensive flamboyance. Ontologically, a fake is a real object, as real as anything it might resemble, but it lacks reality on the Platonic value scale chiefly because of its specifically derivative character.[12] Museum fakes often turn out to be works discovered to have been misattributed after production. They are fake only in the sense that they are not what they were alleged to be, but there is no doubt of their existential reality.[13] Any suspicion of them has to do with their degraded relation to other objects. Their inauthenticity is relative only to their status in a value hierarchy. In a manner of speaking they are impostors, though not through their own fault. Since museum objects, especially works of art, are notably prized for their uniqueness, fakery is not easily detected. An object that bears no comparison to anything at all cannot be identified either as authentic or inauthentic, real or fake. "One of a kind" is quite simply the only one. If its existential reality is not subject to doubt, an object's reality as "genuine" or "authentic" must refer to some suspected feature that can be determined only by examining the object in relation to other known paradigms. This investigation may entail microscopic or chemical analyses or, in the case of art, evidence of continuous ownership or stylistic homogeneity. Notwithstanding the affirmation of connoisseurs that they "know it when they see it," "reality" in the sense of "authenticity" is not directly discernible; it is a term of art that reflects normative conventions governing what will count as a thing of the given kind.[14] These conventions are negotiable, and the boundaries of identity are not indelibly fixed. Yesterday's fake may indeed become tomorrow's find—and not by misattribution. Its physical structure is not thereby affected, but its relation to the authenticating record is altered, and museums are deeply invested in the maintenance of these normative standards.

Forgeries, like fakes, involve resemblance to something else with the invariant additional condition of intention to deceive as to the history of the forged object's origin.[15] A forged work may be an exact copy of an original, or it could instead be imitative only stylistically, thereby distorting the concept of the body of works to which it pretends to belong. Like the fake, a forgery is a real object existentially, but false with respect to its historical claims. Museums document the provenance of the objects they collect to guard against all errors and misrepresentations, whether deliberate or inadvertent.[16] Verification makes use of appropriate disciplinary and technical skills that probe such questions as: Is this painting a real Titian—i.e., was it in fact painted by Titian? Is this object really a mastodon bone—i.e., is it certifiably part of the body of a member of that species of ancient animal? or, Does this item really come from the Persian court of Timur—i.e., can the object's history and identity be traced to that time and historical place? The object's current material state must yield appropriate evidence that warrants confidence in its being the "real thing" it is purported to be. Physical tests, such as carbon dating, used to discover the antiquity of an object, or chemical evidence linking a work's manner of production with the technical capabilities of a historical era, are authenticating to a limited extent. The tests are informative as to the possible place, time, and circumstances of the object's origin and its probable material history, but these features are not always sufficient warrants of an object's cultural reality.

Real paintings produced in the twentieth century by the Dutch artist Han van Meegeren were able to pass the physical tests identifying them as the work of the seventeenth-century Delft master, Johannes Vermeer, and were stylistically convincing as well. The van Meegeren forgeries' "real" identity was not revealed in such tests, however, but was disclosed at last by their author.[17] The relevant history in this case not only was linked to the works' physical production but also incorporated an unusual conjunction of public and private events, intentions, and experiences. Vermeer's and van Meegeren's paintings, all of them existentially real things, affected one another's "higher level" reality through the recursive intersection of their respective cultural and political histories.

The metaphysical puzzles posed by such museal objects intrude into the domains of ethics, social history, and economics. They are grounded in taxonomy and the order of logic but not reducible thereto. The acclaim awarded to "real things" and the special protection that museums give to them are functions of several conceptual orders that come together in the assignment of value. Although in agreement that what they declare to be real is good, the different systems arrive at that assessment by altogether different routes.

Reality as Autonomy and Intersubjectivity

Among the aspects of reality that Plato revered was its nonrelatedness, its absolute independence of human affairs. Belief in the autonomy of reality, though never without challengers, persists today as a foundation of realist thought. Whatever subjective attributes may embellish it, reality is still generally believed to be noncontingent on human thinking. This common-sense conviction prevails in Western secular society. According to it, knowledge is accumulated by acts of exploring, gathering, collecting, and probing that disclose the nature of reality to the investigator. Exercise of the "liberal spirit of curiosity," which advances knowledge, has long been hailed as a form of social enrichment. Notwithstanding the material plunder that intellectual inquisitiveness sometimes involves, its aims are generally esteemed as noble. Thus European royal societies of arts and sciences and museums proudly funded voyages of exploration and sanctioned their "guiltless spoliation" of goods and property in the name of wisdom and progress, just as federal agencies, universities, and private foundations continue to do today.[18]

Travel in search of knowledge of new lands and their people and customs was always well rewarded. It is a model of the scientific quest, a journey into the unknown, whether of outer space or the mysteries of the organism. The unknown is pursued as an object of conquest, but once captured, it is sheared of its autonomy. Having become knowable, the unknown enters the stream of human subjectivity and, freighted with its interpretive burden, is ready to enter the museum.

No longer impervious to human consciousness, things known are recast in the form of a generic subjectivity. There are no independently real things to be found on the shelves of museums, but many objects whose human-made identity decides their disposition. These captive things do not "speak for themselves"; their voice is not independent of the semiotic systems that define them. They have been inscribed with the concepts in whose name they were collected and to which they now lend credibility.

Susan Pearce calls the museum object a "message bearing entity," like a bottle at sea with a note in it, which alerts the finder metaphorically and metonymically to the world to which the object belonged in its precollected state.[19] That state was as dense semiotically as the object's current, collected, state. Both are phases of the object's identity. We tend to think of the object's earlier phase as more real only because it seems comparatively independent of our current cognitive intention, but at no time was the designated object conceivable as object apart from any human intention. The successive objectifications that it undergoes represent syntactic shifts, the object's autonomy being premised upon an elusive prior reality. The museum's identifying labor begins with the "discursive object," which presupposes and supervenes upon an ineffable "real thing." This "real thing," however, turns out to be less independent of subjectivity than Plato supposed. Instead, it is a link in a chain of consensually supported and hierarchic subjectivities.

Objective and Virtual Reality

As keepers of objects, museums thus turn out to be depositories of subjectivity. Far from being passive storehouses, however, they actively join in giving currency to the past and, by extension, giving legitimacy to present claims of reality. By naturalizing the notion that generations of humans can communicate with one another through objects that transmit real presences, museums confirm the existence of "essential experiencing individuals" without denying their social reality or sacrificing objectivity.[20] A socialized subjectivity is maintained through the canonization of objects whose objective reality is equivalent to intersubjective communion. In the language of modern idealism, objectivity requires no separate and frozen Platonic absolutes, but only the systemically guided confluence of discretely signifying minds.

New materials and technologies that affect perceptual experience redesign the epistemological conditions that control the collaborative consciousness of reality. Microscopes and telescopes extend vision, and therefore the range of things thought to be real, without conflicting with the faith that vision discerns a separate physical reality. These instruments empower people to see more of reality. Some technologies, however, undermine this dyadic consciousness by breaking through the gap between perception and reality. They expose images that "hang in space" without additional props that vindicate the separate stability of subject and object. Contextless, disembodied experiences, which would once have seemed madly unreal, have therefore now become plausible "real things" and can be encountered without need for additionally validating sensory reinforcement. The grin on the face of the Cheshire cat can persist happily and even be recalled without a feline body to support it.[21]

Contemporary authors have recovered the term "virtual reality" from ancient roots to refer to "artificially produced" phenomenological experience that occurs in the absence of the physical event normally associated causally with such experience. The experience of the apparent reality is a procession of representations, perceived and interacted with as real, but without the constraining properties of physical bodies. Virtual reality is both real and virtual. It is a present appearance that is objectively nonpresent. Neither illusion nor hallucination, virtual reality engages conscious experience in real activity at the center of a simulated and hyperreal environment. It is a collusion of subjectivities that fulfills some, but not all, of the conditions of objectivity.

The Neoplatonic expression "virtually real" referred to occult powers attributed to agencies able to bring about effects without direct intervention. Causation at a distance, the result of undetectable forces, seemed to account for phantasms such as the illusory visual effect, still called a "virtual image," that we know to be caused by convergence of reflected light at a point where the reflecting object is not to be found. The virtual image cannot be touched or projected on a screen. Its reality consists in its conformity to the laws of optics and its realistic appearance, and its virtuality consists in its nonconformity to the usual behavior of objects. Although one can pass one's hand through the image without sensation, virtual images have the uncanny ability to make observers believe that they are face to face with real, substantive objects. Actual objects thus seem superfluous to the experience of their reality, and it is conceivable that reality no longer needs anchorage in the world of physical things. For museums, this hypothesis, long entertained by mystics and visionaries, invites the practical reflection that the historic burdens of physical accumulation and care of objects might be alleviated, and attention may shift to the manufacture of virtually real experiences.

The Production of Real Experience: Emotion and Cognition

The arts are typically celebrated for their creation of virtual worlds.[22] Figures from literature and the plastic arts sometimes seem closer to us than our

neighbors, and fictional situations more intensely real than those encountered in everyday life. Images and characters and even fictitious plots can become so deeply embedded in our lives that they share mental space with
personal memories and experiences and, like them, shape our ethical and
political convictions. Art has the power to displace time and space, to prise
us loose from our ordinary lives, and to implant us spiritually in another
place. Some aestheticians maintain that the "real" work of art is not a physical stimulus but rather is identical with the experience that it mediates.[23]

According to this position, the experience, though mediated by objects,
does not depend on their authenticity. Its own authenticity is the end to
be achieved, the sole measure of art's reality. Arguably, a paradigmatic
"real experience" could be produced by direct stimulation of specific
brain centers, a proposition well exploited by science fiction writers but
not readily implemented by museums. Closer to home, however, is the
simulacrum whose verisimilitude produces a "lifelike" experience.

Consider again the beloved dinosaur: Steven Spielberg's 1993 film *Jurassic Park* gave public prominence to a scholarly controversy that was
previously brewing in the world of paleobiology. Could extinct species be
recreated from recovered strands of DNA? And, if living specimens could
be produced by such procedures, would they be instances of the real
thing? The film did not resolve the question whether or not such offspring,
if generated, would qualify as genuine dinosaurs. This is a matter for philosophers and scientists to decide. But the film's technical proficiency and
allusion to serious scientific research lent credibility to the simulated creatures and made them appear very real.[24] *Jurassic Park* was an adventure
story, contrived to produce actual thrills and evoke terror. The filmmakers
used the artificed verisimilitude of an impossible event to elicit directly in
viewers an experience that was phenomenologically real. Their million-
dollar objective was to cause as many people as possible, individually, to
endure an effect much the same as might be stimulated by placing elec-
trodes in the moviegoers' brain centers. They were meant to really experience real fear—but not too much of it.

Ancient bones and relics have tantalized people for centuries. Museums
that display fossil skeletons extracted from sites where prehistoric animals
roamed promise to impart true information about the past and demonstrate how evidence is used to reconstruct a past reality. The cognitively
induced experience that these exhibitions elicit may be less dramatic, but
is no less real, than that produced by twentieth-century animated robots,
which do not pretend to be evidence at all, only remote simulations.[25]
Traditionalists point out that, unlike the fossilized bones and eggs ex-

tracted from the prehistoric sites, the contemporary replicas are not the "real thing," nor is the thrill they engender the same as that which the real thing would evoke. Both experiences nevertheless qualify as "real."[26] The difference between them is not in the degree of their reality—they are equally real—but in their emotional intensity and quality and their cognitive effect.[27]

In redirecting interest from objects used as evidence to objects that evoke experience, museums combine two contemporary cultural trends. We have noted the shift from object to experience that turns attention from real things to real subjective states. The second tendency, which merges with the first, valorizes emotive over cognitive meaning. It identifies the experiential with the empathic, and in calling for a reality of experience, it covertly gives priority to the evocation of feeling.

Enlightenment philosophy treated cognition as distanced, impersonal, and exclusively rational. According to that doctrine, in order to understand the nature of something, one must contemplate it without intruding private interest or feeling, which would detract from the universal validity of one's judgment. Not the absence of experience, but the exclusion of emotive bias, is what legitimized scholarly authority. Ideally, scholars and students—and museum visitors—were expected to set subjective feeling aside in the pursuit of knowledge and to be emotionally indifferent to its outcome. This idealization does not entail that the pursuit of knowledge have no emotive significance; a passion for wisdom is always in order. But its intention is to detach cognition from personal interest in order to connect it with the intersubjective conditions of reality.[28]

The gulf posited by Enlightenment thinkers between reason and feeling was dissipated in the twentieth century. Today's public does not discriminate sharply between what is known and what is felt, and often it dismisses as cognitively unintelligible a construct that it cannot encompass empathically. Experience is taken to be inherently emotional; indeed, the very idea of affectless experience is sometimes suggestive of a pathological cast of mind. The public demands that ideas be so presented as to make them imaginable. The depersonalization and detachment that formerly defined objectivity and guaranteed its cognitive worth now strike people as both undesirable and impossible. It is assumed, moreover, that all theoretical knowledge, however obtained, is value laden, and therefore, ultimately, that all knowledge is inextricably tied to emotional commitments.

Since feeling, however, is notoriously subjective, its penetration of knowledge has the consequence of subjectifying cognition. The persuasiveness of any given knowledge claim is as likely to flow from its emotional intensity as from the empirical or rational evidence in its favor. If seeing is believing, seeing forcefully may foster a still stronger belief, and a timid or weak presentation can undermine an idea's credibility. Theatricality makes a story more compelling emotively, and so design and the art of spectacle compete with logic and evidence in the inducement of belief. Since strongly held beliefs register as powerful experiences, the production of shared, powerful experiences becomes a means to create a public reality that passes for knowledge.

Dramatic visual representations have been integral to museums for more than a century. Dioramas depicting animals and people dwelling in their natural habitat were introduced into American museums in the mid-nineteenth century.[29] Long before that, huge, circular paintings with the observer placed in the center were displayed, accompanied by stirring music and sound effects.[30] Contemporary technology simply augments the impact of such "realism" with three-dimensional, "walk-in" environments that feature olfactory and tactile sensations as well as moving figures and human or animated actors. All of this is calculated to heighten and intensify the museumgoer's engagement with the exhibition. Science centers and historical museums, especially, have elevated interactivity to unprecedented levels. In holding that holistic engagement through multi-dimensional experience, rather than distanced contemplation, answers a common human need, these museums are taking a novel epistemological and ontological stand. The reality they aim to construct is cognitively and emotively totalizing.

Real Experience

"Get more than a pretty sunset from your next vacation!" runs the advertisement for the Disney Institute, which also offers "over eighty unique experiences every week." Walt Disney World, with its multiple outposts and imitators, is the archetypal theme park today. Theme parks have won extraordinary importance in contemporary society, having subtly influenced the residential and commercial environments—restaurants, hotels, shopping malls, schools and playgrounds, not to mention the redesign of the tourism and leisure activity industries. This success alone would give museums reason to pay attention, but a more elusive feature of theme parks, of which museums are taking note, is their capacity to mass produce and retail "unique experiences" that are phenomenologically real.

Combining technical know-how with enormous resources, exact knowledge, and imaginative genius, Disney Enterprises has effectively invaded history with a new sense of reality. A defender describes the implements of metaphysical construction: "Through the device of themeing and its shorthand stylizations of person, place and thing, an archive of collective memory and belief, symbol and archetype has been created."[31] The obsession with realistic detail is so intense that, as described by Umberto Eco, "Absolute unreality is offered as real presence. . . . The sign aims to be the thing, to abolish the distinction of the reference, the mechanism of replacement."[32] No longer contrived simply to replicate the reality of its source, as in a forgery, the image strives to be a reality, so completely believable that it can shout its artificiality from the rooftops—an expression of unquenchable thirst for more experience that Eco attributes to "an America of furious hyperreality." Such experience need not be of anything other than itself. Hyperreality evokes a sweet, incongruous feeling of nostalgia for something that never was or brings on an adrenalin rush inspired by a fiction so precise that it seems truer than life.

The reality of the theme park is not the reality of the research laboratory. It is a mythopoetic construction that succeeds in gratifying more than 50 million annual "guests," who neither can nor care to analyze its accuracy or compare the experience of the moment to the historically real. The world that Disney creates exceeds the most ambitious museum recreations in providing an atmosphere that totally encompasses visitors and lifts them out of ordinary time and space into a virtual "free zone" where the pressures of living are savored but not endured.[33]

Theme parks are commercial enterprises, primarily dedicated to making profit, a goal explicitly denied to museums.[34] But there are common interests. Although entertainment is manifestly their function, theme parks are finding that well-packaged education is compatible with pleasurable experience and may enhance it. Their wealth enables theme parks to develop and deploy resources for addressing crowds that are out of range for museums. Some museum professionals are aghast at the prospect of learning from such close encounters with undisguised commercialism, but others are hopeful that the Disney techniques might be adaptable to their own purposes. Theme park commercialism and the temptations of profiteering may in fact be less menacing in the long run than a more subtle corruption of epistemological sensibility that precedes Disney's influence. Plato's gloomy imprecations may not have been entirely misplaced.

The constructed reality of the theme parks imposes itself on and overtakes conventional understanding of reality. Its brilliant imagery and the totality of its controlling effect eventually numb sensitivity and restrict reflective capacity, especially among those who never were exposed to the reality that the theme park pretends to represent. Unimprinted with the originals that might inspire nostalgia—or perhaps repel it—their experience is confined to the surrogate, whose artificial realism is stunning as well as readily accessible. By contrast, the past or distant "real thing" looks pale and lacks immediacy, and the difficulty of visualizing it makes its pursuit not worth the effort. Ignorance reinforces the sentiment that there is little point in visiting distant places or finding rare things when one can capture their "essence" with less trouble and less expense. Why preserve grubby old stuff when its "substance" can be holistically reconstituted at will? Disney's practical sentimentalism resonates with American stereotypes that have now been in place for more than a generation and are easily exported. The successor generation cannot share its grandparents' memory of a reality of which it has no direct recollection. Not even the second-hand souvenirs that television may have stirred in their parents will recall "Main Street" or the "frontier" to children for whom theme parks alone are definitive experience. Detached from the links that tie it to a remembered reality, theme park reality is pure hyperreality that depends for its vitality on the power of expressive persuasion.

Disney Enterprises counts on educational as well as marketing research to please the public and vies with museums to produce aesthetically gratifying experience that is evocative and personal and that may incidentally lead to learning as a bonus. Appealing to the public on the same empathic continuum as theme parks, but with more particularized historical reconstructions, are museums such as the Plimouth Plantation at Plymouth, Massachusetts. Here actors perform the roles of seventeenth-century settlers engaged in the daily pursuits of domestic life—farming, beer making, teaching school—and answer queries by visitors in the manner and dialect of pre–Revolutionary America. Well-trained historians, the actors rely on their knowledge and skillful use of environmental props to make themselves into interactive, living exhibits that teach by animating the past. Their task is to entice visitors into the ambit of a historical place and time by representing themselves as of it. As period figures, they disclaim possession of anachronistic knowledge, indulging in only such speculative explanations of their doings as their historic prototypes might venture.

Another Massachusetts historical reconstruction, Old Sturbridge Village, exhibits the American preindustrial labor and domestic economy of the 1840s by using a different theatrical technique. Here too, actors display history, but without "playing" their characters. As in Plimouth, they demonstrate the fabrication techniques and customs of their period and invite visitors to partake of that experience as observers. The actors answer questions from the public, speaking didactically in their own personae as commentators from the present, and with somewhat greater speculative freedom than the actors at Plimouth Plantation enjoy. Placing historic distance between themselves and the moment they represent, the Sturbridge "interpreters" illustrate early manufacturing practices—making shoe soles in batches, twisting straw onto broom handles, dropping molten pewter into spoon forms—and their products may be purchased in the museum store at competitively marked-up prices. The technical demonstrations are the museum experience. When accompanied by conversation, they are "interactive" components of an exhibition that mediates between learning about the past and having a present experience.

Plimouth Plantation and Old Sturbridge Village illustrate two ways of confronting the epistemological problem that is central to the modern museum: how to convey valid knowledge of reality through artificially contrived experiences. Both museums undergird their approach with a profusion of historical research, and the success of each depends on its accuracy as well as its impact. Theme parks, untroubled by that responsibility, aim chiefly to entertain and can lavish full attention on creating self-vindicating experiences. The propagation of knowledge is, for them, a secondary benefit that may but need not enhance an experience whose hedonic tone is sufficient unto itself. Although museums are frankly envious of theme parks' mastery of techniques of engagement, they are bound to acknowledge that the authenticity of experience must not be confused with the authenticated referent to which the induced experience relates.

The authenticity of museum reconstructions is comparable to that of early-music performances in which contemporary musicians, trained to use the techniques of the past (and sometimes costumed accordingly), play medieval, Renaissance, or baroque music on preserved or reconstructed instruments. Some critics insist that modern listeners cannot possibly ascribe the same meaning to such performances as original listeners would have done, or experience them in the same way, however exact the re-presentation. These critics note, moreover, that today's audiences, dressed in modern clothes, nourished on modern food, and habituated to the acoustics, tempi, and sounds of the present environment, necessarily hear early music as "museum pieces," wrenched from their own historical context. Our musical ancestors would, in any case, lack the intervening events that have shaped our own retrospective consciousness and auditory sensibility—just as we must lack their perceptual background. Unavoidably, we hear what was current to them as precursor to what has been superseded by our own musical tradition, which they could not possibly know. The performances we hear and see are "real," but they are not "real history." They are not identical with the performances they reconstruct. Yet, they are not altogether independent of real history, for even if we cannot literally return to or replicate the past, our present experience refers to it and has been affected by the sequence of events that are its consequence. Theme parks are free to exploit that reference, within the limits of plausibility, to enhance today's experience—by touching it with a nostalgic glow, for example, or eliminating unsavory details. Museums are obliged to struggle with more restrictive conventions. The indispensable rules of evidence and legitimation that warrant a museum's credibility prohibit its use of some techniques of engagement—such as those based solely on inducing tears and thrills— that enable theme parks to thrive and prosper.

Museum Experience

Synthesizing experience has, nonetheless, become a major museum project, contributing to a metamorphosed conception of the function of museums. As memorial evocations rather than mere warehouses, museums intentionally arouse feeling and therewith a new dimension of authenticity. Objects work to conjure rather than to signify. The "Blitz Experience" at the Imperial War Museum in London, for example, strives to create in visitors the terrifying feeling of being under siege; and Washington's U.S. Holocaust Memorial Museum relies on a few carefully salvaged artifacts and devices to bear witness to the reality of this—let us hope—irreproducible event. Rational explanation is not the objective here, but with the aid of these powerfully evocative objects and coercive exhibit architecture, visitors are made to undergo something like the feeling of terror to which Shoah victims were subjected. The museum, in addition to its admonitory message, makes available a wealth of documentary material from which the public can learn more about that tragic history; but the primary impact of the memorial is overwhelmingly experiential.[35] Visitors literally shuffle along the dark, narrowing passages, speaking little to one another, and living through disorienting feelings of shame, horror, and incredulity, sparked by the terrible things they see. Neither objects nor experiences are simulated here; they are real and they are referential. As we have seen, however, their realism finds its foremost didactic function not in the dispensing of cognitive information, but in the recall and release of profound feeling.

Of course the experiences generated by such circumstances are multitudinous and idiosyncratic. It is naive to suppose that experiences can be more personally felt and yet also be more subject to external control than the perception of physical objects. Experience is notoriously ephemeral. Traditional museums intentionally addressed only a small segment of the community in which they were situated. They were able, therefore, to take certain perceptual and behavioral uniformities, and perhaps even some emotional regularities, for granted, but that is no longer possible. Museum visitors today cover a much broader social spectrum and hold fewer values in common, and they are less prepared mentally to conjoin familiar objects with preordained experiences. They do not even have a common sense of what is familiar. If it is true that today's audiences are less inspired by the sanctity of the "real thing" than by the emotive surge of a "real experience," they also may be less affected by the conditions of its production, which meant so much to a previous generation. If simulated objects or something altogether different can produce real and satisfying experiences, nothing more may be wanted, and the costly and effortful preservation of real objects can then seem nearly superfluous.[36]

Different types of museums are experimenting with new conceptualizations of the real that functionally displace objects in yet another fashion. Science centers aim to induce people to observe real phenomena—to notice, pay attention to, think about, and make discoveries through them. Some phenomena are too big, small, far away, fast, slow, complex, or incidental to be observed by normal perception or under normal conditions. Museums therefore make available the special apparatus and instruments that scientists use to study these phenomena, adapting them for public use by nonscientists. The objects retain their routine laboratory utility and are not reverentially regarded by the museums as "real things" or as "collectibles." They may, however, represent a considerable material investment and are often cherished by historians and connoisseurs of technology. They require maintenance and care, not at all as "museum objects" but for the sake of their function as tools, and so as means to the production of the real experiences that the museum fosters.

The resulting experiences that museum audiences undergo are rarely unprecedented discoveries. Museum visitors are not pioneers at the forefront of science; their discoveries need not be new to the world to be authentic.[37] To qualify as "real experience," they must only have been genuinely made by the discoverer through his or her own exploration. Matters of common knowledge are thus recurrently discovered by people previously ignorant of them. To the discoverer, that event constitutes a "real experience," and it is genuinely gratifying. The museum provides the conditions under which certain types of experiences may be expected to take place. Their occurrence is therefore real from the vantage point of the person who actually experiences them. It is a hope of science museums that such induced experience may excite visitors to further inquiry. Its designation as a "learning experience" refers to the discovery's potential as a teaching threshold. It is not, as such, an experience of learning. Alternatively, the discovery might terminate simply with pleasurable, aesthetic enjoyment of the experience as an end in itself—a "wow effect," not unlike that stimulated by the theme park or joy ride. If the experience is complex and transformative, it may even resemble a religious epiphany or the rapture of enjoying art. Whatever the wonderment inspired, this experiential awakening of consciousness is highly individuated and independent of what other people may have discovered under the same or different circumstances.

What a visitor's actual experience will be is not predictable and is, ultimately, beyond the control of the museum, whose role is, humbly, to make it possible. The challenge to museums is not to develop greater predictive acuteness or better skills of manipulation, but to provide more interesting options and more opportunities for people to undergo generative experiences sensitively and with discrimination. Creating an environment in which experiences can safely take place is an enormous responsibility. It is important to understand the potential risks and benefits to individuals and to society, and to compare these with the risks and benefits entailed by the old-fashioned stewardship of objects and collections, which traditional museums claimed as their ultimate responsibility.

André Malraux conceived the "museum without walls," an idea that reveals how the past is metamorphosed by new technologies.[38] As he observed, a dialogical human history discards nature as the foundation of the museum experience and replaces it with process. Pictures and visual signs still do carry evidentiary force and elicit belief, but new techniques of reproduction and the possibility of manipulating images have undermined confidence in that belief. We no longer rely on representation as veridical witness; invention and fantasy are livelier substitutes. Though unwilling to give up the secure sense of reality that a monological view of nature seemed to protect, people now seek reality elsewhere: in immediacy and spontaneity, in emotional intensity, in intersubjective agreement, and, most paradoxically, in the acceptance of a polylogicality that appears to do away with all conventional grounds for judgment.

Museums have made a difficult adaptation to this revisionist metaphysics of diversity. Without abandoning their pride in the "real thing" or their claim to authenticity, museums have shifted their allegiance from real objects to real experiences. Accepting the premise that every experience is equally real, and that no experience has prima facie priority over any other, we must now ask how museums can fulfil their commitments without ranking experiences according to some arbitrary value system. To answer this question we are obliged to move, with Malraux, outside the museum walls, into a dialogue with human history. And, just as human history cannot be assessed without exploring the ideals of the good life, so in the case of the museum, we cannot understand the nature or purpose of that institution without a closer examination of the values that guide it.

6.   Museum Ethics
The Good Life of the Public Servant

Where do the values that guide the museum come from? Is there an institutional persona whose "good life" expresses the museum's identity and moral character? Are there uniquely museal obligations and responsibilities to match its special capacities? And, if so, how is the ethical nature of the museum made manifest and advanced by the people who, collectively, compose it?

Like other legally constituted corporate entities, museums have an expressed mission and policies, which dictate the duties of their employees, the rights of benefactors, and the responsibilities of boards of directors. According to that model, the museum is a construct, an abstract entity legislatively defined, and distinct from the actual human beings who combine in its formation and do its work. But such reduction of the museum's status to legal fiction fails to take account of the substance it has accrued throughout the history of its formation, as the museum conformed to a succession of cultural paradigms. Alongside its impressment of people, the museum is marked by its uniquely allocentric, or "other centered," and continuously intense relationship to *things*. Beyond their mere use or exchange value to individual possessors, things, divorced from their immediate value or utility, are the foundation of the museum, and museums are among the few sites where objects are so valorized.[1]

Museum workers are required, temporarily at least, to attend to objects without reservation and with the selfless devotion normally accorded only to beloved persons. Within the museum, care for objects is sometimes as outrageously exaggerated as the concern shown by luxury health resorts to pampered clients. This benevolent scrutiny, conscientiously fixed upon objects, is the crucial ingredient of museum work that distinguishes it from other modes of caretaking. Are there consequent ethical demands that apply in singular fashion to museums, imposing on them a moral identity uniquely their own?

Whose Obligations to What?

The Western philosophical tradition, for the most part, ascribes ethical behavior, its prescription, merit, and judgment, only to human beings. Objects have no direct moral status. Moral obligation is a human institution predominantly owed by persons to one another.[2] Although rules of ethical conduct are sometimes claimed to derive from supernatural sources, and obedience to them is ordained for the sake of spiritual reward, the commandments ordained generally pertain to human interactions. Only rarely are exhortations and prohibitions extended to actions that do not have human origins and consequences, and these are almost never addressed, except metaphorically, to nonhuman (or nonsentient) beings. Environmentalists claim exception on behalf of rights for nonhuman animals, plants, and even inanimate objects such as rivers and mountains, but these claims are singularly isolated, and often they covertly reintroduce a human factor by alluding to potential future generations for whose sake the things in question are to be protected.[3]

Philosophers usually predicate moral desert on the real or potential capability of percipients to experience suffering and to understand what it is to inflict it, thereby excluding whatever lacks that sensibility from moral consideration.[4] By this criterion, most museum objects could still command respect under the heading of property, but not as morally deserving agents in their own right. The suggestion that people have moral obligations to things apart from their human connections, or out of a general exhortation to care and frugality, is countered by pointing to the apparent lack of reciprocity between persons and things. Things can injure and be injured, and one can cherish them and grieve their loss. But things cannot act from deliberation, and barring unusual legal circumstances, things are not held responsible for what they do.[5] The conclusion commonly drawn is that only those beings capable of genuine moral agency are proper recipients of moral regard, and thus the capacity to be moral is restricted to creatures with human consciousness. Notwithstanding their aesthetic, economic, historical, educational, or sacred worth, objects, including those preserved in museums, are therefore excluded from primary moral discourse.

But what of the museums that house these objects? Are they not bound to their content with an obligation every bit as profound as that which they owe to present and future human agents and to the preservation of human memory?[6] Curators are appointed as "keepers of collections," a title meant to evoke a more pastoral than custodial responsibility. Museum staff members often refer to this charge reverentially, more as a moral calling than a professional duty, and are at pains to remind themselves and others of the thrill and the responsibility that go with handling the "real thing."

To whom is this unusual moral concern for things enjoined and to what does it extend? The human agents associated with museums are not exempt from ordinary normative expectations toward persons. Moreover the range of persons to whom their obligation extends exceeds that to which either private or corporate persons are normally committed. Their charge is not confined to stockholders or customers. Varying with the type of museum and the nature of its content, ethical reference can be to the original producers (e.g., of ancient or modern artifacts), to exemplary members of past cultures on display or to their descendants, to current holders of particular religious or moral persuasions, to neighbors and citizens of the community in which the museum is situated, to museum donors and lenders of objects, to exhibition sponsors, to fellow professionals, to the museum staff, to the visiting public, and to future generations affected by the museum's collection. Obviously, ethical conflicts among people can arise where such a complex variety of interests is at stake. The difficulty is compounded by the absence of criteria by means of which conflicts might be resolved, or of standards that would justify a given resolution. How shall the presumed claims of past creators be weighed against those of future descendants? Or these against adjacent householders? How, in the face of the wants of variously ranked people, shall the needs of objects be balanced?

Since museums must make choices among objects and situations, they inevitably reflect and act upon value judgments. These, even where conscientiously intended by some person(s) at some time, may not always be rational or morally coherent, and they may be unknown to the people who are subsequently required to act in conformity with them.[7] Moreover, the multiplicity of objects and transient situations implicated in such interactions renders any real moral consistency improbable. Standards have also changed drastically, and today's public institutions are accepting accountability for the social impact of what they do in accordance with values that differ markedly from those that guided their predecessors. Environmental protection, for example, was simply not a significant issue for museum officers prior to the 1960s. It is, furthermore, debatable whether the same or any of the principles of normative ethics that apply in the private sphere are strictly operative in a public context. Traditional moral theory has been chiefly concerned with the "good life" and the "virtue" of the private individual, leaving public morality to the dubious domain of politics.[8]

Collective midlevel units, such as cities, families, churches, and professional organizations, are composed of individual persons related by a common bond. Their aims are more specific than those of the social whole, but neither as varied nor as specific as those of any given individual. Institutions intersect with, but do not completely absorb, the lives of the people they encompass. They work as a mediating device that connects private life with the public world. By virtue of their institutional affiliation, people acquire certain privileges as well as duties and obligations beyond those assumed privately and sometimes incompatible with them. Ethical theorists have been interested in the moral conflicts encountered by individuals that arise out of multilevel and multiple group membership. Resolving these moral dilemmas is not simply a matter of personal choice between explicit rights and wrongs, or between higher and lower order commitments. Some value structures are incommensurable; the loyalties and conduct that one framework prescribes are logically independent of those dictated by another. It is an existential tragedy for individuals when membership in one community conflicts with belonging to another one. But the need to reconcile the moral discontinuities of different institutional identities is a fact of modern life.[9] People who are part of the museum world and the community it encompasses are not alone in facing this demand. They do, however, bear the unusual burden of accommodating the museum's unique object-oriented history.

Professionalism

Professional ethics prescribes behavior to the individual practitioners of specific professions. Codes of ethics are drawn, appropriately, to fit particular circumstances—access to confidential or sensitive information, security, opportunity to cause physical injury or to give and withhold care, control over valuable property or the means of expression—and the ability to regulate certain types of activity. The codes are directed to the persons who practice the professions and not to the professions as such, although there are also formal laws governing professional structures (e.g., tax laws, laws of incorporation.) A profession is not identical with an organization, but professions often do comprehend communities that are bound by common history and interests. Museum workers belong to a self-described profession, with affiliate organizations and personal subscribers, but this is also associated with a historic institution, the museum, whose existence predates the profession.

Like many other occupational groups in which people form a self-selected community to foster certain skills and provide certain services, museum people take pride in their achievement and have an interest in the maintenance of high standards. Their professionalism is a bond of commitment and fellowship among qualified individuals. Their voluntary adoption of a professional code of ethics does not displace the ordinary moral expectations that exist among private persons but rather introduces additional moral associations related to specific, goal-oriented, collective activities. These activities and the agents that perform them constitute a moral domain that differs qualitatively from the moral context in which the same persons are implicated when functioning only as individuals.[10]

Professionalism as such relates to the performance of a type of work that requires specialized training.[11] Commensurate with the social value of the work, those qualified to perform it receive rewards of prestige and other advantages. Most importantly, they are granted authority over their own field and are in a position to monitor and train successors who gain entry to it. This is how, over time, they are able to form a relatively closed subsociety, sometimes regarded as an elite that lives by its own rules. Professional self-governance can work as a subterfuge to evade scrutiny of deviations from ordinary morality. But the purpose of professional codes of ethics is not to protect scoundrels or to safeguard the professional community and insulate it from society at large. Rather, professional codes are meant to integrate the practices of the specialized group with the good of the larger community, concentrating in particular on features that might enhance or lead to tension with that common good. Professional codes of ethics emphatically do not legitimize behavior that is morally indefensible privately, since professional practice is presumptively pledged to preserve the common welfare.[12]

Museum workers in the United States have repeatedly come together to construct a professional code of ethics, and their efforts reflect not only the particular circumstances of the profession at the time, but also the prevailing moral spirit of American society as a whole.[13] As this society re-

sponds to such pressures as demographic shifts, technological development, and catastrophic events such as war and economic crises, the moral
values it lives by are tested, and the ethical codes of the several subgroups
included within society must also be adapted. The moral tone of the three
major publications of museum ethics that were propagated in the United
States during the twentieth century plainly reflect the shifting values of the
ambient world. Each reflects the current conceptual and ethical fashion of
its time. Each has subsequently been judged inadequate as those fashions
passed into disuse. None of the codes addresses all of the complex concerns that periodically confront museums. Consequently, each of the
codes is a partial and incomplete portrait, too vague in some respects, and,
in others, trivial in its specificity. Generic exhortations to honesty and integrity, for example, have insignificant points of attachment, and explicit
proscriptions, like dress codes, become quickly out-of-date or would be
better regulated by broader public legislation. The enterprise of code making, though well intentioned, has therefore been only marginally successful. Nonetheless, as a step toward professionalism in the museum world,
it represents an acknowledgment of public responsibility and care superior to the clannish and paternalistic pattern of museum founders in centuries past.

Museum Codes of Ethics

The American Association of Museums first adopted a professional code
of ethics at its twentieth annual meeting in 1925. *The Code of Ethics for
Museum Workers* was based on the premise that museums serve a public
function as "institutions which hold their possessions in trust for mankind
and for the future welfare of the [human] race."[14] Reflecting American
commitments to populism, pragmatism, and education, the code stressed
the dissemination of knowledge throughout all levels of society. In accordance with the vision of society prevailing at that historic moment, the museum was meant to be an instrument of community betterment and not a
citadel of scholarship or entertainment exclusively for the privileged few.
The code set forth broad general principles and, in addition, made certain
explicit injunctions—that museum workers not accept gifts or commis-
sions from business enterprises, that museums refuse to acquire objects obtained through vandalism, that trustees use discretion in discussing
administrative and executive matters with staff members.[15] Museum work
had been the province of a small group of individuals, for the most part

well known to one another, who could rely on each other's honor and judgment. The code dealt with conduct within and between museums, their trustees, directors, and personnel. In keeping with the mores of its closed society, it assumed a benevolent hierarchy in which employees could be expected to faithfully carry out the orders of employers and certainly would not presume to formulate policy.

Museum directors and curators were typically amateurs who had collected long before acquiring their official designation as "keepers of collections." Their prior experience with and love of their subject was what qualified them for their specialized employment. Trustees, too, tended to be men (often under the influence of women) who were motivated by a deep knowledge of and affection for the objects the museum held in trust. Many had helped fund the expeditions that studied and brought back the items ultimately to be included in the collections. Their contributions to the museum were substantive and substantial and were not limited to money and business know-how.[16] Nevertheless, reason dictated that allowing them too close involvement with museum practice and policy might come to have adverse effects; and so, where a tradition of charitable magnanimity and sense of noblesse oblige had been a sufficient ethical foundation, now a new society demanded a more exacting standard of public trust.

The 1925 code fell into disuse with the shifting tide of social and aesthetic norms and a proliferation of museums with divergent aims. In the 1950s, the postwar rise of the American avant garde and the turn to formalism, especially in art and criticism, led to a renewal of interest in method, scholarship, and, once more, to an aesthetic of elitism, though of a different character. Museums focused again on collection, but now with an altered social consciousness. The AAM responded at its 1974 meeting with the appointment of a committee on ethics, charged with the task "to identify the ethical principles underlying museum operations in the broadest sense as viewed by the profession at this point in history."[17] This committee issued a report in 1978—*Museum Ethics*—including four general headings: Collection, Staff, Museum Management Policy, and Museum Governance. Education of the general public appears to have been a less-prominent concern and was left to the care of a subordinate segment of museum staff. Far greater attention was given to internal self-regulation of the museum community and to the explicit formulation of professional practice.[18]

The 1978 statement assumes the conventional primacy of the individual person and his or her responsible agency, and thus references to "the museum" and to "its" duty or obligation must be taken as applying elliptically to employees, volunteers, trustees, or their representatives. The moral relationship of persons to things is acknowledged in the report's declaration that "each museum's obligation to its collection is paramount"; but effectively this duty, expressed as "stewardship," is secondary to the "public trust" owed to "our successors" (i.e., to other people), to "transfer . . . when possible in enhanced form, the material record of human culture and the natural world."[19] This formulation of the museum's duty not only restricts ethical relationships to persons but also deemphasizes the physicality of the museum collections. The language of the new code doubly downgrades things; for what it recommends for transmission is a body of information—a record. This is to be meticulously maintained, and with due respect for its authenticity; but, with no suggestion of irony, the code also indicates various nonphysical interests and influences that might modify or reinterpret that record. There is no allusion at this point to the subservience of objects to experience that would later subjectivize the museum's content even further to the condition of ephemera; however, an instrumentalist attitude toward objects is already evident.

The 1978 report is marked by attention to professionalism, conceived as it was at that time as "specialized personal expertise." The authors of the report were as eager to restrict abrasive performance by people fulfilling their diverse functions as to promote cooperative interaction among them. As composite entities, museums necessarily enlist the collaboration of a number of distinct and overlapping competencies, and the report did not suggest a supervening "museum morality" that belongs to the institution independently of individual moral choices. Rather, it implied that, although a nonspecific "gentlemanly" code of conduct had sufficed heretofore to achieve harmony among those officers conducting the museum's business, pragmatism now called for efficient organizational procedures.

The 1978 statement was therefore careful to separate private from public collecting, the individual from personal collections and interests. Although it admitted that collecting, consulting, lecturing, and writing learned studies might enhance a staff member's professional knowledge as well as the reputation of the museum, the statement warned against conflicts of interest and insisted that, in the conduct of their private lives, employees must be mindful of the status of their institution. Because of the high visibility of museums and the importance of their retaining public esteem, trustees and employees could be required to curtail activities that appeared to exploit, conflict with, or bring discredit on the museum. At a moment of increasing demand for public accountability, professional prudence dictated self-regulation.

Activism that might be construed as political advocacy on the part of the museum was forbidden. However lofty its fundamental ideals, the museum could by no means pretend to speak for all those associated with it; neither should any of them speak on its behalf in any manner except that for which they were officially authorized. Intellectual honesty, the statement held, though it prohibited the perpetuation of myths or stereotypes, imposed upon the museum professional the severe restraint that "he must clearly understand the point where sound professional judgment ends and personal bias begins" and "must be confident that the resulting presentation is the product of objective judgment." This argument, made in the name of objectivity and professionalism, demanded self-restraint and personal detachment. It adhered to the corresponding and widely held belief that intellectual judgment must be dispassionate and disinterested. Museums were to be sanctuaries of political neutrality.[20] Opponents of these constraints protested their use as a way of temporizing in order to avoid offending powerful museum donors or jeopardizing favorable tax consideration.[21]

At the highest level of discussion, there was conflict over the meaning of *integrity* or, more precisely, over the nature of the museum's role as a public institution that transcends the individual preferences and prejudices of the people it encompasses. But such philosophical speculation rarely became part of the professional discourse.[22] It was hard enough to reconcile the institution's officially declared mission with the disparate interests of benefactors, scholars, the cultural community, and the public, while remaining sensitive to increasing restiveness throughout society concerning such externalities as cultural expropriation, degradation of the environment, racism, and the blight of cities.

Museum Ethics was more like a report on a general climate than an operational directive. The atmosphere that it surveyed was governed by market forces and by a doctrine of balancing interests. It did not have the singular moral certitude of the 1925 *Code of Ethics for Museum Workers*. As its chairman admitted, "On matters of both substance and wording, the committee members were in total accord on few if any issues."[23] Instead, they compromised by endorsing a final draft of the report, which counseled individual museums and professional subgroups of the museum community to formulate their own guidelines and codes of conduct. Following that advice would particularize professionalism to an even greater degree but also would encourage exploration of museum standards at grassroots levels and make their implementation more possible. While the task force that produced *Museum Ethics* was doing its work, several of the subordinate professional museum groups, in compliance with the committee's recommendation, drafted statements that applied more specifically to themselves. Thus were produced "A Code of Ethics for Curators," "A Code of Ethics and Standards of Practice for Conservators," "A Code of Ethics for Registrars," "A Code of Ethics for Museum Stores," "A Code of Ethics for Public Relations," and "On the Ethics of Museum Education."[24] These policy statements have enabled the museum community to deal collectively, as a profession, with some of its more egregious abuses, in some instances enlisting the aid of courts and attorneys general in enforcement, in others using the sanction of accreditation and its denial as a goad.[25]

Broad issues such as the acquisition of objects and their deaccessionment were intensely discussed in the 1980s, especially in light of attempts by some museum officers and accounting agencies to view their collections as convertible assets that could be liquefied in times of economic crisis.[26] In the years to follow, these matters assumed an entirely new character as attention shifted to the disposition of cultural property and, in some cases, demand for its return to original sources. Americans were awakening to the moral as well as the economic connotations of global citizenship.

The demand for repatriation of human and cultural remains reflected a growing consciousness of national expropriation and tribal dispossession among those more often depicted than served by museums. Ironically, the market-driven quest by museums for larger audiences was in part responsible for the growth of discontent with their collection and exhibition practices.[27] Politically sensitive and multicultural audiences, whose views of themselves were not derived from museum displays and who did not have the traditional museumgoers' reverence for the institution, felt insulted by the manner in which they saw themselves portrayed and resented the paternalism of the conventional museum style. They demanded the right to be consulted on their public representation. At the same time, critics within the academic and scholarly community were offering parallel challenges to the dominance of the European tradition and the canons of taste that had produced the museum.

Their objections coincided with new initiatives sponsored by some private foundations in the 1970s and undertaken by museums seeking ways to link education with programs for public outreach. Sparked by innovative theories of learning, especially in science teaching, museum professionals were beginning to think systematically about ways in which museums could use objects to educate the public.[28] Pluralism and the programs for its promotion drew attention to object literacy and the use of material objects for symbolic expression. A movement simultaneously underway to develop museum practices that were sensitive to multicultural-ism would eventually lead to the formulation of an inclusive code of ethics for the new century.

The New Museology

The combined effect of these developments was to open up the museum to "existential scrutiny" and "phenomenologically oriented inquiry." The museum had passed through phases that historian Neil Harris calls "authoritarian condescension" at its beginning, "authoritarian experimentalism" early in the twentieth century, and "populist deference" in its approach to the public after World War II. In its subsequent postmodern stage, the museum not only welcomed new audiences but also adopted a new style of self-presentation that was subjective, self-validating, and emotional. No uniform reaction to exhibitions could any longer be anticipated, nor was there an expectation of intellectual closure.[29] This embrace of epistemological relativism would deeply affect the authority of the museum's ethical imperative.

Revisionist readings of museum collections emanated in the late 1980s in a new style of curation, much of it politically motivated. The museum itself had become visible. No longer enthroned as an abstract authority, it was now perceived as a cultural artifact, historically contextualized, and a product of class and economic privilege as well as individual taste. The neutral objectivity and detached scholarship formerly prized as befitting professionals, which had insulated institutions of learning against explicit social engagement, was suddenly exploded in a shower of postmodern fragments. Calling for a "new museology," a cohort of new cultural critics looked at the institutional history of the museum and saw it as part and parcel of a maldistributive system of power and meaning, inseparable from the museum's methods of collection and display.[30] Inspired by Marxian social theory and Foucaultian genealogy to bring about change in professional practice, these critics denied that museum exhibitions had ever been as politically unaligned or value neutral as they now professed to be.[31]

Accordingly, a number of innovative, self-conscious, and self-exploratory exhibitions were mounted (or at least imagined) that challenged earlier assumptions of museum presentation and showed how context historicizes and confers meaning. Some denounced the hegemonic past didactically; others recontextualized the materials contained in museum collections in order to encourage audiences to imagine new interpretive strategies. Many were intended to shock and scandalize the public, and some exhibits sought to undermine the very professionalism that the previous generation of museum workers had carefully nurtured. All of them repudiated the existence of universal and absolute value and embraced local affirmations of power and desire in place of the quest for a monolithic truth.

These exhibitions (and treatises) derided conventional museum standards of truth and value, but they appealed implicitly to other standards and to the public's intuitive ability to recognize them. Where the previous educative role of museums had been invoked chiefly for the sake of conserving a culture and transmitting knowledge of it from past to future, now museums were admonished to become agents of social change rather than conservation.[32] Museums were under attack not only for their failure to portray cultural options, but more importantly, for their failure to acknowledge their own covert exercise of power in the making and withholding of legitimating judgment.

In response to pressures from within and without the museum community, the AAM appointed a new ethics task force in 1987 and instructed it to revise the association's 1978 statement. Following a great deal of field research and grassroots consultation, the panel produced a new code that was adopted by the AAM board of directors on November 12, 1993. This document recommended that each nonprofit museum member of the AAM frame its own customized code of ethics in conformance with a very generic principle by January 1, 1997. The task force also advocated procedures to review violations and to withdraw AAM membership from those museums that remained in violation.[33] The community thus took seriously not only its distinctive identity as a profession and the challenge to it, but also its moral responsibility to police and reform itself in the belief that "if museums did not regulate themselves, others, such as government, would."[34]

Indeed, the specter of governmental intervention was real, though not always in the interest of socially progressive reform. Charges of obscenity and pornography from conservative sources threatened to put an end to congressionally authorized federal funding to the arts and to censor "offensive" museum exhibitions.[35] Legislation had also caught up with the troubling issue of the disposition of cultural property and especially human remains. Under the *Native American Graves Protection and Repatriation Act of 1990*, the return of remains was mandated by law.[36] Although oppositional arguments favoring museums' retention of sacred objects were made, on moral as well as scholarly and practical grounds, museums were compelled to take a careful look at their traditional collection philosophy and to enter into serious dialogue with cultural communities whose convictions and values differ from their own.

The AAM ethics task force understood the language of its assignment to invoke "a standard higher than the law," implying an unfashionable faith in a value hierarchy that might subject the law itself to moral scrutiny. The task force maintained that although only individuals could act ethically, their behavior as pertaining to the museum should be regulated according to standards established by that institution. Everyone is prohibited from committing deception or fraud and is obligated to honor contractual agreements and to respect the basic rights of others, but these are private duties, and the committee was impaneled to decide what additional moral imperatives apply to museums simply because they are museums. An ethical institution must be distinguishable from those institutions whose sole obligation, beyond conformity to law, is to themselves or to their investors and constituents. Ethical behavior is taken to be on a higher plane than professionalism or the mere avoidance of legal liability. Perhaps that is why it resists encapsulation in a formal code. The museum community called upon itself once again to refine and validate its ethical mission.

Collections and their care no longer seemed the central preoccupation. Noncollecting institutions, such as science centers, were by now prominently included within the museum community, undercutting the hypothesis that responsibility for precious objects is the essence of the museum's uniqueness.[37] Moreover, despite the persistence of the language of "stewardship," museums' relationship to the objects they held in trust was changing. A diminishing sense of their materiality was expressed in abstract rhetoric that referred to existing collections as "a natural and cultural commonwealth," whose diversity museums were pledged to foster and preserve. Meanwhile, museums were devoting attention to augmenting audiences through public programs and outreach activities. Visitor surveys and evaluative studies did not lag far behind, as museums assumed their extroverted task as "nonprofit organizations that serve the public" by providing gratifying experience conducive to leading a "good life."[38]

A New Museum Identity

What is the "good life" that the postprogressivist museum promotes? Unlike department stores and storage depots, museums have always had a more than utilitarian relationship to the objects they preserve. Now an added value consideration celebrated things for the experiences they engender as well as for the ideas they transmit. If the material benefits of collection were in doubt—and indeed material acquisitiveness had become morally problematic in a postmodern, post-scarcity-driven world—museums must consider alternative self-rationalizations as paths to virtue.

Viewed in a contemporary light, it seems that the museum's function has become largely catalytic, to render experiences available to visitors without overdetermining the actual nature of those experiences. Catalytic agents typically remain apart from the reactions they propagate, accelerating their progress and then disengaging without effect to themselves—but museums may not enjoy that privilege of detachment. The brokering of experience is not ethically more selective than the collection of objects. Neither is it intrinsically more intelligible. Undergoing an experience can be aesthetically satisfying or dissatisfying, emotionally exciting or dull, instructive or enervating. It can also be injurious or productive of harm. Experiences are inherently neither moral nor immoral. But experiences have moral consequences, and those who induce experiences are responsible for what they do.

An ambiguating note therefore haunts the museum's shift of interest from collecting materially real objects to providing real experiences and from the reversal of their ranking. If the reality of experience takes precedence, then that of its productive means or cause becomes "merely" instrumental, and eventually such value can be expressed solely on a one-dimensional scale of utility. The complex circumstances out of which the "reality of experience" emerges come to be defined operationally in terms of the experiencing subject's potential arousal.[39] Did the earth tremble? Ordinarily, one experiences *something*. One undergoes an experiential event related phenomenologically to an inferred reality. A "real experience" that is not *of* something is metaphysically crippled. There is a weird novelty in the manufacture of such truncated metaphysical monsters, and the technology of "virtual reality" is certainly reaping its benefits. Museums that substitute the virtual for the real, however, risk altogether negating the reality that virtuality presupposes. Once again, we meet the discorporated smile of the Cheshire cat.[40]

The philosopher Jean Baudrillard traces the self-devouring path of simulation, beginning from the radical authenticity of lived experience and ending with its contraction into sheer medium. Evincing some moral revulsion, he articulates the demise of reference and therefore of standards against which reality may be judged.[41] Simulation does away with reality by replacing it—and, with the death of reality, all pretenders are likewise killed. Only experience remains, but its reality is indistinguishable from that of appearance, i.e., of nonreality. Infatuation with experience has filled a vacuum left by the insubstantiality of objects. Thus we persist in valuing a perceived "real"—the reflexivity of experience—regardless of what it is or stands for. Enough that there be brain waves in a conscious subject!

The museums' fascination with technically reproducible experience prolongs and faintly echoes their historic dedication to physically "real" things. In their zeal to achieve phenomenological veracity, museums have come upon the empty process of realizing. At the risk of moralizing, I suggest that this love affair with the manufacture of real experience is nihilistic. A generation raised on "spin" and "morphing" is whimsical in its taste for happenings and easily confuses the immediate with the real. But preserving reality is not a trivial pursuit: the museum's survival depends on it. Without a meaningful distinction between things that are real and their more or less adequate representation, neither truth nor falsehood remain to wrest experience from uninflected being.[42]

Institutional Morality

Discussions of professional or institutional ethics often focus on the moral discontinuity between public and private life, as if the ultimate choice were between individual integrity and the conflicting demands of political or professional interest.[43] In my estimation, the museum is a suprapersonal entity, subject to moral imperatives that are qualitatively distinct from those that apply to individuals. More like the theater than like a mausoleum or department store, the museum is bound by institutional performance standards that affirm moral responsibility for transforming people's feelings and judgment.[44]

The committee that formulated the AAM's 1992 *Code of Ethics for Museums* ascribed to the museum a capacity that "promote[s] higher and more consistent ethical standards that . . . serve[s] the interests of museums, their constituencies and society." Evidently, however, it took these ends to be achievable by regulating the personal behavior of board members, employees, and volunteers. The ethics statement directs attention to the need to respect pluralism, the subordination of private interest to the public good, and collaborative behavior; but no appeal is made to a supervening normative character belonging to the museum as a whole that might assume leadership in guiding individuals toward realizing the "Good Society."

As institutional mediators, museums are positioned to shape as well as

preserve values, but narrowly focused moral codes lack the creative idealism to bring this about. A more inspirational source of moral leadership
may be found in some controversial exhibitions and, especially, in the
public discourse that accompanies their planning and execution. The excitement unintentionally evoked by the reaction to the National Air and
Space Museum's exhibition of the *Enola Gay* fuselage in 1995 reveals the
moral potency that museums possess in principle, even where, as in this
case, the museum yielded to restrictive pressure and backed away from its
original exhibition proposal. Like the exhibition of Robert Mapplethorpe
photographs at the Corcoran Gallery several years earlier, the NASM exhibition elicited public debate and perspicuous discussion of issues whose
moral import could not have been deduced from universal principles or
inferred from obligations prescribed to individuals.

If philosophers attribute moral character to institutions at all, it is only
metaphorical. Even where personal behavior would be uninterpretable
apart from the institutional framework that gives it meaning, the defining
role of the institution is rarely noticed. Perhaps it is inconceivable to people
that baseball, or the stock market, or the museum should originate value,
because these institutions are commonly represented as abstractions—as
conceptual composites of individual agents and administrative bodies. Notwithstanding their literal incorporation, their massive property holdings,
and their political influence, institutions such as these are routinely denied
a life of their own.[45] This limited view of institutions, the one apparently
assumed by the 1992 *Code of Ethics for Museums,* precludes the possibility
that an institution could (or should) have an independent moral outlook or
any character to speak of—good, bad, or indifferent.

The suggestion that institutions might originate and express moral
agency appears to personify and invest them with suprahuman consciousness. We tend to believe that because morality entails intentionality, it therefore requires consciousness. I am claiming that moral character does not
imply consciousness, but rather the capacity to create meaning. Institutions
possess that capacity to an extent exceeding that of any individual.[46] Indeed,
the individuals they employ are merely the vehicles that propagate the
meaning that institutions create and for which they must take responsibility.

The Self-Reflective Museum

Museums express intentions, but not necessarily consciousness of them.
We regularly "read" intentions off of bodies and gestures, and even of

inanimate things, which surely are not conscious of them. In their acquisition, storage, display, and disposal of things, museums consign them to categories of meaning that can endure for generations, sometimes outlasting the objects themselves. The values fixed thereby hover over the objects independently of anyone's individual judgment, setting norms and expectations that become fused with the objects. Generations of users and observers "take in" these congealed intentions as if they belonged to the objects intrinsically. Like size or shape, an object's purpose and value come to appear as perceptual properties that adhere to it objectively, and that appearance is reinforced by conventional museum strategies—placement, security, label copy, docent tours, catalog description, guidebooks, and references in scholarly essays. The museum's role in conferring value is invisible, like that of college survey courses and anthologies, which, in selective teaching, also unconsciously canonize. Just as they exhibit things that are green, six inches long, cast in bronze, or found at Gettysburg, museums also display objects that are deemed great, precious, typical, sacred, foremost or historically important—and thereby naturalize value.[47]

This remarkable power that museums possess to signify and affirm value has recently been exposed by revisionist curatorial and alternative exhibition practices. Expressing their disaffection through the museum's own resources, dissenting curators and critics deliberately reassigned meaning to objects. Though not all oppositional installations have had a political purpose, even the most eccentric of them have shed light on the museum's power to reify. Some exhibitions were created as liberatory expressions of personal autonomy; but others set out explicitly to test the moral fiber of the museum's institutional character.[48]

The installation "Mining the Museum," mounted by artist and freelance curator Fred Wilson in the Maryland Historical Society (April 1992–February 1993), exemplifies this trend. The exhibition is an indictment of a national culture that denies personhood on the basis of race. But it also specifically addresses museums which, by their complicity with that culture, betray their own moral and intellectual vocation. In "Mining the Museum," Wilson culled the museum's collection of artifacts and documents to reveal an episode of American history—slavery—and its perpetuation in racism and bigotry. Moreover, he showed how the entitlement of slaveholders continues to be mirrored in the collection and display practices of contemporary museums. Creatively using some of the museum's own damaged, neglected, obliterated, and carelessly forgotten objects that bespeak a people's dispossession, and juxtaposing these with other items it proudly protects and displays, Wilson produced a truly dialectical exhibition that called the museum forcibly to account.

"Mining the Museum" was not simply a historical retrospective that exposed a shameful practice. The show confronted the museum itself, and the butt of its attack was that institution's character. The exhibition highlighted the contradiction of the museum's principled evasion of responsibility for creating and dissolving values. Wilson charged the museum with a deception, witting or unwitting, that belies its dedication to authenticity. The presumed fact that neither the founders of the Maryland museum nor its current staff took a personal part in the perpetration of slaveholding does not absolve the museum—or them—of moral complicity. By uncritically perpetuating a caste-laden validation of certain material objects from the antebellum period and devaluing others, the museum conjoined its own expert judgment with that of the slaveholders and shared in responsibility for their wrongdoing. Wilson's subversive ways of revealing objects such as shackles and whips, and of delineating persons whom the museum had consigned to oblivion, repositioned them in relation to more conventional treasures and persons.[49]

In demanding of the museum that it face up to its own moral history, Wilson confronted the public as well, questioning its complacent acquiescence to that history. Some detractors from the public found this intrusion upon their subjectivity more immediately offensive than the wrongs of which it reminded them, and there were urgent complaints. But if museums are sites for objects to speak, then, when eloquently displayed, they will speak of past and present wrongs as well as rights. A code of ethics for museums that permits selective silencing is logically, as well as historically, incoherent. Effectively, it short-circuits the communication between generations that the museum is dedicated to preserve. This observation, however, applies to the museum as institution and does not pick out professional derelictions on the part of individual museum workers. The neglect and damage to certain objects and the oversights that Wilson's exhibition brought to light, like the abuse of people to which it witnessed, were not due to conservatorial lapses or the carelessness of some museum staff members. Incomplete provenance or the unconfirmed identity of artists and subjects in these cases were not caused by curatorial incompetence or the inattention of registrars. The "errors" uncovered were not occasioned by individual improprieties at all; they were the sanctioned result of the bad faith of the institution. Individuals other than Fred Wilson might have intervened at some earlier point or protested against practices seen as breaches of professionalism—but they did not, nor would that have been expected of them or rightly understood had they done it. There might have been objections on grounds of personal moral integrity—but there were not, nor would that have been expected. Presumably no comprehensible standards of professional correctness or ethical codes were violated. The moral fault lies elsewhere. It is an institutional wrong, a symptom of bad character or moral blindness in the museum that does not flow from individual misbehavior alone and that cannot be corrected simply by the regulation of professional guidelines.[50]

The Museum as Public Servant

At the time of its mandate to the Committee on Ethics, the AAM also commissioned a task force on museum education. In 1992 this committee issued a report, *Excellence and Equity: Education and the Public Dimension of Museums,* which broadens the reach of the codes of ethics, addressing the museum holistically as an institution with a moral function. This report places public service and education at the center of the museum's mission and diffuses the appeal to highly specialized professionalism that characterized the previous statements. Education, it affirms, is the business of the entire museum and not the province of a discrete staff that is only minimally involved with other aspects of the museum. Furthermore, education is not confined to children and school groups; it reaches out to everyone of every age and every level of society. Acknowledging past tensions between the concerns of collecting, preservation, and research and reaffirming the importance of public access, the report calls for a rededication of the museum that unambiguously embraces diversity and public service. *Public* is here understood pluralistically and democratically, and *service* refers to the museum's educational mission. The educational objective is "to nurture an enlightened, humane citizenry that appreciates the value of knowing about its past, is resourcefully and sensitively engaged in the present, and is determined to shape a future in which many experiences and many points of view are given voice."[51]

Skeptics may find this a rather bland moral commitment, yet it does mark a timid and secular faith in human civility and the possibility of communication. It speaks for the good of human society and declares the museum's investment in and commitment to achieving that good. It promises to strengthen and build on the particular aptitudes of museums, inviting public participation in that endeavor without fear that professional status will thereby be compromised. The statement expresses willingness to assume leadership and to accept responsibility without, in turn, expecting to exercise absolute control. These are hopeful moral declarations. They pledge active fidelity to a good to be realized, rather than passive obedience to a platform of rules and prohibitions. Expressing unsentimentalized regard for the concept of human dignity and for its creative expression, the report affirms its commitment but abjures specific moral entitlements on the museum's part.

A somewhat different tone is taken, approximately at the same moment, by another author, who, with no less moral conviction, remains tenaciously attached to the belief that "collections, and the objects and specimens within them, will always be, and should always be, at the heart of the museum operation." Speaking circumspectly and in a spirit of great humility, Susan Pearce strives to reconcile the current erosion of objectivity and value with her belief that objects nonetheless "constitute social life and . . . help to create value." Museums have a moral part to play in the maintenance of social life, she observes, and in perpetuating the means that give it meaning.

> If we pretend to be what we are not and to possess powers which we do not have we are practising magic, not curatorship, and dishonesty of this kind sins particularly against the central, traditional standards of curators and their kin. Equally, the anarchic and nihilistic post-modern position which denies our human ability to achieve any measure of coherence or satisfaction finds no echo in the ways in which our minds or societies, work. Perhaps if we are willing to live with more uncertainties than our predecessors, and to accept intentions rather than beliefs, we may see our way to behaviour patterns, negotiated rather than imposed, which allow a limited harmony and a provisional agreement. In the process curators have their part, as important mediators of social knowledge and value to society at large.[52]

As I understand what Pearce is saying, she is speaking not of curators alone, nor of other museum workers, but of the intentionality that belongs to the museum—an institution with a life and project of its own, whose ethical character is not reducible to that of individual people. Yet it requires the goodwill of many people to fulfill its mission as public servant.

7.   Museums and Education

In the 1990s, the directive to public service implied an educational obligation. Claudine Brown, then a Smithsonian deputy assistant secretary, exhorted her fellow museum educators to "pose thoughtful questions that speak to the human experience," at the same time reminding them that no one can meet all of the needs of all of the public at any given time.[1] Teaching has always been a struggle to reconcile individuals within a community, and Brown's reminder emphasized the increased breadth and intersecting complexity of the multiple communities that museums now address. At the end of the twentieth century, museums generally accepted the democratic principle that all people have a right not only to a share in the public culture but also to an active part in its formation. This means that museums must listen and respond, as well as speak, to the public—a requirement common to all democratically ordained educational institutions. Museums are historically distinct from the others chiefly because of the central place they have assigned to objects as sources of education.

On one side, object centeredness is sometimes seen as giving the museum a unique educational advantage. Not only are linguistic restrictions bypassed, but objects are held to be "lacquered less with layers of interpretation" than films, history books, television documentaries, photographs, or songs.[2] On the other side are those who argue that, once placed in the museum, the artifact becomes irretrievably a rhetorical object, as thickly lacquered, and with the same discursive layers of interpretation, as any book or film. Indeed, they point out, the sheer placement of objects in a museum expresses the intention to distance ourselves from them—whether to encapsulate the past and put it behind us, as do the many Holocaust museums and memorials that have emerged a half century after the event, or to glorify a memory, as does the "temporary" Seoul museum marking the fiftieth anniversary of the foundation of South Korean nationhood. The artificial preservation of events, processes, and entire eras by means of stories told in assemblages of museumified objects is typically fairly static; however, as we have seen, museums today are moving to a quickened pace, using interactive and theatrical devices to generate experiences.

The displacement of objects by experiences, however, risks compromising the uniqueness of the museum's educational agency. Experiences are notoriously private and unpredictable. But the museum's reliability as educator depends on the ability to modify experience to achieve as great a degree of commonality as objects can represent. If museums have only recently come to terms with being mediators of objects as sites of variable meaning, how much greater is the challenge of battening down what is even more ephemeral? If experiences, not objects, are to be their stock-in-trade, museums must reconsider their claim to educational singularity and ask such deep and perplexing questions as how and why experience is educationally useful in the first place.

That experience is broadening, that we learn from experience, and that there is no teacher like experience are all clichés—but not all experiences are equally educative, and some are downright counterproductive. Moreover, it is not obvious how or what we learn from experience, or what follows from the very private process of undergoing an experience. Experience becomes educationally meaningful only when it ceases to be private and acquires shareable form.[3] The technologies that museums employ to produce experiences are not the same as those that fabricate or display objects. Making museum objects confers public visibility on them; the viewer is caused to accept something as externally given. Making museum experiences must likewise have a public face, although it necessarily turns museumgoers inward upon themselves. Experiencing is a performance, subjectively undergone, with oneself as audience. Until that experience flows outward toward a common domain, it has no more educational efficacy than uninterpreted objects do.

Learning is the means by which infants and strangers are brought into a public sphere, where they join others in common discourse. Private experience is often a retreat from that realm. Why then should museums labor to produce something that appears to be regressively isolating and potentially alienating? The answer is drawn, on one hand, from a residual faith in the communality of objects, and, on the other, from a yearning for the unity of human nature. Underlying the promise of experiential communion, and despite the appeal to "diverse" audiences, the epistemological conviction remains strong—in museums as elsewhere—that ultimately there is one truth and that a single (and well-controlled) stimulus will recall it. Thus some of the glory of objective reality, the vindication bestowed by belonging to the public sphere, overflows onto the secluded experience that is intensely yours or mine. Even as we stand, side by side, simultaneously undergoing our separate experiences, "shaped" by a museum environment, we are prompted to carry away the judgment of a "same" and publicly acknowledged reality. This is the object to be learned.

Learning from Objects

Exposure alone is rarely sufficient to guarantee that anyone will experience an object in a particular way or derive a predictable idea from it, but objects never are experienced in isolation. Whether in the world or in a museum, they are presented in a context, shaped by a culture, and whoever experiences them does so through a complex, learned, assimilative process. Cultures teach their members how to experience and understand objects informally, through use. Users will also bring their personal history to experience, but that too is framed within a culture. Certain formal sciences study cultural artifacts from a "depersonalized" vantage that detaches the objects from their primary users. Traditional museums have favored this perspective without recognizing that it also represents a type of cultural "use" and a community of users at one remove from the culture of the primary users. As sites for the reexperience of objects, museums generate a context unlike that of the primary user, but tangential to it. Thus to learn from museums, one must become acculturated to them and to the second-order competence they instill. Sometimes called "museum literacy," that competence includes the ability to "read objects" and also to benefit from all of the additional, higher-order physical and programmatic services that museums are capable of providing.[4]

The legibility of objects is the professional domain of researchers of material culture. Their decodings parallel the accounts extracted by historians of verbal documents. Historians of objects have developed concepts and methodologies for systematic classification and typological analysis that are now everywhere accepted as authentic historiography. Obviously, things are as semiologically thick as words, and therefore museum collections are important research sites. Proponents of the teaching of museum literacy regard their subject as a means of understanding human interactions on a very broad scale: "Museum literacy, at its core," writes Thomas J. Schlereth, an outstanding scholar in the field of material culture, "is but another form of human literacy, another mode of knowing, another grammar of understanding for reading others and ourselves."⁵ Material culture study is thus a humanistic discipline, and Schlereth recommends that museums teach the public how to transform artifacts into legible objects that hold personal significance. To do this would require museums to take visitors behind the scenes, effectively initiating them into the work of the museum professional, much as a college professor guides students through a disciplinary apprenticeship. Although such intensive training would certainly relieve their museum illiteracy, most people are not interested in such concentrated learning. People do not visit museums to become museum professionals, and few regard the ability to decipher museum objects and artifacts as an end in itself. If museums are to be educational, they must help visitors apply what can be experienced in the museum to the world outside.

The presumption on the part of museums that they teach people "to see" has mystified those who take "seeing" simplistically, as a normal consequence of looking. It is true that visible things do not communicate an unambiguous tale. Learning to interpret them is as necessary an ability for everyone as learning how to use numbers or how to speak and listen, but it is far less commonly recognized. Formal schooling works largely with symbolic frameworks that can be taught abstractly and are easily transferable, or at least the pedagogic procedures for generalizing them are well in place. We learn about things at a distance, through mediating systems that have no inherent location and can be reproduced at will—in books, television, lectures. The written or spoken word and the rules of transmission will suffice. Of course museums also use these technologies, but in addition, as specialists in the care and exhibition of objects, museums put people immediately in the presence of things, to learn from or through them. "Reading" things assumes a degree of particularity and requires a personal encounter with them. That personal encounter is the ground of an experience, and museums bank on it to fulfill their educational promise.

Objects are a resource for individual reflection that institutions can influence but cannot entirely control. To illustrate with an experience of my own: Some years ago, I visited an exhibition of fabric production in colonial America at a New England textile museum. With a shock of understanding, I "saw" how domestic labor claimed every member of the family, giving useful tasks even to three-year-olds and solidifying the family's sense of mutual dependency and responsibility. On the same occasion I "saw," through examination of the machinery, how nineteenth-century industrialism radically transformed the nature of work, rendering it rational rather than simply replicative of human practice, and how subordinate concerns, such as the profitable disposition of waste products, were introduced by this rationalization. At that point, the demands of labor exceeded the capacities of small children, forcing a separation of families into workplace and domestic functions. I now remember these as thrilling and alarming discoveries, enhanced by the fact that they felt like mine alone. That they were not the lessons the museum intended for me to learn was evident from the auxiliary signage that was confined to describing the techniques of clothmaking. Perhaps by studying conventional texts on industrial history, I could have learned the social and economic history I had extracted, but I doubt the impression would have been made so indelibly. In this case, I believe, I learned directly from the experience stimulated by the museum objects. There is no doubt that the museum was responsible for the collection and arrangement of those objects, but it did not foreordain the particular character of my experience. If anything, my educational "insight" was achieved despite the experience intended by the museum's exhibition program.[6]

From direct experience of immediately sensible properties of objects, with the help of suggestive display, one can infer the implied causal means of production, functional value, social purpose, cultural environments, historical development, stylistic influences, and symbolic significance and also make comparisons with possible alternative constructions.[7] Not all artifacts are equally interpretable or readable on the same scale, and rare indeed is the museum exhibition that would try to address all parameters at once. Nevertheless, learning theorists and environmental psychologists have concluded that certain conceptual and developmental commonalities do exist and that knowledge of these would enable museums to shepherd the experience of their audience to achieve some degree of uniformity.

Clinical observation of museum visitors has shown that neither adults nor children readily give up their naive preconceptions about the world.[8] We tend to reinforce what we think we already know or want to believe. Another type of research on cognition describes different intelligence types, which appear in variable configurations in different individuals. This typology leads to distinct models of problem-solving and learning styles, and the researchers recommend museums as ideal sites for experimenting with individually centered learning paradigms.[9]

Individual cognitive difference must certainly account for some perceptual dissimilarities, but acculturated class, race, and gender differences constitute more formidable grounds for variation in people's perceptual judgments. Museum collection and exhibition is historically associated with a particular culture and with an epistemology that is far from universal. Members of the public who do not share the museum's epistemic point of departure may be repelled by an invitation to partake in its practice of spectatorship. What appears as benign collegiality to the host may seem a paternalistic act of condescension to the guest, who may feel compromised by the very suggestion of complicity with it. Urging radical deconstruction of the museum and its philosophical presuppositions, a group of irreverent explorers has taken a hard look at the epistemology of collection and its institutions. Citing Virginia Woolf's *Three Guineas,* one critic advises: "Let us never cease from thinking—what is this 'civilization' in which we find ourselves? What are these ceremonies and why should we take part in them? What are these professions and why should we make money out of them?"[10]

Applying that critique to the museum and to its pedagogy suggests that promoting scientifically supported and methodologically neat "literacy" also imports social codes and strategies, which enshrine the values of the culture that gave birth to the museum. Tools dispensed for empowerment may not, in fact, liberate their recipients but instead indoctrinate them into tool-using subservience—all the more opaquely for the apparent transparency of the tools. This charge cuts to the very identity of the traditional museum and raises the question of the relation between teaching and authority.

A comparatively new museum model, the "ecomuseum," aims to overcome the cult of expertise and exclusion that the epistemology of objectivity engenders. Categorized as a "minority" museum, this type of museum is actually no more parochially localized in time and space than other museums, but it explicitly does away with universal claims and overtly focuses on the local society and its culture:

> Objects here are family and community memorabilia. . . . In a local museum, "here" matters. Either one has traveled to get here, or one already lives here and recognizes an intimate heritage. Of course, every museum is a local museum: the Louvre is Parisian, the Metropolitan a characteristically New York establishment. But while the major museums reflect

their city and region, they aspire to transcend this specificity, to represent a national, international, or human heritage.[11]

Ecomuseums are, more or less, community centers:

> Rather than serving as a storehouse or a temple, both of which isolate objects from ordinary people and require professional assistance for access and understanding, an ecomuseum recognizes the importance of culture in the development of self-identity and its role in helping a community adjust to rapid change. The ecomuseum thus becomes a tool for the economic, social, and political growth and development of the society from which it springs.[12]

This model rejects the typical pedagogic assumption that every museum visitor is an untutored interpreter. It effectively removes the gap between "inside" and "outside" the museum that the proposal to teach "literacy" implies. The local museumgoer is considered a co-owner, rather than a visitor, and is a stakeholder in the institution's success. Some minority museums profit from their interdependency by trading technical workshops in "outsider skills" for dialogue that elicits hidden cultural knowledge from within the community. Attendees learn how to be the curators of their own stories, and teaching and learning take place nonhierarchically among all the members of the community. Exhibitions grow organically from small beginnings as their development jogs memories and invites further amplification by additional community members. Such "dialogue-driven" museums are still relatively scarce, but they are beginning to appear, especially in social communities that, denied a voice in traditional museums, figure frequently there as objects to be studied.

New York's Chinatown History Museum is a good example. John Kuo Wei Tchen, its director, has adapted techniques of teaching literacy, developed by the Brazilian educator Paolo Friere, to the museum's purposes. In 1984, this museum, collaborating with the New York State Museum, mounted a bilingual exhibition: "The Eight Pound Livelihood: A History of Chinese Laundry Workers in America." The exhibit was developed through interviews, community workshops, and dialogues "resonant with local individuals' personal experience." It helped American-born children understand their Chinese-born parents and enabled ethnic Chinese with very different backgrounds to respect one another's histories. It produced knowledge from a variety of standpoints, including Chinese and non-Chinese interpretations. Reflecting on what is to be learned from exhibits such as this one, the director anticipated profound changes in museum structure that would empower people to smooth the transition from past to present and improve their lives in the multiple worlds they inhabit.[13]

The Education Bandwagon

Education has always been everybody's business, but the commodification of education in recent decades has given that concept new significance. Education has become truly big business, and museums are more than ever in the position of competing, as well as collaborating, with other institutions to reach the hearts, minds, ears, and pocketbooks of the public. Legislation in 1965, under the Johnson administration, mandated equal educational opportunity, supplementary educational services, and special education for the disadvantaged, which put new burdens on public schools to develop new programs.[14] School systems turned to museums for help in designing alternative procedures that would enrich formal teaching curricula appropriately. Leaders of various illustrious cultural institutions were brought together to reflect on fundamental pedagogic questions as well as specific, fundable proposals. Their discussions ranged over the history of museum pedagogy, the preeminence of artifacts over documentary evidence, the nature of research, the comparative merits of art and science, the rewards of individual versus group visits to museums, and, finally, the nature and purpose of education.[15] A consensus emerged, favorable to government support of museums and to the fostering of collaboration between museums and institutions of formal education at all levels, as well as among museums themselves. In a decade of optimism new museums sprang up throughout North America, and old museums underwent drastic restructuring and revitalization. The U.S. government's creation of the National Endowment for the Arts and National Endowment for the Humanities (NEA and NEH), with their subsidiary state arts councils, and the eventual establishment in 1976 of the Institute for Museum Services under the Museum Services Act, gave legal substance to the public affirmation of museums' educational potential.[16]

Within museums, professionalism flourished. Teachers enjoyed a newfound respectability. Graduate certification programs to prepare museum educators were linked to recently founded museum studies institutions, and a journal for museum educators, *Roundtable Reports,* was launched in 1973.[17] Emerging from the shadows of what had been a fairly marginal appendage to the museum's chief occupations, museum educators suddenly were compelled to play an increasingly self-conscious part in a broad-based, knowledge-producing system. New governmental and foundation guidelines pronounced education to be the core of the museum's identity, and museums had to justify their existence to prospective funding agencies by proposing imaginative educational programs.[18] By the mid-1980s, education was cautiously called the "spirit" of the museum, and just a few years later, an internally appointed committee of the AAM admonished museums that they "can no longer confine themselves simply to preservation, scholarship, and exhibitions independent of the social context in which they exist. They must recognize that . . . the public dimension of museums leads them to perform the public service of education . . . in its broadest sense to include exploration, study, observation, critical thinking, contemplation, and dialogue."[19]

Rethinking Education

Perhaps the most significant change that had occurred was not in the nature of museums, but in the concept of education. Educators and theorists of education in the late 1960s were beginning to take a radical turn away from a didactic system of pedagogy, the "banking model" of deposit and investment that seemed to have been legislated by behaviorism and a positivistic epistemology. According to the new model, teachers were not expected to impart knowledge to students, filling them as empty vessels; but, more modestly, to expose students to ideas and to stand by as auxiliaries to the process of their assimilation. This approach to education was not entirely innovative, having been advocated many times over in the past— by, among others, Jean Jacques Rousseau in the eighteenth century and Maria Montessori and John Dewey at the beginning of the twentieth. Nevertheless, a change was in the air in the 1960s, which focused on people and process rather than on fixed subject matter and which was to expand educational outreach in terms of both the human and the nonhuman resources that it embraced. In this regard a closer affiliation of schools and museums seemed worth pursuing.

In museums, the change was largely a shift in emphasis. The Smithsonian Institution itself had been founded in compliance with the ambiguous injunction of its benefactor, James Smithson, to effect "the increase and diffusion of knowledge among men."[20] Early disputes among its appointed leaders had been unable to resolve whether this was an exhortation to private research and scholarship or whether it mandated a more public program of collection and dissemination.[21] The idea that museums have a responsibility to educate the general public and not just a privileged few was deeply embedded in the American museum movement from its earliest origins. But several presumptions were entailed in that judgment, most notably the unchallenged asymmetry in the authority relationship between teacher and pupil.

The pious belief that art and culture are uplifting needed no defense in the nineteenth century. Educators today are more cautious in asserting that "Our work is good for people," although they still cherish the scaled-back conviction that "in teaching people discernment, museum educators are . . . revealing how decisions about what is good [in art] are made . . . so that [people] can eventually make informed decisions for themselves."[22] The sloganlike refrain repeating contemporary museums' commitment to "public service" hardly conveys the confused moral, political, and spiritual conviction that an earlier dedication to educational "upliftment" represented. Today's concern is more pragmatic if no less confused. It centers on whether or how museum exposure links visitors to ideas and events, and whether or how museums are able to cultivate taste, discrimination, judgment, and sensibility.

A view of museum education that still commands respect was succinctly articulated by George Brown Goode, third secretary of the Smithsonian Institution, who held that "an efficient educational museum may be described as a collection of instructive labels, each illustrated by a well-selected specimen."[23] A very different and equally confident view, ardently supported by Sherman E. Lee, former director of the Cleveland Museum of Art, prizes aesthetics more than efficiency. Lee describes the museum as "a living source of original visual knowledge, available to all, which must preserve so long as possible those images worth preserving so that the still living art of the immediate and distant past will remain visible."[24] The educational innovators of the late 1960s and 1970s were less certain of the universality of any standard, perceptual or intellectual. Under the influence of psychologists Jean Piaget, L. V. Vigotsky, and Jerome Bruner, and some pragmatically inspired curriculum reform movements in England and the United States, these midcentury educators defended the "discovery method" of learning and teaching. Central to this approach is the idea that learning is a self-directed activity of exploration and invention, whereby the learner autonomously arrives at desired conclusions. The teacher's job is to create situations in which learning can take place.[25] Obviously this is not as simple as it appears, for the mere provision of schoolrooms and books is not enough, and not all discoveries are of equal merit. Learners do not all begin at the same place and certainly do not begin with a mental blank slate. They come, whether as children or adults, with distinct capacities, cultural formation, and interests. Moreover, the discoveries they make, like my own in the textile museum, follow cognitive dispositions shaped by the learner's concrete history and experience.[26] In order to ensure educational success, schools and museums are inclined to stack the deck, overcontrolling the range of possible discoveries so that what observers find will actually illustrate what they were intended to see. Although it assigns a central educative role to the learner's experience, the discovery method may, therefore, hark back covertly and in no less patronizing fashion to the undisguised didacticism endorsed by George Brown Goode.

Behind this educational model, the foundationalist conviction remains that learners will come, in time and with the help of social negotiation, to solutions that are correct. "Discovery" implies that there are real truths or facts to be discovered, and the method ensures that, upon discovering them, students will be gratified with a sense of ownership. In an environment promoting "relevance" in teaching and personal responsibility for learning, educators were less alarmed by student ignorance, which is a normal condition, than by the decline of student interest in learning. Faced with the prevalence of boredom or—a greater evil—students' passive and passionless acceptance of ready-made answers, teachers wanted to animate student thinking. Discovery connotes an element of excitement. Even if what is discovered is neither original nor new, there is the thrill of finding it on one's own, and educators expected that this would be sufficient motivation for learning. In advocating "minds-on" learning, they did not inculcate the transmission of exact data from one terminal to another, but something less precise. The radical deconstruction of knowledge was also not what most of them had in mind. Especially the scientists among them, many of whom were pioneers in the application of the discovery method, wanted nothing more than to awaken people's curiosity and natural intelligence, to promote sound investigative methodology, and to encourage the exercise of independent judgment—conditions they regarded as primary necessities for the advancement of science.[27]

The multilayered, object-rich museum seemed an ideal environment in which to engender discovery experiences. Precisely because the rules of managing experience were unwritten, and the authoritarian associations with education could be evaded, a museum was an excellent venue in which self-initiated learning could take place. Museums were, after all, tiny corners of the world. They had been repositories in which the things of the world were kept; now they would disseminate safe and illuminating experience of them. Joining the movement that was turning schools into "learning centers," museums were to become "cultural centers," and both institutions were dedicated to creating an environment for personal growth and social interaction. Whereas the museum had the means to stimulate spontaneous curiosity, schools could maintain the regularity and discipline that fruit-bearing research demands. It seemed like a happy marriage.

But old strictures are not easily shaken off, and the disciplinarian, schoolmarm image of the teacher remained an obstacle to full collaboration. Traditional patterns of authority within museums, coupled with a heroic representation of scholarly research, reinforced a pedestrian vision of "mere" teaching as a lesser goal and inhibited the acceptance of educators as equals in museums. Education in the 1960s was still a poorly paid, low-status occupation whose practitioners were mostly women. Regardless of their good works, teachers were seen as solemn handmaidens or technicians, whose job, befitting their capacity, was to dispense watered-down lessons to the "nonspecialist" public.

To the curatorial hierarchy, and therefore to most museum directors who came from its ranks, education was not a substantive discipline. It did not entail expertise in a selected area of history, science, or art history, and it seemed to call for only that general, motherly instinct that is normally held in contempt in professional circles. Ironically, those who were most vociferous in their insistence that the entire museum is educational in its nature, were often most dismissive of educators as "adjuncts" to the museum staff.[28] Clearly a change in attitude would be necessary before genuine cooperation could take place between schools and museums.

Integrating Education into the Museum Hierarchy

As both museums and schools began to adapt to a "learner-centered" philosophy, they turned for theoretical support to findings from the social sciences. If education is not simply the delivery of subject matter but is a multitermed form of communication, then disciplinary expertise is not sufficient preparation for teaching, and those who know most about a field are not necessarily the best teachers of it. Behavioral and cognitive psychology, sociology, and developmental studies must help to explain how learning takes place. What happens to the learner became a basic concern of curriculum planners in schools and of audience surveyors in museums. In addition to making quantitative and demographic studies of who comes to

museums, evaluators throughout the 1970s tested and measured public response to exhibits and struggled to describe the phenomenology of the educational events that happen there.[29] Top priority was still assigned to
delivery of a message, but there was growing interest in the integrity of its
reception.

Representing themselves as "advocates" of students and museum visitors, educators lined up against the partisans of subject matter and objects. Some defended this shift to a human-centered focus of attention as
a social revolution, and it surely was an intellectual one. It shifted weight
away from content and from programmed learning, repetition, and inquiry driven by external reward, all of which ignore the identity of the
learner. It recognized the learner, not as empty receptacle, but as an agent
voluntarily engaged in self-transformation. Directing attention to the interest of the learner coincided with the aims of the proponents of the discovery method, but also, to a degree, with a consumer-based market
model whose research is designed to create a delivery system that "gives
clients what they want."

Audience development is only circumstantially related to market development, and what they have in common formally—point-to-point transmission—is overshadowed by their difference in goals. Communication
theory shares with the theory of marketing an interest in transmitting a message efficiently from a source to a receiver. Successful reception is measured
by appropriate behavior on the receiver's part—buying in the case of con-
sumers and learning in that of students. The reaction of students to teaching
and of potential buyers to product promotion merits comparative study;
teachers and manufacturers are equally likely to perform more effectively if
they understand the needs of the addressee. Persuasion is an element of both
situations, but whereas profit is the incentive of the market, teaching is
guided by a more nebulous aim. Moreover, the evidence of learning is
harder to assess than that of purchasing. Especially in museums, where no
transaction such as submitting homework or passing tests takes place, the
behavioral counterpart of learning is obscure. As Frank Oppenheimer,
founder of the Exploratorium, often remarked, "Nobody flunks museums." Indeed, nobody does, but in the absence of a concept of failure, there
is also no meaningful measure of success.

Confusion regarding the nature and importance of different segments
of the educational process led to their theoretical segregation. "Learning,"
said one educator, "is not the product of teaching."[30] His statement could
be understood as an aphoristic denunciation of teachers, snidely excusing
museum administrators' exclusion of educators from the arenas of power

and influence.[31] But it might also be taken, and probably was intended, in a broad philosophical sense, to mean that learning is essentially a self-activated process that continues throughout life and throughout the reconstruction of one's own experience. Museums do have much to offer if learning is taken in this light, for they afford ample opportunity for reconstruction of experience.

Which of these positions might have been on the minds of the members of the AAM-appointed Commission on Museums for a New Century is uncertain, but they devoted an entire chapter of their 1984 report to the topic of education. The commission, sponsored by a number of foundations, corporations, and museums, undertook to "study and clarify the role of museums in American society, their obligations to preserve and interpret our cultural and natural heritage, and their responsibilities to an ever-broadening audience."[32] Their report drew attention to confusion over the "learning function" of museums and attributed it to a variety of factors, significantly including the absence in museums of the programmatic trappings of the formal teaching institutions. They pointed also to the well-known "tension of values inherent in the very mission of museums," which pits the concerns of preservation against the demands of public access. Agreeing in principle on the museum's duty of public service, they chose to speak of "learning" rather than "education," to divert attention away from a narrow, conventional understanding of that word and to "encourage museum professionals to see learning as a museumwide endeavor."

In addition to expanding the general concept of learning in museums, the AAM's commission worried about the increasing professionalism of museum education and the risk of its "intellectual isolation . . . from exhibitions, research and other museum activities." The report emphasized the "spontaneous, individualized" process of learning yet warned against "imposing" it on visitors. Innovatively placing educational responsibility on curators, the report required that their graduate education ensure that they have "a full understanding of the public side of their responsibilities." The apparent intention of this remark was to underscore the pedagogic effect of exhibition and to bolster that with good visitor experience. Implicitly, this was a step toward generalizing the "learning function," by removing it from the exclusive control of "teachers" and reconceiving it as the obligation of the entire staff—indeed, the mission of the museum as a whole. Effectively, this was a way of reconceptualizing curatorship. Exhibition, never its primary task, had been second to the production of catalogs and scholarly monographs. Whatever momentary rewards an exhibition's public acclaim might bring, these ultimately would be outweighed by more

permanent cultural contributions. The short-term interpretation of exhibitions to the public could, therefore, be consigned to the allegedly lesser skills
of the museum's educational staff.

For their part, the educators were well aware of the gap in communication between the curatorial point of view and that of the visiting public
and knew themselves to be its mediators. Consequently, they reacted with
some alarm to the sanguine assertions of the AAM commission that
seemed to diminish their importance and even to characterize their work
as somewhat pernicious. A group of educators published a response that
combined vigorous protest with an imaginative reconstrual of the commission's findings. Taking to heart the recommendation that learning be
fully integrated into all museum activities, the educators concluded that,
far from forcing them to the sidelines, the report was a call to action. Educators must be part of all the museum's internal operational structures,
as well as planning and executing its public programs and exhibitions.
This, they affirmed, demanded of them the mastery of "an armada of
skills and knowledge," and they urged museum educators to hone and
refine a professional identity, thoroughly attuned to that defined by the
museum's mission and in harmony with the ambitious spirit of the commission's recommendations.[33]

Encouraged by a statement of professional standards made by the International Council of Museums (ICOM) in 1987, and by the AAM's publication of *Museum Ethics,* museum educators mobilized themselves nationally
to devise their own statement, *Professional Standards for Museum Education.*[34] In it, they allied themselves with the generalized conception of education that the 1984 commission had proposed and addressed, inclusively:
"All museum professionals, paraprofessionals, and volunteers who are involved in helping visitors have an enriching experience in the museum."
The statement pledged to uphold the traditional values of the museum—
with deference to the integrity, authenticity, preservation, and quality of the
objects—but designated the educator's unique professional priority to be
the presentation and interpretation of the museum's collections to the public. The statement unilaterally terminated subordination to curatorial authority and declared the first responsibility of educators to serve the public
as "advocates for museum audiences." In the language of the document,
"audience advocacy" means understanding its diversity and its needs, a
project that entails cultural sophistication as well as the study of psychological processes and learning theory. At the same time, educators must know
their museum's collections and be informed in the history, theory, or practice of the relevant fields of study. Adopting the metaphor of building

bridges, they placed themselves between the visitors' expectations and those expectations "that emanate from a museum's collection." To adjust one to the other, they must collaborate *as equals* with other members of the museum staff and outside communities, and must play a responsible part in the original planning of exhibitions and programs through which the museum introduces its collections to the public.

The educators' statement was a bold and mature repudiation of their "ugly duckling" segregation and a bid for comprehensive engagement with all facets of the museum's operation. Their effort and their well-made arguments did meet with some success as, increasingly, museums abandoned hierarchical exhibition strategies and switched to a team approach to exhibition making. Educators, along with curators, designers, professional evaluators, and specialists of various types, are now routinely a part of the exhibit development process, and it is widely understood that "informal education" is the chief business of the museum.[35] Educators have also advanced their political presence within the museum structure. Members of their ranks now occupy important administrative positions, serve on boards of trustees, and often represent the museum officially to the world outside.[36]

Substantive Conflict: The Getty Report

Remarkably, a study completed two years after the AAM commission's report, *Museums for a New Century,* reflects little acquaintance with the work these educators had done. Two academic art educators, Elliot W. Eisner and Stephen M. Dobbs, published a report, *The Uncertain Profession: Observations on the State of Museum Education in Twenty American Art Museums,* which had been commissioned by the J. Paul Getty Center for Education in the Arts to examine "how the potential of museum educators might be more fully realized."[37] The authors interviewed only the directors and chief educational officers of twenty art museums across the United States. Although their observations were limited, they drew some general conclusions about museum education and made recommendations that stirred controversy throughout the profession. Eisner's and Dobbs's initial observation was that little consensus exists among museum professionals regarding the basic aims of museum education. Although there were differences between the museums they examined, they attributed the confusion they found to a lack of understanding of the meaning of education *tout court.* They had little sympathy with the view that merely shining a light on a painting was an "educational event," and they derided descriptions of programs that simply cast more light on a larger scale. They expected to find clear classifications of goals and taxonomies of functions of museum education, but instead they found unresolved and conflicting pressures to dispense knowledge of art history, on the one hand, and on the other, to help museumgoers experience works of art meaningfully. Where they looked for a theoretical foundation of an intellectual discipline, they saw only practical strategies conceived in haste to meet current necessities.

Taken aback by the philosophical discord and bitter hostility they found between curators and museum educators, Eisner and Dobbs urged their conciliation. Their own patronizing tone, however, and the limited reach of their interviews only to upper staff echelons did little to enhance that alliance. They scolded museum administrators for their paucity of new, imaginative ideas, without questioning their budgetary allocations, their preferential treatment of donors, or their tendency to let education departments struggle and starve. They blandly approved thematic contextualizations of artworks as if this intensely disputed deviation from modernist art-historical procedure had never before been seriously proposed and awaited only the Getty team's happy discovery. Observing a gap between "community interest" and the museum's professed dedication to public service, they charged the museum with its lack of relationship to the educational resources and institutions outside the museum and remarked on the limited contact between museum educators and the officials who shape the museum's external policy. It is difficult to accept the credulity with which Eisner and Dobbs endorsed the "social vision" expressed in a statement by one museum director whom they cite: "The role of the museum is to expand the elite"; or that of another: "I think we are a nonpolitical institution that can be involved in social change. Fundamentally our museum is an institution which is involved with the redistribution of wealth, not only cash wealth, but the wealth of ideas." The dissemination of sentiments such as these, vapid at best, and surely paradoxical, nevertheless galvanized museum educators once again to seriously examine the place of museums in American education and to press for the role of museum educators in realizing it.

Eisner and Dobbs left their initial questions unanswered. More than a decade later, some of the same confusions about education in museums persist. There is still uncertainty about what a museum can do to help works of art (and all museum exhibits) "live in the experience of those who encounter them." Conflicting research studies have found that some visitors reject "learning" in museums altogether. They want docents and explainers (in science centers) to "facilitate understanding of the exhibits" but not to "teach" them. According to one study, visitors come to museums to "have fun," and whatever learning takes place, they believe, is incidental and not the result of didactic explanations on the part of museum staff.[38] Another study finds that some visitors do come to learn. Learning, it concludes, is but one of several types of experiences that people expect to have in museums.[39] This unclearness on the part of visitors is duplicated by museum educators, who are sometimes perplexed by their clients' incidental or "wildcat" learning of things unrelated to the explicit purpose of exhibits. Regrettably, self-initiated learning forays by imaginative visitors are seen as a failure of an exhibition's objectives. Thus, according to a report in the *Boston Globe,* some staff members of the Boston Science Museum were displeased to find a visitor "misusing" an exhibit designed to replicate Galileo's famous experiment atop the Leaning Tower of Pisa. Rather than using the exhibit's machinery to test the rate of descent of falling bodies, a student applied it to measure his own reaction speed. Instead of applauding his resourcefulness, the museum chose to consider its exhibit a failure because the visitor had not employed it in the manner intended.[40]

The attempt to characterize what museum education is or should be exposes several sources of disagreement. What is to be taught, how, and by whom—if anyone—marks different priorities held by distinct factions within the museum profession. The curatorial and administrative functions, especially of art museums, were traditionally coordinated with the acquisition and ownership of highly prized objects, and this linkage was the basis of the museum's social prestige. The museum and by extension its staff were a public surrogate, a collective stand-in for private ownership of valuable property. Education pertaining to that property was necessarily collection centered and expository.

The task that now befalls the educator, as described by Danielle Rice, is to dilate that center and displace the system that values art as property with one that values ideas. The educator has the moral duty, she says, to "navigate through institutional contradictions in order to bridge the gaps between the value systems of the scholars who collect and exhibit art and those of the visitors who come to the museum to look at and perhaps to learn about art."[41] Here again, the educators' bridging role in a community is cited, but the metaphor is given a new twist. Rice points to qualitatively distinct value systems structurally embedded in art and in the museum's history. The diversity of these systems, she believes, rather than the unequal reservoirs of scholarly and visitor knowledge, is the motive power of museum learning. Rice's model of the museum's educational transaction emphasizes the mutability of value. Ideally, museums are well placed to reveal the human value systems that underlie different institutional structures, she believes, even where these are ill assorted or incommensurable. Precisely because of the multitude and variety of their collections and the incredible array of ideas they express, museums are in a position to open people's minds and help them overcome the impoverishing tendency "to assume that everyone else sees and thinks exactly the same way they do." And precisely because of that same multitude and variety, the plurality of visitor reactions to museums should be taken optimistically as a sign of vitality.

The learning that Rice proposes is not of fixed subject matter, but of an aptitude for discernment and judgment. It is an aesthetic skill, experientially based, whose focus is on people, not things; yet things serve as scaffolds on which judgments by and of people are made. Since its origin and end lie in people, experienced-based learning cannot be contained within the museum: nor should it be. Learning in museums opens the door to the world outside the museum.

Museums are probing the boundary between learning that is "fun" and fun that is "merely" entertainment. Between them lies the grotesque hybrid, "edutainment," which is neither. We may conclude that museums are neither a footnote to formal education nor wholly independent of it. Their mission should be distinctly their own. Long absorbed with the embodiment of value in things, museums are now seeking fresh ways of expressing value and transmitting it in nonmaterial constructions. Effectively, museums are places for learning to learn. They teach us to treasure experience, and though experiences are not collectible treasures, it may be that the experience of learning is what museums now curate and preserve.

8. The Aesthetic Dimension of Museums

We have good reason to look to the discipline of aesthetic theory for help in understanding the shift to the subjective that museums are undergoing. Traditional philosophical aesthetics has made a parallel turn from the study of objective beauty to an interest in subjective experience. Ancient philosophers believed that Beauty exists apart from human judgment. They sought intellectual understanding of the conditions of Beauty, much as scientists aimed to understand the laws of nature, whose presence was evident in the world's phenomena. As long ago as the eighteenth century, however, aesthetic theory turned first to the perceptual basis of aesthetic enjoyment, and then to the phenomenology of feeling and subjective gratification. Contemporary aesthetic theorists tend to differentiate between theories of art and theories of the aesthetic, but both types of theory examine a particular sort of experience and the conditions under which it occurs. Although aesthetics is closely related to other branches of philosophical thought, especially those pertaining to value, it is unique in its preeminent focus on the immediate, felt quality of experiences, and their intrinsic worth.

Aesthetic theory presupposes aesthetic awareness and the capacity for aesthetic enjoyment. The same capacity is implicit in the very notion of a museum, of whatever variety. The museum's ambiguous tradition of passionately studious attention and solicitude for "selected lumps of the physical world" discloses an attitude that combines selfless absorption with intensely personal pleasure. As a broker of such satisfactions in a world of things, the museum is conceptually bound and beholden to aesthetic theory.[1]

We have observed the lability of things in museums. Their multiple objectifications would be of little interest, however, if the resulting experience were not intrinsically appealing.[2] Unless objects or the act of collecting them delighted someone at some time, they would never have been assembled at all.[3] This is not to deny that their initial valuation may have been for other reasons, but as collectibles, museum objects are liberated from whatever primary function gave them birth and are released into a new life.[4] Aesthetic interest inducts an object into a realm of privileged inutility. To arrive in a museum, an object must, at least once, have fascinated someone sufficiently to cause them to contemplate it apart from its immediate context. It does not follow that every item found in a museum will continue to please forever or that it can have no further use, but, having become a "museum object," the item is launched onto a slope of meaning transformations that could go on metamorphosing indefinitely.[5]

In the museum the objects enter a new environment where among their significant reference points are other museum objects, and henceforth they are part of a new historical and ecological system. They are newly surrounded by friendly and hostile elements that affect experience of them and therefore modify their identity. The sheer accumulation of objects in one place and their simultaneous exposition in the absence of formerly "normalizing" conditions forces them into novel interactions. Some critics despise the "disengaging" and "neutralizing" effect of these displacements; others complain of antagonisms evoked among the objects when coerced into "promiscuous proximity." In fact, their proximity is almost never coincidental. However diverse the items in a collection may appear to be, and however surreal their juxtaposition, they are bound by someone's selective system, which the museum enforces by aesthetic means.[6]

The museum's authority, in turn, depends upon the willing acquiescence of experiencers—visitors, staff, scholars, connoisseurs—who simultaneously shape and are shaped by that same authority. Their subjective experience implicates museumgoers in forging the identity of the objects that they observe within a restricted circle of permitted interpretations. The museum provides a framework that legitimizes as it aestheticizes multiple understandings of things in the world.

Let us not underestimate the aesthetic efficacy of the museum. We live in pragmatic times that stress the functional, including the symbolic and the evidentiary. Authority depends on more than a pretty face, but unless museums satisfy aesthetic interest, their inconvenience and the high cost

of maintaining them are likely to outweigh the value of their public service.[7] Museums fix structures of value presentationally, and the first line
of presentation is aesthetic—through architecture, the arrangement of in-
terior spaces, the dress and demeanor of museum staff, the display of mer-
chandise and restaurant choices, and, above all, the selection and
disposition of objects for display. The consistency of a museum's material
presentation and the enclaves of contrast and agreement it fosters are conveyed aesthetically through clues initially accessible to perception, even
where they are unintelligible to thought.[8]

The Paradigm of the Work of Art and the Art Museum

Although aesthetic concern is manifest in all museums, most do not advertise their aesthetic objective as an end in itself. The gratuitous pleasure they
evoke is enlisted in the service of social and intellectual purposes. Only art
museums are sometimes singled out as having no other function than aesthetic gratification, a role often mystified in spiritual or quasi-religious
terms. It is puzzling that these anomalous latecomers upon the museum
scene should have so captured the common understanding that art museums have now become iconic. The art museum, exalted as archetypal pro-
vider of aesthetic experience, is emblematic of all museums, just as the
work of art has come to stand for the entire category of all objects that
afford aesthetic satisfaction.[9]

In my estimation, the conflation of all museums to a single paradigm is
misguided and does a disservice to all of them. Assimilation to the model
of the art museum misconstrues the significance of aesthetic experience
and misreads its generality. Every museum is effectively coerced by that
confusion to aspire to the experiential goals of the art museum and to
measure its own success in terms of inappropriate aesthetic values. The
paradigmatic role assignment, moreover, reflects badly on the art museum
as well, because it too is compelled to modify itself in a desacralizing spirit
of compromise.[10] In order to understand how the art museum came to exercise such authority, we need to examine the somewhat circular process
by which certain objects have been sanctified as "works of art" and then,
by a philosophical sleight of hand, allowed to serve as standards for all
aesthetic attribution.[11] Museums play a major role in this process.

The philosopher Monroe Beardsley suggested that art museums have a
social obligation to preserve "aesthetic welfare."[12] Believing that aesthetic
experience is intrinsically good, he argued that its advancement should be

a matter of public policy. Museums, he thought, are responsible both for developing the capacity for aesthetic experience in individuals and for the democratic distribution of its satisfactions. As public institutions, therefore, museums should contribute to the growth of aesthetic capital.

But the promotion of large-scale aesthetic gratification, let alone social justice, has rarely been a primary aim of any type of museum. Aesthetic pleasure, considered a privilege of a select few, was often closely tied to the trappings of power and its consolidation. The social historian Nathaniel Burt points out that museums dedicated to the display of art purely as aesthetic object, i.e., as a source of pleasure rather than as a source of historical knowledge or moral inspiration, are relative newcomers: "What was once pure knowledge—ethnography, anthropology, archaeology—turns into esthetics," he writes. Gradually, the art "crept over them," presumably covering more practical functions with a surface of aesthetic glamour.[13] Pierre Bourdieu amplifies this point with the argument that the aestheticized art museum conceals a consolidation of power and social status, in which the cultivation of an aesthetic outlook plays a useful and subversive part. Bourdieu's thesis is that, far from facilitating universal access to pure aesthetic experience, museums are structurally implicated in a class-segregating conspiracy, which invents a species of experience for the sake of maintaining social hierarchy. The art museum thus projects a practical end that supersedes the aim of proliferating aesthetic enjoyment.[14]

Beardsley was a formalist who believed that gratification is aesthetic "when it is obtained primarily from attention to the formal unity and/or the regional qualities of a complex whole, and when its magnitude is a function of the degree of formal unity and/or the intensity of regional quality."[15] This gratification, he believed, is preeminently provided by works of art, and especially by those celebrated in the modern art museum, which disavows all but a narrow aesthetic nimbus that surrounds and protects its content against nonart associations.[16] This rarefied and self-conscious aestheticism, which presumes a single, universal response to form, style, and beauty, marks a modernist phase of museum theory that disregards both the more promiscuous museum practices of preceding centuries and the current trend toward unlimited aesthetic gourmandise.

According to Beardsley's modernist assumption, the intrinsic goodness of aesthetic gratification, properly grounded in appropriate objects, is sufficient reason for its social promotion. This formalist defense of "aesthetic welfare" rests on the presumption that human experience, cleansed of local specificity, is uniform. Like many pleas for democratic causes, aesthetic universalism requires an optimistic faith in the generality of human nature. It assumes that, under optimal and uncoercive conditions, everyone would come to see and think the same thing. Aesthetic pleasure, on a universal scale and as a potential of common humanity, is thus arguably defensible as a human right. Progressive advocates have been at pains, however, to discriminate between different kinds of pleasurable experience, not all of which are equally desirable. Very few people recommend the indiscriminate pursuit of unregulated pleasure or are indifferent to its source.[17] The merit of aesthetic experience is that its value is taken to be intrinsic. It is an end in itself, enjoyable without reference to further consequences, complete within itself. Although available in many contexts, such pleasure, in its purest form, is alleged to occur in the presence of autonomous works of art. These objects, designed to be experienced gratuitously and without real-world contamination, are therefore ranked as exemplary sources of aesthetic experience, and the museums that collect and preserve them are viewed as exemplary pleasure palaces. But few experiences exist in a void. We can hardly contemplate pleasures so divorced from worldly existence that they modify nothing and no one, and such contextless satisfactions would surely be short-lived.

John Dewey, still the most prominent partisan of aesthetic experience and of art as a means to it, judged the value of experience "on the ground of what it moves toward and into."[18] Dewey endorsed only that experience which leads to further growth and helps the individual to integrate a world of external conditions that are social and real. Well known as a foe of the misguided quest for static certainty, Dewey was nevertheless no friend of pointless experimentation or purposeless activity. A pragmatist, he believed that every experience modifies the one who undergoes it and thus affects the subsequent experiences of both this person and all her or his communicants. This very communicability of experience undergirds the potential for growth that Dewey esteemed. Dewey and his followers appreciated the potential for growth through art, but they had little use for the concept of art for art's sake or experience as an end in itself. Concluding *Art as Experience* with a nod to Shelley's defense of the poet as seer, Dewey declares: "While perception of the union of the possible with the actual in a work of art is itself a great good, the good does not terminate with the immediate and particular occasion in which it is had." Far from being an experience encapsulated within itself, the work of art, as Dewey understood it, enlarges the scope of human relations in common experience.[19] Today's proponents of aesthetic experience, who focus on the radical subjectivity instead of the publicity of that experience, ignore the very conditions that transform it into art and make aesthetic experience worthwhile.

Museums today face a similar dilemma. Paradoxically, those that abdicate objective expertise, in order to affirm plurality of experience, escape the burden of authority only to risk destroying the intersubjective network that gives aesthetic value its meaning. Having enthroned experiential privacy as a condition of aesthetic legitimacy, these museums sanction communion between the individual and the work of art, rather than among communicants. This narrowed aestheticism, confined to an individual's subjective and self-affirming experience of the artwork, however, draws implicitly on a history of faith in a common experience.[20]

The traditionally authoritarian art museum validated the judgment of certain people and confidently imprinted their aesthetic sensibility on the public at large. The objects these tastemakers singled out set a standard of "taste" as a quasi-judgment made by a faculty of aesthetic discrimination. The museum that presented the objects for appreciation as "works of art" became an arbiter among museums. Its prescription, to go forth and experience likewise, was intended for a homogeneous clientele and must cause bewilderment when extended to diverse audiences and institutions.

The imperative of the art museum to preserve aesthetic quality was fixed in the nineteenth-century world for which these institutions were designed, but its meaning became unintelligible outside the culture that invented it. The mythology of the art museum is so infectious, however, that once within its walls, an object mysteriously attains the imperious status of artwork, and visitors feel compelled to confirm its judgment within the parameters of their own experience. Where this resonance is lacking, people take its absence as a personal defect. Visitors expect to sense aesthetic merit as they would perceive an object's shape or size, and traditional aesthetic theory gives them reason for thinking so. If they do not experience what must be "there" to be experienced, the fault must be their own. They must be afflicted with something equivalent to blindness.

"Seeing" the quality that makes something a work of art, however, is a bit like "getting" a joke. To grasp the humor is not a matter of direct sensation, but requires acquaintance with a code and with a class of things whose apprehension demarcates a community of initiates. And like jokes, works of art are to be shared, but not universally. The art museum protects and propagates the community of its adherents. It is not open to all alike, regardless of its admission policies. It does not authorize every experience, notwithstanding its nonjudgmental rhetoric. Its claims to project a democratic appeal arise from confusing the universality of a capacity for aesthetic experience with a capacity for a universal aesthetic experience. The former is probable, the latter nonsensical.[21]

Denial of a universal aesthetic experience is not to be taken as a declaration that all subjective experiences are therefore equally valid or that there is no basis for choice among them. Selection is a function of interest, which often includes the aesthetic as a primary or auxiliary component. Objects now appearing as works of art in an art museum might, at another time or place, be presented as something other than art. Differently warranted, a single physical object could be a cultural artifact, a historical memento, an illustration of technical proficiency, or a model that demonstrates a scientific principle. All these modes of apprehension are unaffected by the object's aesthetic quality.

Some aesthetic affirmation is nevertheless inevitable. Every formal structure has an aesthetic core, which is the epistemic basis of its identity. This condition of conceptual "collectibility" is as vital to history or science, which depend equally on pattern formation, as to artistic unity. Confusing things that evoke aesthetic experience, a common happening, with works of art, which may or may not do so, mixes distinct logical categories and has produced some misattributions. One result is the apparent neglect of the aesthetic by most nonart museums. Another is an overemphasis on aesthetic excellence by art museums.

Alternative Museum Aesthetics

In all types of museums, museumkeepers have built their collections with the zealous appreciation of the art lover, but most have been moved by different aesthetic principles than those that shaped the art museum.[22] All museums rely on aesthetic "hooks" to make exhibits initially attractive and additional aesthetic "holds" to keep the interest of their audiences. In this, museums employ the same strategies as commercial or other enterprises whose aim is persuasion. Aesthetic stylization has long been used to charm perceivers, often, as a pedagogic device that complements mediated rational argument or displaces it with immediate sensory and emotive force. The aesthetic vehicle is a direct transmitter of complex notions that are difficult to express or analyze abstractly.[23] Ideas are conveyed through repetitious behavior, through kinesthetic resonance, by sensory isomorphism and contrast, by emphasis, and by associative aural or visual suggestions that illustrate or symbolize the content of the idea. The impact of these aesthetic techniques is intellectually indirect, but powerful, and all cultures use them to inculcate behavioral conformity. Through table manners, dress codes, holiday celebrations, grieving rituals, slang expression, and other forms of behavior, aesthetic indoctrination takes place inconspicuously and relentlessly—at work and play—at all times and everywhere. As we have seen, museums are part of the system of cultural formation and utilize a variety of aesthetic instruments to accomplish their ends, but this common aesthetic practice neither sets them apart from other cultural institutions nor distinguishes them from one another. Neither reliance on aesthetic process nor protection of aesthetic quality uniquely defines a museum genre.

Some museums that purport to present cultures from a detached vantage point depict certain styles of aesthetic expression as "typical" or "deviant" within a particular culture.[24] History and anthropology museums do this without declaring a preference when they identify a stylistic signature by means of which a society, an era, or a community can be recognized. We learn, for example, to recognize Byzantine or baroque representations by certain qualities of line and curve, regardless of whether or not we happen to like them. The aesthetic form in such cases is wrongly understood as an end in itself. Rather, it is objectified as an interpretable meta-entity, albeit an abstract or stylistic one, that can be analyzed, classified, and assessed as exemplary of its kind independently of its specific aesthetic merit.[25]

The power of aesthetic statement is well understood by majority museums, and some are using it to reshape their paternalistic image of grandeur. The Pompidou Center in Paris is a good example of a contemporary museum that, with its utilitarian exterior and ragged fringe of jugglers and fire-eaters, is striving for an appearance of nonjudgmental egalitarianism. Its popularized content and vernacular architecture are on an aesthetic plane with a democratic image of humankind. The museum seems to repudiate ancestral authority, purporting instead to mirror a multiple vision of itself back to a pluralized public. Its stylistic shift from temple to bazaar, and from the depiction of a linear past to a fractured, timeless present, lends the museum a tone of nervous energy accentuated by the endless replications and reflections in its gleaming metal and glass surfaces. The museum broadcasts all its stations with equal assertiveness, vibrating as a dazzling whole that violently rejects the aura of intimate mystery that Walter Benjamin took to be the hallmark of the work of art—and, by association, of the museum that houses art—whose loss through reproduction he prophesied.[26]

The Pompidou Center makes its self-immolating statement by aesthetic means. Likewise, the political lessons conveyed by Fred Wilson's exhibition, "Mining the Museum," are achieved entirely by way of aesthetic displacements. Drawing all of his exhibition material from the collection owned by the museum in which his installation appeared, Wilson made minimal modifications—nothing more radical than shifting the position of a spotlight on a painting to reverse foreground and background—and with that reversal to foreground the cultural perpetuation of endemic social wrongs. Using similar aesthetic displacements and reversals applied to formal museological strategies, Wilson revealed the "invisible" complicity of the museum. He turned polished statues to display their roughly unfinished backs and highlighted accession numbers like ugly tatoos to reveal how objects are commodified when they become museum property. He exhibited damaged works betraying the neglectful and disrespectful museum practices that are normally hidden from the public, protecting what the museum does not choose to display. There are many stories that museums could tell—and do not—and Wilson's telling depends as much on his aesthetic choices as on the literal truths he imparts.

We typically take science museums to be dispensers of unvarnished truth, ignoring their reliance on aesthetic techniques to bring about the effects they hope to produce. Like all museums, they use aesthetic spectacle to attract and hold attention, and frequently the beauty of a natural phenomenon suffices to do that without additional embellishment. Laser shows, Van de Graaff generator demonstrations, wave machines, and crystal formations are mainstays of science halls—the bigger and more dramatic the better. Natural history museums and aquariums rely on the attraction of brilliant plumage and the iridescent splendor of ores and scales. Most of nature's beauties require no embellishment, only some help from the museum to bring to consciousness what is ordinarily hidden from the unpracticed eye and the unprepared mind.

Science museums also make other deliberate aesthetic choices. Some integrate works by artists among the exhibits to illuminate natural phenomena or to make complex scientific concepts more concretely accessible. Models and metaphors play an important part in the mediation of ideas. But the deep aesthetic of inquiry is by far the most interesting feature of science museums—the forming of questions and designing of answers. The intellectual role of aesthetic curiosity in scientific research is insufficiently acknowledged by any educational institution. Yet, though it eludes standardized programming, it is well documented by scientists, and a few museums are trying to elucidate the pleasure of gratifying curiosity for the public.[27] Curiosity abides in the hearts and souls of museum visitors too, but it must be kindled with care. It is easily eclipsed by the inquisitorial correctness of logic or defeated by trivializing its origin in aesthetic experience.

Many a scientist remembers coming to her or his profession through a pleasurable discovery of the order of the heavens or of numbers, or by finding the inherent beauty of plants, animals, and minerals. Many made that discovery in a favorite natural history or science museum.[28] Some confess to having been drawn to science by a quasi-religious feeling of grandeur or of awe at the immutability of cosmic law, recalling the motivation of the earliest didactic museums to celebrate, in microcosm, God's plan for the whole of the physical universe. In recent times, most museums have dispensed with the theology, but they continue to foster an aesthetic appreciation of natural order and magnificence that conduces to a feeling of oneness with the universe. A range of aesthetic devices is enlisted to that end. Some border on gimmicky sensationalism, borrowing ideas from theme parks and science fiction drama, but even these can be tastefully used to stimulate thought. A very successful exhibition at the American Museum of Natural History incorporated film clips of *Jurassic Park* to pose questions of genuine scientific interest. Could dinosaur DNA be preserved by a blood-engorged mosquito preserved in amber? Could it be reconstituted? Could the animal survive today? The film was the bait, but the exhibition was the hook that made the inquiry vivid.[29]

Science museums reproduce the natural world by using the technological advances of their time. From the earliest "lifelike" arrangements in glass cases to contemporary "walk-in" installations, the aesthetic fascination of mimesis has been prominent. Now, many museums aim to capture the vivacity of experience as well as its causes. Phenomenologically evocative exhibitions address the science museum visitor through subjectively "authentic" encounters, much as works of art in art museums engage viewers in aesthetically evocative experiences. Visitors want more than to learn information about the grizzly bear's great dimensions and habitat; many want to feel the terror of his fearsome visage as well. Some will also want to take part in the experience of studying the animal. Their wonder addresses the doing that guides the knowing. Their questions concern the process of science.

Interactive exhibits, like those meant to stimulate curiosity, generally assume a common phenomenological urge that infects the visitor with the "feel" of "doing" science. Here the aesthetic satisfaction is presumed to lie in the process of intellectual pursuit that undergirds the cognitive result. The process is characterized as collective, for the work of science is not so much the probing by an individual as a meeting of many minds, and so its accomplishment is public, however private the participatory experience. Things work as place markers for visualization and often as opaque conductors of thought.[30] Since the exhibited objects thus play an essentially vehicular role, it is ambiguous and somewhat misleading to say that visitors to science museums are in the presence of the "real thing."

In a sense, all science exhibits are conceptual or "virtual." They are meant to lead the museumgoer, in thought, to the world outside. The experience they elicit is both in the museum and inside the visitor's head, but also in the natural world of phenomena where phenomenological experiences normally take place. One really does see illusions and afterimages that in one sense are "unreal," just as one really feels an electric shock or hears the changing pitch of the Doppler effect. The things in the museum that elicit these experiences are really there, but the experience elicited is not of those things. Unlike the paradigmatic work of art in the art museum, which draws the viewer's contemplation to itself, science museum exhibits "work" when they are no longer concretely present to the viewer. Whatever aesthetic delight they may incidentally afford, these exhibits are not "aesthetic objects" as that expression is applied to works of art. Aesthetic pleasure is, however, a significant ingredient of a successful encounter with them.

What if science museums and their exhibits were taken as the aesthetic paradigm for all museums? What if the self-transcending public event that takes place in the science museum were aesthetically normative, instead of the self-contained work of art, an object, or the private, subjective experience that it promises? If the aesthetic pleasure of "doing science" were a model, what lessons in appreciation might flow from the science museum to the art museum and to all other museums?

An Aesthetic of Doing and Thinking

"What makes some molecules beautiful?" asks Roald Hoffman, who proceeds to answer his own question: There are many factors—their intricate geometry, their unexpected and complex ability to bring about ends, the capacity to surprise with their novelty and to incite new thinking. "Molecules can be beautiful because of the wondrous quantized motions they undergo, truly a music played out in tones, harmonics and overtones that our instruments, now measuring instruments, hear. The music they hear is a music of the mind. The pleasures of the chemist are felt emotionally—the molecule is loved—and the satisfaction it invokes parallels that of seeing relationships, of knowing essences, of soaring with the wind."[31] Though their ostensive aim is cognitive, science museums aspire to make people hear the beauty of the "music of the mind."[32]

Like artists, scientists have stylistic preferences. Their work is aesthetically distinguishable and provokes dissimilar aesthetic responses.[33] Like art, science does not terminate in a single experience; neither is a single experience at its origin. Some science museums connect aesthetic pleasure with the cognitive spur of related exhibits that lead visitors from one to the next with a self-propelling logic. Other museums find ways to captivate visitors with the aesthetics of doing research. The Boston aquarium has made a fascinating exhibition of its hospital facility. Visitors can observe the animals undergoing treatment and assist staff members' study of the organisms through interactive computer programs. Interacting with these exhibits is meant to be fun as well as instructive. We are familiar from infancy with the aesthetic satisfactions of "getting it right," and science museums are reminding their visitors of the continuity between such delights as mastering the art of tying one's shoes and the happy absorption in scientific research.

There is good reason to believe that an aesthetic of discrimination, selection, response, and absorption guides art making, as it guides science, and provides at least some of the pleasures of both art and science museums. The harsh disciplinary segregation of science from art, met with in schools and affirmed by popular mythology, obscures their congruence and also has arbitrarily separated the several types of museums. The artwork paradigm and the exaltation of the art museum as archetypal source of aesthetic experience have driven all other museums to measure their own aesthetic potential only by comparison to the art museum's example. But other museums have their own aesthetic value and their own ways to realize aesthetic pleasure, which should not be lost on art museums.

The Value of Aesthetic Value

Experiencing art makes no art, but it influences the way people act in the world and may cause some of them to become artists. Insofar as art enlivens one's sensibility and consciousness, it makes the world more interesting, inspiring those who study it as well as those who simply live. Just as making art is not for the art world alone, so do science and the historical disciplines seek patterns of doing that are not exclusive to those disciplines. Aesthetic value and the multiple modes of its expression form a bridge between disciplines. Experiencing science, likewise, makes no science, but appreciating the aesthetics of science might yield lessons for art; and the art museum might gain from taking the aesthetic values of science to heart.

Describing a science teaching project at the Boston Children's Museum, its former director, Michael Spock, discussed a kit that the museum designed to teach classification. The staff, having determined to use specimens of real birds and film loops of bird behavior in the kit, began asking themselves questions about what they hoped would happen to students:

> Do we really care about whether the kid can name the bird? Is she good at observing detail about the bird? Can she explain something about bird adaptations? Can she describe something about bird behavior? Can she draw a bird accurately? (In college biology, a student has to draw things to observe well, and the question isn't whether or not the student is a great artist but whether she is a good observer.) Is she good at finding sources of information about birds? . . . Does she choose voluntarily to read books about birds? Does she choose to go on bird walks? Does she decide to have a pet bird? Does she keep a life list?
>
> Would she be comfortable if a bird landed on her shoulder or if she held it in her hand? Does she understand what ornithologists do when they spend their lives being ornithologists? Can she make sense out of information in ornithological journals? Can she prepare a study skin (used to preserve data but without necessarily making the specimen look life-like)? Could she prepare a realistic mount? Has she become an ornithologist? Has she become the ornithology curator at the Peabody Museum at Yale?[34]

Notice that these questions soon leave the child's cognitive reaction to the kit behind and focus more broadly on what she does in the world. Science exhibits, we have seen, move us out of the museum and into the world. The most effective of them have a certain transparency that leads the museum-goer to pass through and beyond them, extracting what may be applied elsewhere. Spock cites a favorite quotation that expresses the goal of science exhibits: "Playing with clay makes no pots, but playing with clay makes potters."[35] Do we understand now that the pleasure that draws one to science might be related to the pleasure that draws one to art? And the value experienced in both instances is aesthetic.

The question of aesthetic motivation, Why do people spontaneously do what they do not have to do? has excited the scientific interest of the psychologist Mihaly Csikszentmihalyi. He labels "intrinsic motivation" that nonutilitarian, self-rewarding investment of energy into a subject, which causes one to hold the course in the absence of extrinsic rewards and even under stressful conditions.[36] Csikszentmihalyi wonders why so many scientists seem unfazed by difficulty or tedium and persist in their work independently of the hope for money, prestige, status, or any other compensation—ostensibly with the same nonconsequential excitement that brings people to compose music, climb rocks, dance, play chess, or paint pictures. Aesthetic gratification seems to surmount all obstacles.

Museums of all kinds have an interest in tapping into this capacity that humans have for what Cszikszentmihalyi calls "flow experience." Even where the museum's professed mission is educational or social, this motiveless motivation seems apposite, since people generally come to museums voluntarily, with the expectation of enjoying themselves, and are disappointed when they do not. Science museums are as eager as art museums to provide people with optimal experiences that are self-rewarding. Cszikszentmihalyi suggests that the challenge to different types of museums might not be as specialized as we have been led to believe. He finds certain conditions common to all instances of "flow experience" under very different circumstances. These include an optimal balance between the person's competence and the challenge presented to it, a clear indication of the person's goal (which may be performative), and feedback throughout the experience concerning the person's approach to the goal. In addition, Cszikszentmihalyi notes as a feature of the experience a concentration so intense that people lose consciousness of time and lose their sense of self.[37] The spell is broken when they are reminded of clock time or made to return to self-consciousness.

These features, described as "conditions of optimal experience," are surely not the whole of what anyone undergoes in aesthetic enjoyment, whether the specific incident be appreciating or making art, rock climbing, or scientific inquiry. Csikszentmihalyi's point is that such experiences do occur and are not so rare that we cannot know them, even from the quotidian events of normal living. Aesthetic satisfaction is often overlaid with pragmatism in the case of science and with mysticism in the case of art, so that the spontaneous enjoyment common to both is concealed along with their connection to ordinary pleasure. Museums are committed to the provision of such pleasure, but because of their historic associations and the heavy cost of maintaining them, even their most ardent defenders tend to underplay the aesthetic satisfactions that all but art museums afford, and to yoke the others to more stereotyped pursuits.

Only art museums are persistently credited with the production of spontaneous and unalloyed gratification, and this achievement becomes a benchmark for other museums to emulate. Museums themselves must bear some responsibility for the perseverance of that monolithic standard, but they should be open to its revaluation in light of new trends. Not the least of these is the shift from the museum's object-centeredness to an experiential base, which must include, but is not confined to, aesthetic experience. If the value of aesthetic welfare remains, as Beardsley described it, a good, and its promotion a desirable public policy, then all museums do have something to give to the public. Providing aesthetic experience is a public service that all museums, not art museums alone, can fulfill. No one has a monopoly on the conditions of "flow experience." All museums can augment the aesthetic resources available in the world by helping people to experience the world more aesthetically. And they can teach one another how best to reinvest and multiply the aesthetic goods that each displays in its own way. Teaching people to experience the world aesthetically is not sufficient to make it a better place, but it is a necessary condition for undertaking that task.

9.   Conclusion
The Museum in Transition

Like most contemporary institutions, museums have descended from the heaven of authoritative certainty to inhabit the flatlands of doubt. That move could have inspired venturesome individuality and exploratory novelty; in most instances, however, doubt has led to cautious self-censorship and timid understatement. It has brought progressively more uniformity as museums hedge their bets by covering all possibilities. The more they celebrate diversity, the more indiscernible museums have grown from one another and from other public institutions; the more emphasis they place on professionalism, the more standardized their practice becomes. It is not likely that the eccentric amateurs who founded the great traditional museums of the nineteenth century would have asked themselves such questions as, Why do we exist? What do our visitors and supporters consider of value? What are our strengths as educational institutions? or What do we have to offer our communities?[1] They would have been confident in their ability to judge, and their judgments would have seemed self-evident. We may regard their self-assured sense of entitlement and overt didacticism as arrogant and excessive—and frequently wrong. There is no doubt that it was patronizing, but it was, in many instances, coupled with an equally strong sense of moral purpose and civic responsibility.

Multiperspectivalism spreads the burden of responsibility that formerly encumbered the work of cultural conservation. Although its redistributive intention is beneficent, the endeavor to achieve pluralism has a flattening effect that diminishes individual accountability.[2] Nowhere is this more evident than in the demotion of curatorship to bureaucratic status. Denied their traditional authority and devoid of the passionate connoisseurship of the independent amateur, curators must now be client-oriented team players, harnessed to exhibition teams as "resource persons." Candidates for curatorial positions are still expected to give evidence of scholarly ability and of the capacity to cultivate patrons and museum supporters; but in addition, they must write for and speak to the general public, collaborate with teachers, and reconcile their disciplinary judgment with the more pragmatic aims of exhibition evaluators, public advocates, market specialists, and "project managers" whose skills may or may not include subject expertise.[3]

A popular metaphor among museum professionals today is the giant, multicolored beachball kept afloat by the hands of many separate players. Each player bats the ball from what is alleged to be a unique perspective, but the vision of each is impaired by the vast ball, and so no one clearly apprehends the perspective of the other players. Yet everyone is careful not to disrespect or discount the views of the other players, whose perception is, of course, presumed as valid as one's own. The beachball homily suggests that keeping the ball afloat is the sole and sufficient goal of every player's activity. It does not question the merit of that objective, nor does it invite scrutiny of the individual and collective aims of the players or their mutual compatibility. Keeping a museum afloat, however, is not a recreational pastime.

Museums arose out of centuries of passionate human longings. They should not be diminished to a condition of self-perpetuating subsistence. To their devotees, museums still represent a personal commitment that approaches a sacred calling. And despite their descent from elite circles to the denser public sphere, single-issue museums with small budgets and minuscule staffing continue to have a loyal following of lobbyists and specialists to maintain them. In the late 1960s, museums were given a decisively populist spin. Many of them had effectively turned into community activity centers, informally providing innovative education without benefit of the tax concessions available to formal educational organizations.[4]

Since then, museums have reinvented themselves as institutions whose foremost function is "public service" defined as education. Where previously they catered to collectors and scholars with specialized research interests, addressing the public at irregular intervals chiefly by dispensing edification, now they have placed themselves at the contested centers of cultural interactivity and welcomed democratic debate. Casting their own history up for review, museums invited their visitors (and even nonvisitors) to validate their existence, appealing to "stakeholders"—board, staff, volunteers, and community—to shape the museum's vision of itself, as well as its presentation strategy, through negotiated settlements and managed dialogue.[5]

"Growth," "change," "development," and especially "experience" are the generic bywords that have replaced the substantive visions held by past curators and museum directors, leading them sometimes into fierce struggles over power, succession, and ideology. Gratifying the public translates as programs and exhibitions, and the comparative devaluation of other priorities that followed from that emphasis shows up in concrete ways. Process, associated with a vague sense of experiential product, now determines personnel decisions and financial allocations. Every facet of the museum is affected: its architecture, investment in technology, acquisition policy, storage facilities, provisions for conservation and deaccessionment, management, and governance. Even the "gentlemanly" vocabulary in which its activities were formerly described has given way to the brisk language of organization and enterprise. Fully emerged from its nineteenth-century cocoonlike role as an enclave of private pleasures, the museum, by the end of the twentieth century, has become part of what Tony Bennett calls the "collective hail" of the leisure industry.[6] It belongs to the well-regulated public sphere.

Compromise and consensus were once the ideals that inspired the public sphere, but they have been displaced by a market model that is full of contradictions. Derived from an ancient faith in the universality of reason, which suppresses difference, today's marketplace capitalizes on difference and trivializes reason. Individuals gather in the public sphere to "duke it out" symbolically by whatever means possible. Museums' entry into that domain as sites for multiple experience marks their new partnership with the public, but it does not represent a coherent identity. No single consensual path can be expected to fuse out of the exposure of differences; yet perceptual distinctness among systems is not itself a final truth. When taken seriously, pluralism calls the very meaning of *same* and *different* to account, for the meaning of these words depends on a traditional logical system that does not map precisely onto alternatives and may find no common denominator with other logics.

Some museums have experimented valiantly with the simultaneous exhibition of independent logics, hoping thereby to initiate visitors into the mysteries of interpretive diversity. In 1994 the Boston Museum of Fine Arts mounted an experimental exhibition, "The Label Show," which provided an overabundance of interpretive labels intended to demonstrate both that various ways of understanding artworks are possible and that language influences the manner in which works are perceived. The artworks were grouped according to a mix of conventional and unusual categories, meant to provoke visitors to ask why these, rather than another set of categories, were selected. The show was a fascinating but tedious tour de force, which imposed a neck-straining burden of reading on viewers, few of whom were inclined to endure the cognitive labor required of them or enjoy its aesthetic dissonance. It is difficult to represent the syntactic mismatch of logical systems in visual or tangible terms. Simplified endeavors to do so inadvertently suggest the parallel legibility of a few arbitrarily selected objects used as semantic placeholders—and thus their direct translatability as units that fit handily into any system. But the logics of collection, and, more so, the logics of meaning and production that preceded them, may fail to overlap at all.[7] Exhibitions of this didactic type, though nobly intended, may therefore be self-defeating, perversely as elitist as the practices they mean to expose. Moreover, their message may be no less misleading.

Discord and Dialogue

The spirit of compromise can have other dispiriting consequences where it undermines the clarity of the museum's purpose. We have seen already the clash of history and memory displayed in the contest between veterans groups and academic historians over the Smithsonian's 1995 *Enola Gay* exhibition. That dispute was unhappily resolved in favor of political compromise—a failed attempt to find a common denominator among the contending parties—which ended with the museum's absurd presentation of nothing more than a conventional B-29 fuselage, modified to carry an unconventional cargo. Diverted from their original script, which focused on the use of the atomic bomb in terminating the war in the Pacific, the exhibit producers switched in midstream to a logic of self-observation as they laboriously restored an artifact, the B-29 fuselage.

The drastically reduced *Enola Gay* exhibition was not a peaceable reconciliation of diverse interpretations of the "same" phenomena. There never was agreement on what phenomena were to be exhibited or what the exhibit was "about." Was it a commemorative tribute to American veterans of World War II? Was it an abstract remembrance of a turning point in modern history? Was it evidence of the extraordinary military hardware and strategies for its use in the war against Japan? Or was it a technical illustration of the salvaging of materials that make their way into museum collections?[8] All of these and other constructions might have been legitimate exhibition material, yet each would inscribe the objects that it used differently. Each would convert the meaning of artifacts according to its own logic. Visitors to the National Air and Space Museum who were not privy to the controversy among the contending logics must wonder why the restoration of a single airplane body should elicit such rancorous discussion. The regrettable conclusion to this incident effectively removed the *Enola Gay* from any systemic account and presented an orphaned airplane part in a light that vaguely and ambiguously celebrated its historicality as an authentic object while obscuring its specific historicity.[9]

Museums have the option of portraying a specific point of view clearly and unambiguously together with an admission of its fallibility. Professing a focused interest and an undiluted story line does not discourage the expression of other, discordant positions, and empirical studies have shown that it will not prevent visitors from attributing their own meanings to the exhibition. A purportedly nonpartisan, encyclopedic approach that strives for harmony by covering all fronts is more likely to obscure diversity than to embrace it. When exhibitions are so balanced that every possible point of view is rendered equal, the probable result is that no point of view will be recognizable since all will have been reduced to a single formula.[10]

Museums that capitalize on their uniqueness certainly do face peculiar obstacles. Obscurity, restricted appeal, the charge of eccentricity or offensiveness, and limited funding are only the least of these.[11] There may be no bridging mechanisms or common expressions found universally unobjectionable. Any solution to an impasse will entail making practical choices that preclude other possible choices and are likely to disturb someone. The integrity of objects must sometimes be sacrificed for the sake of physical access to them, and permanent access is sometimes denied out of respect for traditional group values. Decisions of all kinds, including whether or not something should be exhibited at all, must be made on a case-by-case basis by each museum, according to its need and the dictates of its chosen logic. These decisions must not be reached in a manner that deludes the public or desensitizes people to the fractiousness of the world. Agreement is not always the best policy, and it is possible that unanimity is reached only where nothing that matters is at stake.

The Museum Experience

Whatever it may be, "the museum experience" has a seductive ring. Seducers are often deceivers, however, and cannot be relied on to deliver what they promise. Museum experience seems to bring people together, since some kind of experience is obviously accessible to everyone. But it is doubtful that the same experience is communicated to all. The effort to homogenize erases the gradients that make actual experiences interesting. Overcompensating for their differences out of dread of the absence of common ground, some museum professionals aspire to manage a sort of experiential parallelism or "preestablished harmony" among their visitors. Everyone must sing in unison, even at the cost of grossly simplifying the tune. Having conceded the lack of objective reference to something solid and external, exhibit designers try to jump-start visitors' experience predictably with the help of triggering devices.[12] Although mistrustful of conventional cultural significance, exhibit makers trust to visitors' empirically confirmed psychological suggestibility. They have concluded that people assimilate what they apprehend into a matrix of "mental categories of personal significance and character that are determined by events in visitors' lives before and after the museum visit."[13]

This representation of the museum experience, purged of objective reference, purports to highlight the visitor's individual creative freedom of interpretation; but actually, it underlines the manipulative interventions of the museum designers. It trivializes individuated and long-standing social prizings of ritual and material things and obscures the collective past experiences that endowed those rituals and material things with their peculiar social identity. The claim to elevate personal choice over material determinism denigrates the intrinsic value of material nature and wrongly equates the accumulation of things with fetishism or greed—the sheer impulse to possess. But the interest that people express for things in which they have no personal investment of ownership testifies to a nonpathological interpenetration of physical nature with human spirituality that constitutes them both. Who we are is a function of the things we care for; moreover, our understanding of other people is a function of respect for the things that matter to them. Often we are unable to empathize with their caring, but with the help of museums, we are able at least to glimpse the objects that evoke it. In time, our understanding may expand from things to relationships to persons and to the social attachments that their conjunction represents.

I have a suspicion that glorifying "museum experience" at the expense of the objects that make it possible will not be economically profitable in the end. Experiences grow stale. Their shelf life is brief and the cost of refreshing them enormous. Moreover, their synthesis degrades the significance of even the artificed museum experience. Diversity thrives on its nonrestriction, not on a misplaced promotion of it. "Let a thousand institutional flowers bloom!" Randall Kennedy declares, writing in favor of protecting what he believes are obnoxiously exclusive private colleges.[14] The same reasoning applies to the specialized and unconventional minority museums that are struggling to survive against economic odds and pressure toward homogenization. The aim professed by traditional museums was to teach discrimination and discernment; to develop a culturally specific sense of intellectual, moral, and aesthetic values; and to come, by that route, to self-scrutiny and self-knowledge. Contemporary museums could do worse than to adopt that goal, bearing in mind that discrimination and discernment that fail to be reflexive are rightly associated with bias and exclusion. The challenge facing contemporary museums, therefore, is not to seal themselves off from multiplicity, nor to unify and sanitize it, but to invest its complexity with moral breadth, cognitive significance, and aesthetic pleasure.

Museums today fill a different spiritual, if not physical, place in the world from that which they occupied at the time of their foundation. Those constructed to be oases of recreative communion with beautiful and uplifting things have turned into busy centers of recreational and communicative interaction. Those originally meant to instill civic pride now advertise their universalism. Something more than the buildings and their content has changed; the hearts and minds of museum users have been transformed.

Now, as in the past, museums provide relief from the unremitting battering of life. Museums are still places of renewal, where visitors can find stimulation or repose or relaxation through removal from absorption with daily routines. Removal might take the form of inducing meditation, or an almost mystical self-transcendence through art or knowledge or identification with an exoticised past. It is not coincidental that museums are often built around gardens or adjacent to parks, where visitors can extend their contemplative mood to nature, whether in fascination with its material profusion or in submission to a quasi-religious quietude. The museum satisfies a need to "get outside" oneself in much the same way that people have long found solace in abstract studies, in disinterested reflection, or in any inquiry disassociated from practical outcome. Even those museums that exhibit the trivia of ordinary life remove us from the trivia of our own immediate circumstances and promote an allocentric aestheticism that is neither materialistic nor antimaterialistic.

The philosopher Hannah Arendt suggests that to be fully human one must occupy the public sphere. In the ancient polis, she says, only brutes and slaves (and women) were consigned to constant preoccupation with the necessities of survival. With one's snout in the ground, one is mired in sameness. Only public existence makes possible the awareness of distinguishable selfhood, which alone makes community with one's fellow humans possible.[15] Museums are among the institutions that lift people into the public sphere where they are free to be both selves and different. This opportunity to detach from the needy self is now presented to the public in somewhat standardized form as a healthful "othering," not from self alone, but from other "others" as well. Self-transcendence, unromantically depicted as self-definition, sustains equilibrium in a world of many options. It positions the individual among galaxies of counterpositioned and identity-conferring categories of things. Real people find themselves located among real things in meaningful spaces. Museums help to assign and preserve those meanings. Traditionally they have done this through the mediation of things, linking marked styles of embodiment with public memory. No other institution does this on so vast and orderly a scale. We must consider, finally, the merit of this practice, and whether its abandonment in favor of currently fashionable modes of simulation denotes the end of the museum.

Savoring and Saving the Museum

What is left of museums when the objectivity of objects disintegrates, the self reverts to privacy, and the separateness of others is merely an accidental projection of one's own consciousness? Should we care that anything be remembered or cherished? The lazy language of "keeping the beachball afloat" implies motion randomly imparted and reactive to whichever currents and eddies prevail. "The beat goes on." I have argued that museums are composed of more than present impulses and casual encounters. They retain an aura of substantial reality, a re-collection that holds up against the more spectacular effects of re-created experience or "virtual" reality. Those manufactured effects—for all their claims to hyperreality—defer to a known and preexperienced reality. Museums, however, have the potential to disclose heretofore unknown realities and to awaken new thoughts. They have the power to wrap thought in a substantially denser reality than that of passing experience.

It is important that museums have the lucidity and courage to define their own objectives, submitting them to honest criticism, and, where irreconcilable with the aims of others, agreeing to pursue their ends forthrightly and independently. Museums need a memorable identity. Frequent fliers today all too often confuse the exhibition they saw in San Francisco with one they saw in Milan or Singapore. This is not just because major shows are packaged to move from site to site, but because even the permanent installations are designed to formula and have become indistinguishable from one another. It is, of course, valuable for museums to learn from each other what has and has not "worked," to solve common problems, and to realize common ends, but it does not follow that every one of them should replicate the "successful" solutions. If each museum were guided by its own mission and resources, going to a museum would be like choosing to spend a vacation in the mountains or at the seashore: One would prepare accordingly for one site or the other. Museumgoers would thus share with the museum some responsibility for their choice, volunteering by their deliberate act of attention to collaborate with the museum's specific curriculum.[16]

"Curriculum" should not be taken too literally, however. Museums are no more schools than they are amusement parks, and they should not become auxiliaries of institutions of formal education. Although service to students (and to teachers) is an important element of their pedagogic function, the service they provide to the unattached and casual visitor is no less important. Precisely the absence of a curriculum makes the autodidactic and spontaneous experience possible. Museums are among the few remaining oases where the pleasure of heterogeneous and self-selected "flow experience" can still be enjoyed.[17]

I am not advocating disorder or the abandonment of declared values; quite the opposite. I urge museums to reassert their material specificity and to accept responsibility for its diverse reception. Where differences in outlook exist, they should be illuminated for the sake of understanding, and neither trivialized nor romanticized. Differences are real; they are sometimes difficult to accept and should not be obscured for the sake of bogus harmony. Unlike the institutions of law and justice, museums have the luxury of inaction. Their job is to make things accessible. They are not obliged to prescribe or to choose between incompatible alternatives, but they can illustrate how choices are made. They are not forced to sift out truth from fiction (except with respect to the accuracy of their research claims), but they permit the articulation of many tales. They have no investment in the closure of discourse but are dedicated to keeping it open and are prepared to collect and reconstrue evidence indefinitely. As many of their mission statements declare, museums are places for inquiry and exploration, which issue no degrees or certificates of graduation. The rewards museums offer are delight and the satisfaction of curiosity. That arousal is self-rewarding even in the absence of further satisfaction. It would be a tragedy if museums, in their zeal to secure arousal, were to become engines of experiential sameness. Few other sites are left in the world that do not suppress the differences between us. Museums have the power to keep them radiantly alive.

Notes

Preface

1. There is a long speculative history of "possible worlds" explored by philosophers from Leibniz to W. V. O. Quine, H. Putnam, and David Lewis. One approach that is particularly pertinent to museums is taken by Nelson Goodman in *Ways of Worldmaking* (Indianapolis, Ind.: Hackett, 1978).

2. An explosion of interest in museums has recently spawned the academic discipline of museum studies and generated a flurry of historical and analytical texts on museums.

3. There are signs of change in this regard. A recent conference at the Boston Museum of Fine Arts (April 1998), in conjunction with an exhibition of objects from the Victoria and Albert Museum, brought together a rare combination of museum practitioners and theoreticians of culture and cultural institutions. Malcolm Baker and Brenda Richardson, eds., *A Grand Design: The Art of the Victoria and Albert Museum* (New York: Harry N. Abrams, with the Baltimore Museum of Art, 1997).

4. See my essay, "Institutional Blessing: The Museum as Canon-Maker," in *The Monist: an International Journal of General Philosophical Inquiry* 76, no. 4 (October 1993): 556–73.

5. No one claims that education is the sole function of museums, but it is a primary one. Education theorists who are in agreement that learning is predominantly experiential also agree that it is one of the experiences that visitors come to the museum to get. See Zahava D. Doering, "Strangers, Guests or Clients? Visitor Experiences in Museums" (paper presented in Weimar, Germany, March 1999; unpublished manuscript, Washington, D.C.: Institutional Studies Office, Smithsonian Institution).

I. Introduction

1. Doubts about the legitimacy of cultural property are not confined to its authenticity. Recent cases more frequently involve the criminal diversion of confiscated property, piracy, looting, and other possible violations of international law where the authenticity of the object is not in doubt. These cases often demand the deaccession and return of the disputed object, but the generic response that museums might make in all such instances matches the paradigm offered here.

2. Estimates run as high as twenty-five thousand accredited museums worldwide, more than eight thousand of which are in the United States. Susan M. Pearce, *Museums, Objects, and Collections: A Cultural Study* (Washington, D.C.: Smithsonian Institution Press, 1992).

3. ICOM Statutes, sec. 2, art. 3, adopted by Eleventh General Assembly, Copenhagen, June 14, 1974; cited in Stephen E. Weil, *A Cabinet of Curiosities: Inquiries into Museums and Their Prospects* (Washington, D.C.: Smithsonian Institution Press, 1995).

4. U.S. Code, vol. 20, sec. 968[4]. This definition corresponds to that of the American Association of Museums, *Museum Accreditation: Professional Standards* (Washington, D.C.: 1973).

5. S. Dillon Ripley, "Museums and Education," *Curator* 11 (March 1968): 183–89.

6. A number of recent books of all genres, which are not about museums, nonetheless capitalize on such associations in their titles: e.g., Donald Hall's book of poetry, *The Museum of Clear Ideas,* exhibits his ideas as jumbled artifice, reverberating the poet's past and present. John Updike's short story, "Museums and Women" the first of a book of stories by that name, suggests tantalizing, mysterious, and not quite possessible items that mutely wait, incorporating a touch of prurience that is also emphasized by Jean Baudrillard in "The System of Objects," in *The Cultures of Collecting,* ed. John Elsner and Roger Cardinal (Cambridge, Mass.: Harvard University Press, 1994); and Baudrillard, "Le système marginale," in *Le système des objets* (Paris: Editions Gallimard, 1968). Ellen Handler Spitz traces a thread of meaning through a collection of occasional thoughts and aesthetic pleasures; Spitz, *Museums of the Mind: Magritte's Labyrinth and Other Essays in the Arts* (New Haven, Conn.: Yale University Press, 1994). In a philosophical exploration, Lydia Goehr traces the historical concept of a musical "work" with reference to repeatable musical events that can be notated and cataloged, just as objects designated "works of art" were emancipated by their inclusion in museum collections from their functional engagement in the lived world; Goehr, *The Imaginary Museum of Musical Works: An Essay in the Philosophy of Music* (Oxford: Clarenden Press; New York: Oxford University Press, 1992).

7. The degree of sensitivity of this issue was highlighted by the discovery of the wreck site of the RMS *Titanic* in waters outside the jurisdiction of any nation, and therefore subject to private salvage. Objects salvaged from the wreck by an American company were exhibited in the United States in 1997, and earlier in Europe and Britain. Within the museum community there were expressions of consternation that excavated items would be dispersed and sold before an

adequate archaeological report could be produced. "If nothing is done to record and collate these data now, they might as well never have been collected in the first place," wrote a member of the International Congress of Maritime Museums; Kevin J. Fewster and John R. Valliant, "Titanic: Delving beneath the Surface," *Museum News* 76, no. 3 (May–June 1997): 29–31, in response to "Titanic: An In-Depth Look," *Museum News* 76, no. 2 (March–April 1997).

8. Some definitions include the specification of nonprofit or noncommercial status, meaning that museums are not in the business of buying and selling for private gain. Poverty as such is not a necessary condition, and the suggestion seems ludicrous in light of the enormous value of the collections that some museums contain. The point, however, is that the museums have a fiduciary relationship to these objects. They do not have proprietary rights over them but hold them in trust as servants of the public.

9. This book addresses questions concerning the continued primacy of collection by museums as they become more experientially directed. That focus has long been challenged in practice by children's museums and more recently by science centers, which often do not feature large aggregations of objects, although they may include some typical or valuable ones. The phenomenon of simulation poses a different type of doubt as to the museum's essential function of accumulating material things.

10. Joseph Veach Noble, "Museum Manifesto," *Museum News* 48, no. 8 (April 1970): 16.

11. Veach Noble, "Museum Manifesto."

12. According to the director of the academy of sciences in a major urban center, the number of visitors to that institution increased four-fold during the display of the "Dynamation" exhibit, which featured these reconstructions of prehistoric animals; private communication to author.

13. Credit for this movement is also due to the J. Paul Getty Conservation Institute and to its well-funded training program.

14. Among the most successful of these was P. T. Barnum, who, in 1850, with his partner, Moses Kimball, purchased the building and collections of the foundering Peale family museum and brought to the museum enterprise a new spirit of entertainment, titillation, and voyeurism. See Neil Harris, *Humbug: The Art of P. T. Barnum* (Chicago: University of Chicago Press, 1973). See also Gary Kulik, "Designing the Past: History-Museum Exhibitions from Peale to the Present," in *History Museums in the United States: A Critical Assessment*, ed. Warren Leon and Roy Rosenzweig (Urbana: University of Illinois Press, 1989).

15. The ambiguity of their position continues to be a source of confusion and controversy, as is evident from such recent public debacles as the Corcoran Gallery's 1989 cancellation of its planned exhibition of the work of Robert Mapplethorpe, which had been funded by NEA in other locations, and the Cincinnati Contemporary Arts Center's 1990 ordeal in consequence of having shown the same exhibition. As Stephen Weil has pointed out, direct forms of government subsidy are more vulnerable than indirect forms such as income tax deduction for charitable donation, which is therefore an important source of revenue for the

arts. Weil, *Beauty and the Beasts: On Museums, Art, the Law, and the Market* (Washington, D.C.: Smithsonian Institution Press, 1983).

16. Aestheticians in the tradition of John Dewey, *Art as Experience* (New York: Capricorn Books, 1959, 1934), hold that works of art are subjective experiences that may be occasioned by artifacts produced for that purpose by artists. According to that view, a work of art is not realized until it is subjectively experienced. Since individuals respond to objects differently and bring their distinct preparedness to such encounters, there are no objectively unique artworks, but as many authentic works as there are real experiences. The present museological position appears to attribute a similar subjective identity to all museum objects, equating their reality with the multitude of experiential encounters of museumgoers.

17. Cultural objects have also been removed from public display for the very different purpose of avoiding offense to those groups or persons whose culture they represent. Such removals instantiate a different paradigm, which has features in common with that discussed in paradigm 1.

18. Walter Benjamin, "The Work of Art in the Age of Mechanical Reproduction," in *Illuminations,* ed. Hannah Arendt, trans. Harry Zohn (New York: Harcourt, Brace and World, 1968; reprint, New York: Schocken Books, 1986), 221.

19. The originals are stored away in climate-controlled chambers, but even these offer limited protection against floods, rodents, and even occasional theft.

20. It remains to be seen whether or not, as those museums willing to negotiate with the software developers are hopeful, the images will bring audiences in to look at the "real thing." Jonathan Adlai Franklin, "Image Control," *Museum News* 72, no. 5 (September–October 1993): 39, 53–56.

21. See Nelson Goodman, *Languages of Art* (Indianapolis, Ind.: Hackett, 1976).

22. These questions of philosophical aesthetics go to the heart of the discipline as grounded in the eighteenth-century perceptual theory of Alexander Baumgarten, the founder of modern aesthetics. Present-day theoretical explorers of the ontology of art include Nelson Goodman, Joseph Margolis, Arthur Danto, and many others. The practical constraints on the museum, however, place metaphysical reflections on the identity of the art object in a sharply new context, where their ethical overtones are all the more poignant.

23. Some schools of scholarship in art history concentrate on socially contextualizing features of works of art, which depend less on direct aesthetic experience of the works than on independently obtained knowledge. These features can be observed through the study of simulacra and auxilliary documents without recourse to the actual phenomena.

24. The philosopher Jean Baudrillard maintains that although *dissimulation* is a concealment of reality that implicitly affirms it, *simulation* is a substitute for a reality that comes, in time, to take its place. The original may be entirely forgotten as the simulation acquires its own history and creates a reality of its own. Baudrillard, "The Precession of Simulacra," *Simulacra and Simulation* (Ann Arbor: University of Michigan Press, 1981), 6.

25. Marshall McLuhan coined the phrase, "The medium is the message," which brought him instant media fame. Less attention was given at the time to the underlying metaphysical concern that this scholar from the Medieval Institute

in Toronto intended to address; namely, that the medium was in fact erasing the message. McLuhan, *Understanding Media: The Extensions of Man* (New York: Signet Books, 1964).

26. "The 'tribal' objects gathered on West Fifty-third Street have been around. They are travelers—some arriving from folklore and ethnographic museums in Europe, others from art galleries and private collections. They have traveled first class to the Museum of Modern Art, elaborately crated and insured for important sums. Previous accommodations have been less luxurious: some were stolen, others 'purchased' for a song by colonial administrators, travelers, anthropologists, missionaries, sailors in African ports. These non–Western objects have been by turns curiosities, ethnographic specimens, major art creations. After 1900 they began to turn up in European flea markets, thereafter moving between avant-garde studios and collectors' apartments. Some came to rest in the unheated basements or 'laboratories' of anthropology museums, surrounded by objects made in the same region of the world. Others encountered odd fellow travelers, lighted and labeled in strange display cases. Now on West Fifty-third Street, they intermingle with works by European masters—Picasso, Giacometti, Brancusi, and others. A three-dimensional Eskimo mask with twelve arms and a number of holes hangs beside a canvas on which Joan Miro has painted colored shapes. The people in New York look at the two objects and see that they are alike." James Clifford, *The Predicament of Culture* (Cambridge, Mass.: Harvard University Press, 1988), 189–90). See also Eugenio Donato's reduction of the historic museum to a pile of bric-a-brac, in "The Museum's Furnace: Notes Toward a Contextual Reading of *Bouvard and Pecuchet*" in *Textual Strategies: Perspectives in Post-Structuralist Criticism,* ed. Josue V. Harari (Ithaca, N.Y.: Cornell University Press, 1979).

27. "The truly unique object,—absolute, entirely without antecedent, incapable of being integrated into any sort of set—is unthinkable. It exists no more than does a pure sound." Baudrillard, "The System of Collecting," in *Cultures of Collecting.*

28. The phrase is borrowed from William James, but the phenomenon of world making through collection is most exquisitely depicted in the fiction of his brother, Henry. See *The Golden Bowl, The Spoils of Poynton,* or *The Ambassadors.*

29. "Museums are like the family sepulchres of works of art." Theodor W. Adorno, *Prisms,* trans. Samuel Weber and Shierry Weber (Cambridge, Mass.: MIT Press, 1981), 175. Also, S. Dillon Ripley, *A Sacred Grove: Essays on Museums* (New York: Simon and Schuster, 1969).

2. Museum Typology

1. Vera Zolberg (citing Joshua Taylor), "'An Elite Experience for Everyone': Art Museums, the Public, and Cultural Literacy," *Museum Culture: Histories, Discourses, Spectacles*, ed. Daniel J. Sherman and Irit Rogoff (Minneapolis: Minnesota University Press, 1994), 49–65.

2. Aquariums, arboretums, art museums, botanical gardens, children's museums, computer museums, craft and folklife centers, discovery centers, ethnic museums, historic houses and monuments, libraries, military and maritime

museums, natural history museums, outdoor living history reconstructions, museums of science and technology, science centers, wildlife reservations, university museums and galleries, and zoos are included. Some came by their acknowledgment only through struggle (science centers), and there continues to be controversy over the status of other institutions—e.g., Walt Disney World's Epcot Center (Experimental Prototype Community of Tomorrow), described by Neil Postman as "the world's largest animated diorama" in "Museum as Dialogue," *Museum News* 69, no. 5 (September–October 1990): 55-58.

3. As of 1993, with roughly the same annual budget, the Boston Museum of Fine Arts employed approximately twice the staff but received only half as many visitors as its neighbor institution, the Boston Science Museum. The MFA treasures and conserves the nearly half a million objects that are its raison d'être. The Boston Science Museum owns and preserves around thirty thousand objects (including living animals), which require care and maintenance, but most are valued chiefly for their instrumental function and not as treasures in their own right. The two institutions came into being under dissimilar circumstances and with distinct missions, and they employ their staffs and their resources very differently according to their needs. For an alternative classification system that emphasizes the importance of difference in scale, see Stephen E. Weil, *Rethinking the Museum: And Other Meditations* (Washington, D.C.: Smithsonian Institution Press, 1990). Still another classification scheme is suggested by Alma S. Wittlin, who divides all museums into two classes: (a) storage centers and (b) display centers, and then further subdivides these in terms of their intended audiences. Wittlin, *Museums: In Search of a Usable Future* (Cambridge, Mass.: MIT Press, 1970).

4. Tourist bureaus, chambers of commerce, and local newspapers do feature these museums as regional attractions. The cultural supplement of the *Boston Globe* recently recommended the Shoe Museum; the National Plastics Center and Museum, which features pink lawn flamingos; the Museum of Sanitary Plumbing Equipment; and the Museum of Bad Art (Calendar, January 8, 1998.) A newly planned arrival is the Seabee Museum, to be constructed by veterans of the U.S. Navy Construction Battalion (CB) at their former base, adjacent to the Quonset Point Naval Air Station in Rhode Island. It will house uniforms, weapons, tools, blueprints, photos, and other memorabilia donated by members of the World War II veterans group. Paul E. Kandarian, "Seabees," *Boston Globe,* November 8, 1998, B17.

5. See, for example, Detroit's Museum of African-American History, reopened in April 1997. Designed by Ralph Appelbaum and Associates, it features walk-through exhibitions, library and computerized research facilities, several theaters, "contemplation areas," a restaurant, an internationally stocked museum store, and comparatively few collected objects or space for their storage.

6. Private and princely collections preceded museums by several centuries, but the public rarely saw those treasures. The Medici allowed restricted visits to their collections, later to be housed in the Uffizi Palace at Florence, as early as the sixteenth century, and limited public admission was granted in the eighteenth century to famous collections in Rome, Naples, Vienna, Dresden, Basel, Versailles, Paris, and London. Access to such collections was declared a right

of ordinary citizens only after the overthrow of the French monarchy, on August 10, 1793, when the National Museum, a "Monument Dedicated to the Love and Study of the Arts," was opened to the public at the Louvre. Edward P. Alexander, *Museums in Motion: An Introduction to the History and Functions of Museums* (Nashville, Tenn.: American Association for State and Local History [ASLH], 1979), 24.

7. Not everyone has the same fond remembrance of museum visits. Paul Valery, in "Le Problème des Musées" in *Pièces sur l'Art,* remembers them with displeasure, comparing the experience of a gallery full of intentionally unique works of art with the sound of ten orchestras playing simultaneously. The philosopher Theodor Adorno ruminates on the deadening effect that museums have on the objects displayed within them; "Valery-Proust Museum," *Prisms.* The American artist Robert Smithson accuses museums of murdering and entombing works of art, which are torn from their natural environment, neutralized, and "lobotomized"; *The Writings of Robert Smithson: Essays with Illustrations* (New York: New York University Press, 1979), 132, cited in Stephen E. Weil, "On a New Foundation: The American Museum Reconceived," William Cook Lecture on American Studies, University of Michigan, April 14, 1993. See also Gustav Flaubert's remarkably prescient mid-nineteenth-century study of human stupidity (*sottiserie*), *Bouvard et Pecuchet.* Having discovered the discipline of archaeology and determined to pin down historical fact, Flaubert's characters turn their house into a very theatrical museum of antiquities. Striving to tell a story through old things, they are continuously interrupted with new events. They conclude that "things can lie" and that history will never be fixed. At last, the two dilettantes abandon their museological enthusiasm and turn instead to psychology and literature.

8. The possession of such a collection thus symbolically marked its princely owner as sovereign over the world of men. Assembling great collections was no mere recreation; it was a political act, and the commissioning, display, and exchange of works of art represented a significant part of diplomacy. Thomas DaCosta Kauffman, "From Treasury to Museum: The Collections of the Austrian Habsburgs," in Elsner and Cardinal, *Cultures of Collecting,* 137.

9. Since Hegel believed that the path to self-realization was a spiritualization, a movement from the Material to the Ideal, he also believed in a parallel hierarchy of the arts that advanced from the most materially grounded—architecture—through the plastic arts from sculpture to painting, eventuating in music and finally poetry. Ultimately, even this mode of abstraction would surpass itself, and art would achieve its self-cognizant apotheosis in the death of art. Museums, of course, stop short of that self-immolating celebration. *Introductory Lectures on Aesthetics,* trans. Bernard Bosanquet (1886; reprint, London: Penguin Books, 1993). Although museums today no longer credit Hegel's evaluative ranking, they have not entirely abandoned his view of progressive history. A more subtle and lasting contribution made by Hegel to modern museological theory is his understanding of 'objectification'. According to Hegel, the self, or subject of consciousness, engenders itself by alienation, i.e., through the identification of an 'other', an externalized object, which it then reappropriates by eating, knowing, observing, or otherwise absorbing it. *The Phenomenology*

of Spirit (1807), trans. A. V. Miller (London:Oxford University Press, 1977). This phenomenological thesis underlies the museum's historic preoccupation with the possession of objects, whose being—and therefore authentic presence—it understands to be inseparable from their meaning and therefore from the selfhood of the subject consciousness that objectifies it.

10. G. Browne Goode, *Smithsonian Institution Annual Report* (Washington, D.C.: 1891); Sherman E. Lee, *On Understanding Art Museums* (Englewood Cliffs, N.J.: Prentice-Hall, 1975).

11. Pierre Bourdieu and Alain Darbel with Dominique Schnapper, *The Love of Art: European Art Museums and Their Public,* trans. Caroline Beattie and Nick Merriman (Stanford, Calif.: Stanford University Press, 1990).

12. "Thus, the sanctification of culture and art, this 'currency of the absolute' which is worshipped by a society enslaved to the absolute of currency, fulfills a vital function by contributing to the consecration of the social order. So that cultured people can believe in barbarism and persuade barbarians of their own barbarity, it is necessary and sufficient for them to succeed in hiding both from themselves and from others the social conditions which make possible not only culture as a second nature, in which society locates human excellence, and which is experienced as a privilege of birth, but also the legitimated hegemony (or the legitimacy) of a particular definition of culture." Bourdieu, *Love of Art,* 110.

13. In the United States, that objective was explicitly advanced in 1973 by the NEA-sponsored *Wider Availability of Museums Act.* The reauthorization of NEA in 1970 and 1973 included language stressing "improved accessibility of the arts" and "wider availability of the arts" as among the goals of the Endowment. These concepts served as the basis for funding to a number of museum education and outreach programs. I am grateful to Julie C. Van Camp for information on these resources. Expanded accessibility was also promoted privately by the Kellogg Foundation, the Howard Hughes Foundation, the Annenberg Foundation, and others.

14. The same principle is operative in such national spectacles as bullfighting and baseball. Players are ungrudgingly awarded enormous salaries and are permitted outrageous breeches of good conduct because the public identifies with them and sees in them the realization of collective fantasies and dreams. Large-scale architecture, such as that of the great cathedrals as well as the monumental structures of fascism, similarly appeals to a collective identity whose grandeur absorbs the triviality of lesser beings and returns it to them brilliantly magnified.

15. Philosophers from Plato to Herbert Marcuse have recognized the irreplaceable value of aesthetic indoctrination and the legitimization of pleasure as an instrument of civic control. People with aberrant tastes are immune to coercion by many social pressures and do not easily succumb to normal blandishments. Their desires must be brought in line for social stability, and this is accomplished comparatively gently and subtly by the institutions of culture. The engines of law and executive power work with less benevolent sanctions to achieve the same ends.

16. Sherman E. Lee, "The Idea of an Art Museum," in *Past, Present, East and West* (New York: G. Braziller, 1983), 24.

17. Carol Duncan and Alan Wallach, "MOMA: Ordeal and Triumph on Fifty-third Street," *Marxist Perspectives* 1, no. 4 (winter 1978): 28–51.
18. These pressures are coming from, among other sources, feminist aestheticians reared in the traditional philosophical discourse, and from new appreciations by "nontraditional" scholars and connoisseurs of artifacts formerly not dignified as art. Christine Battersby, *Gender and Genius: Toward a Feminist Aesthetics* (Bloomington: Indiana University Press, 1989); Vera L. Zolberg and Joni M. Cherbo, eds., *Outsider Art: Contesting Boundaries in Contemporary Culture* (Cambridge: Cambridge University Press, 1997).
19. Of the ten favorite science museums described by eminent public figures in the November 1993 special issue of *Discover,* six are natural history museums.
20. Shelton, "Cabinets of Transgression."
21. Shelton, "Cabinets of Transgression," 186. The gist of Shelton's argument is that although Renaissance collection abandoned the God-centered worldview of the Middle Ages, the human-centered replacement view did not include New World inhabitants as equally human. Native artifacts and customs were brought back to Europe as evidence of the paganism of the New World. These collections thus generated a category for the comparative classification of indigenous material cultures and, implicitly, justified the colonial subordination of the New World culture.
22. Alexander, *Museums in Motion,* 44.
23. Pervading both science and humanistic thought from ancient Greek times until well into the twentieth century was the Neoplatonic notion of the Great Chain of Being. According to this view, the universe is a grand plenum, hierarchically arranged, descending from its source (God, according to Christian revisions) downward to sheer formless matter. The scale is so minutely graduated as to leave no gaps between its rungs, and so an ideal replica—the perfect museum—would include a token of every possible type of being within the absolute whole. Arthur O. Lovejoy, *The Great Chain of Being* (Cambridge, Mass.: Harvard University Press, 1956).
24. Susan Stewart, "Death and Life, in That Order, in the Works of Charles Willson Peale," in Elsner and Cardinal, *Cultures of Collecting,* 204–23. Londa Schiebinger, a feminist historian of science, challenges the objectivity and universality of the Linnaean classificatory system. She points to the anthropomorphic sexualization of botanical reproduction and suggests that the ascription of morphological gender domination to plants may be a projection of (male) human desires. *Nature's Body* (Boston: Beacon Press, 1993). The gendered botanical illustrations depicted in museums would certainly enhance and popularize the Linnaean scheme. For discussion of an exhibition that casts the Linnaean legacy in a more contemporary light which underscores both a changed conception of knowledge and a new understanding of objects as sites for experience, see Lisa C. Roberts, *From Knowledge to Narrative* (Washington, D.C.: Smithsonian Institution Press, 1997).
25. Alexander, *Museums in Motion,* 12.
26. Natural history museum professionals distinguish between their own work of collection and that of amateur collectors or aesthetes on the basis of documentation. An object without location in history or theory, regardless of how pretty

it is, is a worthless orphan in a museum of natural history. The carefully tended identity that it acquires inside the museum, however, is not the same as it had outside. This figurative rebirth pertains, of course, as much to works of art, torn from their real-world moorings, as to objects in scientific collections. With respect to scientific specimens, the physical and chemical effects of their capture and preservation cannot be ignored, but their significance poses intellectual problems entirely distinct from those encountered by the art collector.

27. Keeping things in running order is of paramount importance, so science centers employ a comparatively large maintenance staff. Since the public is constantly manipulating exhibits, the staff must give priority to the health and safety of visitors over that of the objects. Traditional museums ultimately have the same responsibility, but it is less frequently put to a test.

28. Victor Danilov, *Science and Technology Centers* (Cambridge, Mass.: MIT Press, 1982). Museums in the earlier phases of the movement illustrated the historical development of science and technology and also included the collection and preservation of artifacts (e.g., Palais de la Decouverte, South Kensington Museum). In the second phase, models were shown in operation, together with diagrams and demonstrations of scientific principles and applications (Deutsches Museum). Third-phase science centers (e.g., the Exploratorium, Ontario Science Center), because they do not feature collections, were not officially recognized as museums by the American Association of Museums until the mid-1970s, after having formed an advocacy organization of their own, the Association of Science and Technology Centers (ASTC). These institutions are less concerned with the history and applications of science than with the exhibition of the often invisible phenomena that science explores and the physical and conceptual apparatus by which it does so. Hein, *The Exploratorium: The Museum as Laboratory* (Washington, D.C.: Smithsonian Institution Press, 1990).

29. Addressing this manner of thinking about science, the Boston Museum of Science has developed an exhibition strategy that successively introduces visitors to their own capacity to observe, investigate, formulate hypotheses, devise tests for their confirmation, weigh evidence, and formulate theories. This is a long-term project that compels the museum to reexamine its entire exhibition history and philosophy and, gradually, to replace it with one that addresses museumgoers experientially.

30. Patents and copyright laws may apply to certain cases, but science centers normally (freely or for a price) distribute recipes for their exhibits and even build them for other institutions. See the Exploratorium's series of cookbooks, which give detailed instructions how to reproduce and even improve upon its exhibits.

31. For example, the Sikorsky helicopter and other products of industrial design in the New York Museum of Modern Art.

32. Examples of both the generic and the specific are to be found in the Smithsonian Institution's National Air and Space Museum (NASM). Wilbur and Orville Wright's *Flyer,* the biplane in which they made their historic 1903 flight in Kitty Hawk, North Carolina, is as unique as Leonardo's *Mona Lisa;* NASM's World War II gallery contains typical specimens of various Allied and Axis fighter planes that illustrate aviational advances. The 1995–98

NASM exhibition of the *Enola Gay,* the airplane that dropped the first atomic bomb on Hiroshima in 1945, was problematic both logically and historically. The displayed museum object was a portion of an ordinary B-29, a type of airplane that was in common use during World War II. Its uniqueness was therefore not technological (apart from some adaptations that fitted it to carry the bomb), but as a piece of military and social history. Furious disagreements over the circumstances, wisdom, and morality of the use of the bomb led to the museum's abandonment of its intended presentation of the object in historic context. As a result, apart from its ceremonial aspect, the exhibit was essentially generic. It depicted an airplane of a type commonly used in World War II bombing raids, along with its crew and the staff that reassembled it. The result was a perplexing and hybrid exhibition that satisfied no one.

33. A significant instance of that shift can be observed in the major exhibition, "Information Age," which opened at the National Museum of American History (NMAH) in 1990 with the help of a number of information technology producers and other corporations, including Disney Enterprise Company and its corps of "Imagineers." The expressed aim of the exhibition and its sponsors was to show the impact on people's lives of the telegraph, telephone, television, computers, and other communication networks. The more recent Smithsonian exhibition "Science in American Life" (1994) more emphatically foregrounded some of the political and ethical controversies that constitute the social environment of such technological developments as the birth control pill and the atomic bomb.

34. Consider the political and economic impact of railroads, the cotton gin, the automobile, and computers. Arguably, these have been the primary engines of our social and cultural formation.

35. Lee Kimche, "American Museums: The Vital Statistics," *Museum News* 54, no. 5 (October 1980): 52–57. See also Leon and Rosenzweig, *History Museums in the United States,* xiv. Here history museums are broadly defined as "institutions that display historical artifacts, or even reproductions or representations of artifacts, in the formal effort to teach about the past."

36. In their introduction to *History Museums in the United States,* Leon and Rosenzweig point out that history museums generally attract about a hundred million annual visitors. Few scholarly works reach such numbers; yet the latter are scrupulously reviewed in academic publications, while the former are all but ignored by them. Film and television series, such as Henry Hampton's programs on the civil rights and Depression eras, likewise reach enormous numbers of people, many of whom will never have any other source of historical knowledge. These popular programs, like museums and theme parks, are shaping the public's consciousness of history, and intellectuals have an obligation to take their impact seriously.

37. The "new social history" refers to the record of such previously neglected subjects as the lives of women, workers, immigrants, slaves, and ethnic minorities. Correspondingly, the significant events and moments of their history demand innovative modes of interpretation and conceptualizion in the absence of the "standard" documentary records.

38. A narrative is "an account in any semiotic system in which a subjectively foc-

alised sequence of events is presented and communicated." Mieke Bal, "Telling Objects: A Narrative Perspective on Collecting," in Elsner and Cardinal, *Cultures of Collecting*, 100.

39. This observation is obviously not meant to apply to objects that are fraudulent in origin, but to an alleged error in their representation that falsifies the story they purport to tell. Colonial Williamsburg, for example, "conspicuously excised the presence of black slaves, 50 percent of its eighteenth century inhabitants." Michael Wallace, "Mickey Mouse History," in Leon and Rosenzweig, *History Museums in the United States,* 158–80. This error has since been corrected.

40. See, for example, Yaffa Eliach's collection of thousands of photographs, taken prior to 1941, of Jewish inhabitants of Ejszyszki, a Lithuanian shtetl. Now housed in a tower that spans several floors of the U.S. Holocaust Memorial Museum in Washington, D.C., the exhibit embodies the life and foreshadows the death of the Jewish community, which ended there in September 1941, at the hands of German SS killing squads. Edward T. Linenthal, *Preserving Memory: The Struggle to Create America's Holocaust Museum* (New York: Penguin Books, 1995), 171–86.

41. Linenthal distinguishes between the "commemorative" voice and the "historical" voice. The first is personal and intimate and speaks with the authority of a witness; the second is more impersonal and studious and can appear condescending. The clash between these perspectives was one basis of the deep disagreement between U.S. Air Force representatives and historians in their dispute over the proper context of the *Enola Gay* in the Smithsonian's exhibition. The former wanted a fiftieth-anniversary commemorative spectacle, but the latter wanted a serious examination, at last, of the policies and events that terminated the War in the Pacific. "Between History and Memory: The *Enola Gay* Controversy at the National Air and Space Museum," *Bulletin of Concerned Asian Scholars* 27, no. 2 (April–June 1995); also see note 32.

42. Of course, works of art, like other objects, can tell "falsehoods." The curators of the Chicago Historical Society's exhibition "We The People" point out that such iconic paintings as John Trumbull's *The Declaration of Independence, 4 July 1776* and Emanuel Leutze's *Washington Crossing the Delaware* are actually full of historical misinformation and were originally intended more for their inspirational value than as accurate representations of fact. Alfred F. Young and Terry J. Fife, with Mary E. Janzen, *We the People: Voices and Images of the New Nation* (Philadelphia, Penn.: Temple University Press, 1993).

43. The Brooklyn Children's Museum, founded in 1899, was dedicated to "helping its young audience to understand themselves and the world in which they live." Mindy Duitz, "The Soul of a Museum: Commitment to Community at the Brooklyn Children's Museum," in *Museums and Communities: The Politics of Public Culture,* ed. Ivan Karp, Christine Mullen Kreamer, and Steven D. Lavine (Washington, D.C.: Smithsonian Institution Press, 1992), 242.

44. "We saw ourselves not just as an activities center but as a real museum, and the base of that museum was collections and some kind of contact with the real three-dimensional material. . . . What was it that made a children's museum different from an adult museum: The folks who started the children's

museum movement saw them as educational museums as opposed to display museums. They were just junior versions of real museums, scaled down in size and complexity. But for me the real break-through came about—and it was staring me right in the face, it was in the title—that the children's museums were not so much about art or about science or about history, but they were for somebody. They were for kids." Michael Spock, interviewed by Donald Garfield in *Museum News* 72, no. 6 (November–December 1993): 34.

45. For example, the Brooklyn Children's Museum exhibition on the cultures of Crown Heights after the tragic confrontations there in 1991 between Hassidic Jewish and African-American residents.

46. The YouthALIVE! program is a national initiative by the DeWitt Wallace-Reader's Digest Fund, cosponsored by the Association of Science and Technology Centers (ASTC) and the Association of Youth Museums, that works with urban adolescents in long-term, out-of-school relationships with museums. Suzanne LeBlanc, "Lost Youth: Museums, Teens and the YouthALIVE! Project," *Museum News* 72, no. 6 (November–December 1993): 44.

47. I do not mean to suggest that conventional collection has gone out of style. As remarked above, museums devoted to the preservation and study of particular kinds of things, from thermometers to potatoes to murder implements, continue to flourish. These will always have their following and generally their private funding; and for that reason, they can remain aloof from the pressures of institutional conformity.

48. Our consciousness is shaped by the objects we produce. "Thus artifacts are sometimes symbiotic with humans, but at other times the relationship is parasitic, and the survival of the object is at the expense of its human host." Cited in "Why We Need Things," *History from Things: Essays on Material Culture*, ed. Steven Lubar and W. David Kingery (Washington, D.C.: Smithsonian Institution Press, 1993). See also Mihalyi Czikszentmihalyi and EugeneRochberg-Halton, *The Meaning of Things: Domestic Symbols of the Self* (Cambridge: Cambridge University Press, 1981).

3. Museums and Communities

1. Robert Harbison, *Eccentric Spaces* (New York: Knopf, 1977; reprint, Boston: David R. Godine, Nonpareil Books, 1988), 150.

2. Since museums are nonprofit institutions with tax privileges as well as local employers, they clearly have an economic position within a community. Moreover, in times of disaster or common emergency they have served as meeting places and technological centers, whose staffs have valuable skills and resources. Neighbors are sometimes offended by traffic congestion and occasional public controversy, but they also benefit from the volume of business attracted to local commercial establishments.

3. Not everyone shares this warm and fuzzy view. Social critics such as Roberto Mangabeira Unger point to the resistance to change, the inequality, and coerciveness commonly found in communitarian societies. Unger, *Knowledge and Politics* (New York: Free Press, 1975). Feminist critics such as Iris Marion Young also point out that the ideal of community often leads to the suppression of difference in order to preserve identity, and this invariably leads to ex-

clusionary practice. Young, *Justice and the Politics of Difference* (Princeton, N.J.: Princeton University Press, 1990).

4. *Abjection* is a feeling of loathing and disgust that generates aversion on the part of a subject but also draws it to the object with fascination. Revulsion is coupled with desire, and the imperiled subject is, Kristeva says, compelled to monitor its separation from the loathed object by exaggerating its distance from it. Julia Kristeva, *Powers of Horror: An Essay in Abjection,* trans. Leon S. Roudiez (New York: Columbia University Press, 1982).

5. Ivan Karp, Christine Mullen Kreamer, and Steven D. Lavine, *Museums and Communities,* 2–3. Anthropologists who study particular cultures frequently use the possessive expression ("my tribe," "my people") to refer to the objects of their study, and very likely they extend that appropriation rhetorically.

6. It is risky because to leave out, for example, shippers, looters, vendors, insurers, packagers, janitors, elevator operators, grounds maintenance people, critics, and reviewers is to treat them as outsiders—but who is more intimately engaged with the entrails of the museum and more familiar with its content? Any demarcation of those who are or are not affiliated with the museum presupposes an identifiable domain.

7. A growing number of museum positions are now held by graduates of museum studies programs, which have proliferated during the past two decades. Previously, museum workers were self-perceived "amateurs," drawn from other disciplines, or were, themselves, collectors. Most received their training informally and on the job. Museum practices were therefore less standardized and more likely to be informally adapted to the immediacies of a particular institution's circumstances.

8. Stephen Weil cites Webster's *New International Dictionary* definition of *profession:* "A calling requiring specialized knowledge and often long and intensive preparation including instruction in skills and methods as well as in the scientific, historical, or scholarly principles underlying such skills and methods, maintaining by force of organization or concerted opinion high standards of achievement and conduct, and committing its members to continued study and to a kind of work which has for its prime purpose the rendering of a public service." Weil goes on to point out that in most fields professionalism also includes autonomy: "the practitioners of the profession . . . actually prescribe and monitor the preparatory training for the field, control the entry of new practitioners, and not only promulgate standards of achievment and conduct, but also enforce these standards by imposing sanctions upon those who violate them." Weil, "In Pursuit of a Profession," in *Rethinking the Museum and Other Meditations* (Washington, D.C.: Smithsonian Institution Press, 1990), 75.

9. Albert Parr affirmed that museum workers were indeed professionals, but not members of the same profession. Although there are common goals, the sheer diversity of the types of work done in museums makes the prospect of finding a single functional unity unlikely. Moreover, the existence of common goals does not entail that those who share them should have preeminence over other interested parties that might have different goals. Parr, "A Plurality of Professions," *Curator* 7, no. 4 (1964).

10. Psychological studies of the phenomenon of collecting hold that it is a mode

of self-identification and assertion by appropriation and control over a portion of the world that is not-self. See Elsner and Cardinal, *Cultures of Collecting,* and Susan M. Pearce, *Interpreting Objects and Collections* (London: Routledge, 1994).

11. Mutual constitution does not entail equality; consider, for example, the unequal position of slaveholder and slave, parent and offspring, husband and wife.
12. Museums only occasionally place living people on exhibit, but they do profess to display "living" cultures. To the extent that actual people who are descendants and perpetuators of those cultures identify themselves with the museum project, they are truly (or falsely) represented, and in that sense they are a part of the collection. Artists, likewise, are represented (or underrepresented) in art museum collections and frequently complain that they are neglected as a community in contrast to museums' solicitude toward dealers and trustees. The taste of the latter is, arguably, also on exhibit, but this is diluted with calculations of marketability. Since museums play a powerful part in deciding the fate of artists and in determining whether or not the things they produce are art, it is not far-fetched to suggest that the artists themselves are part of the collection. This, however, is more obviously the case with galleries, which literally have property rights in the artists they represent. As with the "indigenous resources" that "belong to" anthropology museums, artists have organized to win greater control over their own presence in and involvement with art museums. Discussion of this political movement is beyond the scope of this book.
13. Elaine Heumann Gurian, "It's Not a Small World After All," *NEMA News* 21, no. 2 (winter 1997): 1.
14. Or, as Walt Kelly's Pogo would say: "We have met the enemy, and he is us."
15. Logically, *other* is a relative term that demands another "other" symmetrical with itself. Normative distinction, however, includes social as well as evaluative dimensions that give preeminence to the voice that designates itself as standard. Its own otherness is invisible to itself, and, given its de facto power to impose judgment on the other, that other may accede to the inferior status ascribed to it. Revolutionary seizure of political power by persons marked as "other" expresses their refusal to be so characterized and their rebellious demand for parity in difference.
16. Many museums continue to make these taxonomic distinctions, however, and books endorsing them continue to be used in courses of professional training in museum studies. The following text is typical: "In brief, art museums collect the elite artistic productions of civilized societies—paintings, drawings, photographs, statues, furniture, jewelry, textiles, metalware, and some of the crafts of pre-civilized and pre-urban peoples as well. Major art museums collect and exhibit objects from the ancient civilizations of the Mediterranean and the Near East—Egypt, Babylonia, Greece, etc. These include statuary, jewelry, and other objects of art but also such objects as mummies, tomb inscriptions, metal tools and weapons, and common vessels which have more significance in ancient history and in anthropology than they do in art. Ancient history and classical archaeology have traditionally been included in art museums, however." G. Ellis Burcaw, *Introduction to Museum Work,* 2d ed. (Nashville, Tenn.: ASLH, 1983), 32.

17. James Clifford describes the consultation with Tlingit elders brought in to help install the Rasmussen Collection of Northwest Coast objects at the Portland (Oregon) Museum of Art: "In fact, the objects were not the subject of much direct commentary by the elders, who had their own agenda for the meeting. Not that the objects were unimportant; they were important. But they served essentially as kind of aides-memoire for the telling of rather elaborate stories and the singing of many songs. . . . And in some sense the physical objects, at least as I saw it, were left at the margin." Interview with Brian Wallis in "The Global Issue: A Symposium," *Art in America* 77, no. 7 (1989): 152–53, cited by Constance Perin in "The Communicative Circle," in Karp, Kreamer, and Lavine, *Museums and Communities.*

18. Joel N. Bloom, Earl A. Powell III, Ellen Cochran Hicks, Mary Ellen Munley, *Report of the Commission on Museums for a New Century* (Washington, D.C.: American Association of Museums, 1984).

19. Before the eighteenth century, mere curiosity was a prideful offense akin to licentiousness, but it became respectable along with the aims of imperialism: "Since this new era of civilization, a liberal spirit of curiosity has prompted undertakings to which avarice lent no incentive, and fortune annexed no reward: associations have been formed, not for piracy, but humanity; science has had her adventurers, and philanthropy her achievements: the shores of Asia have been invaded by a race of students with no rapacity but for lettered relics; by naturalists, whose cruelty extends not to one human inhabitant; by philosophers, ambitious only for the extirpation of error, and the diffusion of truth. It remains for the artist to claim his part in these guiltless spoliations." Thomas Daniell and William Daniell, *A Picturesque Voyage to India, by way of China,* London (1810), cited by Nicholas Thomas, "Licensed Curiosity: Cook's Pacific Voyages" in Elsner and Cardinal, *Cultures of Collecting,* 127.

20. Members of minority groups are often selected to serve on boards of mainstream organizations cosmetically, "to satisfy the need for diverse representation, . . . rather than to seek diverse opinions. As a result, minorities are often chosen because their backgrounds match the expectations of those already in the structure rather than because they represent another point of view." Robert Garfias, "Cultural Diversity and the Arts in America: The View for the '90s," unpublished manuscript, July 12, 1989.

21. "Empowerment of African American Museums," in *Gender Perspectives: Essays on Women in Museums,* ed. Jane R. Glaser and Artemis A. Zenetou (Washington, D.C.: Smithsonian Institution Press, 1994), 72.

22. The exhibition included procedures for extermination, protective health measures, and proposals to mobilize an effort to eliminate rodents.

23. Edmund Barry Gaither, "'Hey! That's Mine': Thoughts on Pluralism and American Museums," in Karp, Kreamer, and Lavine, *Museums and Communities,* 56–64.

24. Like the Anacostia Museum's rat exhibit, the Chinatown History Museum organized the exhibition, "The Eight Pound Livelihood: A History of Chinese Laundry Workers in America" (1984), which resonated with an experience shared by many older members of the local community. It also had educational impact and solidified understanding within families, between generations, and

among those of unequal assimilation. "Creating a Dialogic Museum: The Chinatown History Museum Experiment," in Karp, Kreamer, and Lavine, *Museums and Communities,* 294.

25. Some science and even art museums are now following the model of technology and history museums, showing skilled workers, on site, using equipment and sometimes enlisting audience participation in active production. Demonstration of the intellectual process of scientific research or art making challenges exhibition designers to do more than "hands on" manipulation. This is a job for creative curatorship, and scholars might well take an active part in its conception.

4. Transcending the Object

1. Robert Harbison, *Eccentric Spaces* (New York: Knopf, 1977; reprint, Boston: David R. Godine, Nonpareil Books, 1988), 31, 140.
2. Jean Baudrillard holds that an object is a "resistant material body" and inhabits a "mental realm . . . whose function is relative to a subject." He also maintains that in so far as they refer back to the subject, objects constitute themselves as a system that defines the subject's personal microcosm. According to Baudrillard, the functional alternatives of possession and use govern the subject's objectifying system. Philosophical history, at least from Aristotle to Kant, has assigned priority instead to a logical level of identification of objects, which is taken to precede all possible functions. Baudrillard, "System of Collecting."
3. George Berkeley, bishop of Cloyne (1685–1753) was certainly on the right track with his fantastic aphorism, *Esse est percipi;* see his *A Treatise Concerning the Principles of Human Knowledge* (1710). His idealism was restricted, however, by the realism of common sense without the spice of cultural diversity and pluralism.
4. Edwina Taborsky, "The Discursive Object," in *Objects of Knowledge,* ed. Susan Pearce (London: Athlone Press, 1990), 50–77.
5. The word "entity" designates anything that may be spoken of, including figments and fictions, impossible things and falsehoods, as well as possible and past events, relations, equations, and abstract qualities. To distinguish their manner of being from the hard existence of material objects, philosophers have introduced the level-distinguishing expressions "subsist" and "subsistence" into the vocabulary of metaphysics.
6. Cited from a story by Luis Borges in Michel Foucault, *The Order of Things: An Archaeology of the Human Sciences* (New York: Pantheon Books, 1970; Vintage Books edition, 1973), xv.
7. Foucault, *Order of Things,* xx.
8. Arjun Appadurai describes such "life histories" in terms of the distribution of knowledge at various points or phases, from production to consumption. Where biographical analysis is applied only to commodities, such knowledge is largely technical and verificational; but with the emergence of the object as a sign function, a more complexly codified epistemology is invoked. Appadurai, *The Social Life of Things: Commodities in Cultural Perspective* (Cambridge: Cambridge University Press, 1986), 41. See also Mihalyi Csikszentmihalyi, "Why We Need Things," in Lubar and Kinger, *History from Things.*

9. Taborsky, "Discursive Object," 66.

10. Not long ago, the Italian government approved the return of an Ethiopian sculpture that was seized by Mussolini's army during the pre–World War II conquest of Abyssinia. The seizure was meant to symbolize the restoration of Italy to the grandeur of the Roman Empire. In returning the item, Italian representatives declared that they understood the experience of having one's national treasures stolen by invaders and not returned.

11. Francis Bacon's fictional second counselor advises his prince on the contents of a well-equipped philosopher's cabinet. It must include: "A library, a botanical and zoological garden, a goodly huge cabinet, wherein whatsoever the hand of man by exquisite art or engine hath made rare in stuff, form, or motion; whatsoever singularity, chance, and the shuffle of things hath produced; whatsoever nature hath wrought in things that want life and may be kept, shall be sorted and included; and a still-house, so furnished with mills, instruments, furnaces, and vessels as may be a palace fit for a philosopher's stone." *Gesta Gestorum,* 1594, cited in Gerard Turner, "The Cabinet of Experimental Philosophy," in Oliver Impey and Arthur MacGregor, *The Origin of Museums: The Cabinet of Curiosities in Sixteenth- and Seventeenth-Century Europe* (Oxford, Clarendon Press, 1985), 214.

12. Two collectors, who sometimes shared and exchanged collected items, used them in the service of very different ideological projects. The academic Ulisse Aldrovandi (1522–1605) defended the naturalistic hypothesis that social customs are affected by environmental resources and production; his contemporary, Christian cleric Antonio Giganti, organized his collection in pious tribute to the harmony of God's universal order. See Shelton, "Cabinets of Transgression," 177–204. See also Laura Laurenchich-Minelli, "Museography and Ethnographical Collections in Bologna during the Sixteenth and Seventeenth Centuries," in Impey and MacGregor, *Origin of Museums.*

13. Alexander Baumgarten (1714–62), *Reflections on Poetry,* trans. Karl Aschenbrenner and William B. Holther (Berkeley and Los Angeles: University of California Press, 1954).

14. I am attributing the birth of art history to the eighteenth-century figure Johann Winckelmann (1717–68). However, specialists in the discipline give pride of place to Giorgio Vasari (1511–74), more than two centuries earlier. I am grateful to Whitney Davis for calling my attention to this discrepancy.

15. Thomas DaCosta Kaufmann, "From Treasury to Museum: The Collections of the Austrian Habsburgs," in Elsner and Cardinal, *Cultures of Collecting.*

16. Carol Duncan, "Art Museums and the Rituals of Citizenship" in *Exhibiting Cultures: The Poetics and Politics of Museum Display,* ed. Ivan Karp and Steven Lavine (Washington, D.C.: Smithsonian Institution Press, 1991), 94.

17. Strictly speaking, an emanating God could not benefit from a watchful eye. This anachronistic confusion derives from the conversion of a Neoplatonic superfluity of Being, an impersonal effluence, into a Christian Overseer, mindful of every sparrow.

18. Brian O'Doherty, *Inside the White Cube: The Ideology of the Gallery Space* (Santa Monica: Lapis Press, 1976, 1986), 15.

19. A most poignant (and ironic) appreciation of this warfare is revealed in Mark

Tansey's 1984 painting, *Triumph of the New York School,* in which André Breton, ideologue of the Paris School of painting, is portrayed surrendering to Clement Greenberg, the American critic and spokesperson of abstract expressionism. The military garb of the antagonists, dressed in World War I and II uniforms respectively, and their well-known artist adjutants suggest archaic combat and a reference to a stylized battlefield that never existed outside the art world.

20. O'Doherty, *Inside the White Cube,* 41.
21. The philosophical implications of these events were noted by Arthur Danto in a 1964 lecture, which became the foundation of a movement in aesthetics that relativizes the concept "work of art" in terms of an art historical tradition. Danto's thesis was the progenitor of the "institutional theory" of George Dickie, who, however, conceives the art world and its turmoils as a sociological rather than an ontological phenomenon, and the identification of artworks as a matter of arbitrary fashion. The focus of philosophical theory on the definition of art has a long history, which was interrupted by a momentary abandonment of speculative metaphysical theory. It was revived by Danto's expression of malaise over the indiscernibility of the difference between (professed) artworks and real world things, a concern that signaled a metaphysical crisis. Arthur Danto, "The Artworld," *Journal of Philosophy* 61 (1964): 571–84. See also George Dickie, "Defining Art," *American Philosophical Quarterly* 6 (1969): 253–56, and Dickie, *Art and the Aesthetic: An Institutional Analysis* (New York: St. Martins Press, 1975). Arthur Danto, *The Transfiguration of the Commonplace: A Philosophy of Art* (Cambridge, Mass.: Harvard University Press, 1981).
22. Spencer Crews and James Sims, "Locating Authenticity: Fragments of a Dialogue," in Karp and Lavine, *Exhibiting Cultures,* 159.
23. Crews and Sims, "Locating Authenticity."
24. Wolfgang Iser, one of the originators of the theory, asks what happens to the reader when he or she reads something. Prior approaches to literary texts focused on intention (chiefly that of the author), assuming or demanding that something equivalent take place on the part of the reader, and defining the text as a device whose meaning causally links the two. Iser holds that texts initiate performances of meaning that are not everywhere identical with themselves. The reader's response is the act of meaning that completes the text. Since there can be many readers and many acts of reading, and since these are often regulated by social position, there are many possible completions of a text that vary with the reader's real and self-perceived social identity. Iser, *The Act of Reading: A Theory of Aesthetic Response* (Baltimore: Johns Hopkins Press, 1978). The treatment of objects by museums may be analyzed analogously. Curators, whether of artworks or historical objects or scientific specimens, were typically understood to seek recovery of an original meaning (intention, function, natural state) and to display the object in the manner best able to reproduce that meaning in the consciousness of the viewer. Bringing the viewer actively into the equation as constitutive of meaning potentiates the object and makes multiple performances of meaning possible. It transforms the museum from dispatch agent to site of dynamic exchange.

25. *New York Times,* January 11, 1994, C17. See also the interview with Ralph Appelbaum, "On Being an Exhibit Designer," in *Exhibitionist* 13, no. 1 (spring 1996): 15.
26. Even here absolute control is not possible. Individuals vary in their perceptual physiology and not everyone will see the same illusions or images or see them with equal speed or clarity. Nonetheless, there is greater likelihood of agreement among perceivers with normal binocular eyesight about an object's distance than about its beauty or ethical import.
27. Viewers of fine art, habituated to seeing reproductions of "great" works of art, are sometimes disappointed by their experience of the "actual" object, which may turn out to be small and drab in comparison to the blown-up, illuminated surrogate. The philosopher Walter Benjamin wrote that excessive exposure to photographic reproduction dissipated the "aura" of original artworks and undermined their effect. New audiences, however, seem to have substituted other, equally satisfying types of experience that have become available as a result of the technologies of reproduction. "The Work of Art in the Age of Mechanical Reproduction," in Benjamin, *Illuminations.*
28. Typological specificity persists among museums, however, and is evident in their limited capacity to legitimize cross-categorial qualitative judgments. A science museum can exhibit works of art and designate them as such, but it cannot confer the status of art on an object. Correspondingly, a work of art can be used by a science museum to illustrate a scientific concept, but the object does not thereby become an element of scientific demonstration. Aesthetic judgment plays a profound part in scientific understanding, but the beauty enjoyed is that of nature—not of art—and the production of art, however inclusive of scientific understanding, is not an advance within and for science. Thus science museums continue to evoke experiences distinguished as "scientific," and art museums elicit "aesthetic experiences."
29. The anthropologist Arjun Appadurai, following Georg Simmel, argues that exchange is the basis of value. What is exchanged and at what sacrifice is determined at the highest levels by what Appadurai calls "tournaments of values." Their victories and vagaries account for the uneven flow of goods, the renewal of tensions, and the repeated shifts in values among contenders. Appadurai, *Social Life of Things.*
30. Empirical studies have identified certain types of experience that visitors come to museums to achieve. The Smithsonian's Institutional Studies Office (ISO) distinguishes four categories: social experiences, object experiences, cognitive experiences, and introspective experiences. These are general categories that can be associated with both individual preference and certain types of museums. The point of these and other studies that classify museum experiences is to enable museums to deliver wanted experiences more effectively, according to the assumptions that museums are accountable to their "clients" for providing conditions that enhance the experience they seek. Doering, "Strangers, Guests or Clients?"
31. The endeavor to generalize by personalizing is evident in contemporary journalism and film documentation, as well as in the popularity of memoirs and the "humanizing" of celebrities.

32. According to this paradigm, to appreciate science is not to know its results but to make one's own observations, formulate hypotheses, gather evidence, and solve problems. To study history is to reenact historical situations empathically on the strength of inferred inductive evidence; and to encounter art is to succumb to aesthetic stimuli creatively and kinesthetically, as the artist does. Museum visitors are expected to bring to every experience their own knowledge, attitudes, and cultural predispositions and so, in their heterogeneity, to resemble all scientists, all historians, all artists, and to join with them in encountering all other visitors.

33. Physical substances such as drugs and alcohol, direct pressure on nerve centers, and exposure to associative stimuli seem to be the most reliable means, but the pornography industry, horror films, and the literature of violence have evidently mastered the art of packaging certain types of experience as well. These, undoubtedly, are not the ones we would most like museums to deliver.

5. Museum Experience

1. Statement introducing a collection of paintings (1953–54) at the San Francisco Museum of Modern Art, June 1997. Gift of Harry W. and Mary Margaret Anderson 72.26.

2. "The Real Thing," *The Portable Henry James,* ed. Morton Dauwen Zabel (New York: Viking Press, 1956), 151.

3. Adorno, "The Valery Proust Museum," in *Prisms,* 175–85.

4. Peter von Mensch, "Methodological Museology," in Pearce, *Objects of Knowledge.*

5. If Reality is equated with God, as Neoplatonist Christians maintained, the boost up the ladder of Being is nontrivial. Things can then be deemed worthy of care and attention, if not on their own behalf then for their conductivity to the Divine.

6. Plato believed that material objects are at one remove from real Forms and that images, which imitate material objects, are twice removed. They are "mere" appearances, insubstantial shadows that distract the mind from contemplation of the real nature of things. The sensuous appearance of art draws attention to itself, diverting the soul away from the true and more difficult path that leads to knowledge of Reality. Descendants of Plato have softened his harsh judgment of the material world as mere seduction, but sensory experience is still considered superficial and, at best, a threshold to a deeper knowledge. Belief in the inferiority of sensory pleasures has made its way even into those museums whose earthly treasures are their glory.

7. The concept of art's autonomy, or "art for art's sake," derives preeminently from the philosophy of Immanuel Kant, *Critique of Judgment,* 1790. Kant distinguishes the experience of beauty from moral or utilitarian judgments by divorcing aesthetic experience from a concern with existence (reality.) One attends with aesthetic appreciation to a work of the imagination without regard for its origin or consequences. Subsequent philosophers further refined this doctrine, elevating the work of art to a superior realm of imagination, where genius transcends the rules of ordinary nature and produces objects capable of

transporting the appreciator to an exalted state of aesthetic inspiration. See also, Miles Orvell, *The Real Thing: Imitation and Authenticity in American Culture, 1880–1940* (Chapel Hill: University of North Carolina Press, 1989).

8. James Clifford cites Susan Stewart's study, *On Longing,* which shows "how collecting—and most notably the museum—creates the illusion of adequate representation of a world by first cutting objects out of specific contexts . . . and making them 'stand for' abstract wholes." A scheme of classification is next elaborated for the storage and display of the objects, giving the collection an order and reality which overrides the history of the object's production and appropriation. Thus in the Western museum, "an illusion of a relation between things takes the place of a social relation." Clifford goes on to make the generalization: The *production* of meaning in museum classification and display is mystified as adequate *representation.* (author's emphasis) Clifford, "Objects and Selves," in *Objects and Others: Essays on Museums and Material Culture,* ed. George W. Stocking Jr., History of Anthropology, vol. 3 (Madison: University of Wisconsin, 1985), 239.

9. Plato himself was not above manufacturing illusions in the service of power; e.g., the myth of "noble" metals in *Republic,* Book 3. The use of persuasive metaphor and inspirational music is prominent in his philosophy, but he does not rely on the mediation of material objects to achieve rhetorical ends.

10. Plato's archetypal Ideas were singular, nonmaterial, unchanging, eternal, and indestructible. Their imitations, being plural, material, temporal, and subject to change and dissolution, could have only dubious resemblance to them. Any imitation, even one that is qualitatively indiscernible from its model, must necessarily be indexically distinct. Where there was one, there now are two.

11. No warranty is thereby made as to the quality of the original; nor does it follow that intervening changes might not improve upon it or have been intended or desired initially. Authenticity assured through provenance refers exclusively to substantive constancy, or adherence to an original condition, or at least to a documented history of change.

12. Fake things can come to have genuine status, distinct from that of their original. Eventually their value may even exceed that of the original, but only as the fake acquires a history independent of its derivative origin. For example, current fashion, stimulated by environmental consciousness and a touch of perversity, celebrates the wearing of fake furs (the *faux* look), which would have been repulsive forty years ago as a cheap surrogate for the "real thing." Fake furs, like vegetarian edibles, are often valued as much for their resemblance to the "wicked" reality as for their freedom from its wickedness.

13. According to the prevalent ideology of the lone artistic genius, works that have been touched by hands other than those of the "original creator," whether by apprentices, improvers, or restorers, have lost their claim to being the "real thing." Museums are cautiously replacing labels that attribute works to individual artists (e.g., Rembrandt, Reubens) where historical research reveals that the master artists oversaw studios and workshops in which students and assistants carried out large portions of the productive labor. Although these discoveries raise important questions for historical authentication, they do not have to lead to the conclusion that the works in question are fraudu-

lent. Rather, they cast doubt on the conventions of attribution, raising the question of what might be signified by a "real Rembrandt" or "real Reubens." This does not necessarily challenge the entitlement of an object to consideration as a "real work of art" or a "real object."

14. For a pithy dismissal of what he calls the "tingle and immersion" theory, "which has become part of the fabric of our common nonsense," see Nelson Goodman, *Languages of Art* (Indianapolis, Ind.: Hackett, 1976). It seems to be understood that changes brought about in an object as a result of "natural" causes (e.g., through weathering or dirt accumulation) do not affect its "real" identity, but human interventions (e.g., addition of embellishment or a coat of varnish) do falsify the original. There are, of course, disputed gray areas of material change, which may have been positively anticipated by the original producer.

15. Denis Dutton, ed., *The Forger's Art* (Berkeley and Los Angeles: University of California Press, 1983), deals at length with historic instances of forgery and poses the problem of its ethical and aesthetic significance. See also Mark Jones, *Fake? The Art of Deception* (London: British Museum Publications, 1990).

16. The difference between fakes and forgeries is largely a matter of ethical and economic significance. It is not determinable aesthetically. Philosophers, however, have found it fascinating. See Goodman, *Languages of Art.*

17. Van Meegeren successfully produced a series of Vermeer forgeries that fooled the experts. Van Meegeren carefully reproduced the master's style and materials but slightly extended his typical subject matter. The paintings were hailed as genuine, even as enlarging the corpus of Vermeer's work in accordance with certain scholarly expectations. The deception was disclosed only when, in 1945, having sold some of his work to the Nazi collector Hermann Goering, van Meegeren was brought to trial for selling national treasures. In order to exonerate himself of the more serious charge, van Meegeren painted another false Vermeer for the court, thus demonstrating his skill at the forger's art and persuading the judges of the fraudulent "unreality" of his earlier productions.

18. Nicholas Thomas, "Licensed Curiosity: Cook's Pacific Voyages," in Elsner and Cardinal, *Cultures of Collecting,* 127.

19. Pearce observes that although material things have been held in low regard in Western culture, they alone "have the power to carry the past into the present by virtue of their `real' relationship to past events." Unlike words, which can only be about the past, objects, given their intact provenance, are literally a part of the past they preserve. This is the basis of their intense interest. "It is the ability of objects to be simultaneously signs and symbols, to carry a true part of the past into the present, but also to bear perpetual symbolic reinterpretation, which is the essence of their peculiar and ambiguous power." Pearce, *Museums, Objects, and Collections,* 27. The collector selects a part of a whole, retaining that portion of the real according to some motivating strategy, but in doing so reinvents the collected item as a representation. The object retains this dual nature, as signifier and signified, in tension, accounting for both its emotional resonance and intellectual interest; ibid., 38.

20. Pearce, *Museums, Objects, and Collections,* 258.

21. Readers contemporary to Lewis Carroll would have found the smile that remained after the Cheshire cat disappeared uncanny, because they knew it was logically impossible that a smile persist beyond the face that wears it. But to late-twentieth-century readers of *Through the Looking Glass,* the eerie grin is absolute. The notion that something intangible could be suspended in space (like a holograph) without visible means of support is no longer bizarre.

22. Susanne K. Langer identifies for the several art forms—painting, sculpture, music, dance—the specific genre of reality that each "creates." All visual art, for example, produces "virtual space," and music creates "virtual time." Langer considered architecture to be a "total environment made visible" and thus an expression of "virtual" selfhood or of a collective ethnic identity. Langer, *Feeling and Form* (New York: Charles Scribner's Sons, 1953).

23. A vast philosophical literature arrays a number of variations on the theme that art is experience. Leo Tolstoy held the view that only a sincere communication of a profound feeling from one soul to another is a genuine work of art; Tolstoy, *What Is Art?* trans. Alymer Maude (London: Oxford University Press, 1930). The Croce/Collingwood theory holds that the work of art is a mental object created by the artist and transmitted symbolically, so as to be reproduced in the minds of appreciators. Perhaps the theory that resonates best with contemporary students is John Dewey's notion, expressed in *Art as Experience,* that a work of art is newly "recreated" by the perceiver each time it is experienced. On this view, there is not one but an indefinite number of artworks for every work that is created.

24. Using computer-generated images and mathematical modeling techniques, the film was able to achieve a virtual reality beyond the wildest dreams of taxidermists. Taxidermic mounts, though literally composed of the real thing, cannot compete with their electronic counterpart in their virtual effect. *Jurassic Park* was not primarily about achieving historic accuracy, however: The film even took some notable liberties with scientific evidence in the interest of dramatic effect. See Stephen Jay Gould, "Dinomania," in *New York Review of Books* 40, no. 14, April 12, 1993, for a discussion of the film *Jurassic Park;* the original book by Michael Crichton (New York: Random House, 1990); and the book by Don Shay and Jody Duncan, *The Making of Jurassic Park* (New York: Ballentine Books, 1993), which describes the making of the film. Gould also calls attention in his essay to the blurring of popular and professional domains, as may be seen, on the one hand, by the British journal *Nature*'s publication of an article on the extraction of fossil DNA from a Cretaceous weevil timed to coincide with the opening of *Jurassic Park.* On the other hand, the filmmakers sought and followed advice from expert paleobiologists to make their rendition as convincing as possible.

25. A mastodon skeleton figures prominently in Peale's portrait, *The Artist in His Museum* (1822), where such recovered items served the dual function of entertainment and evidence. The London Crystal Palace exhibition of 1851 also featured full-scale models that, then as now, drew hordes of curious thrill seekers. What is known today about dinosaurs is based chiefly on the study of fossils combined with comparative study of contemporary animal anatomy and increasingly sophisticated reconstructions drawn from paleobotany and ecology.

26. Lize Mogel, an exhibition preparator at the American Museum of Natural History, writes of a re-creation made for the museum of an 80-million-year-old Oviraptorid nest: "The . . . model gives life to the silent fossils and sparks the imagination of all who try to visualize life in the time of the dinosaurs." "Hatching an Oviraptorid: Building a Model at the American Museum of Natural History," *Exhibitionist* 15, no. 1 (spring 1996): 36. Of course, no humans or large mammals would have been around at that time in the Gobi Desert, where the nest was found, to enjoy the actual experience of observing the hatchlings. We can only imagine what that might have been like.

27. Paleobiologists and many museumgoers disagree with this judgment. They maintain that the antiquity of the natural object and the knowledge of its history have a deeply moving effect of their own upon visitors, which exceeds whatever excitement might be produced by the cleverly engineered contemporary fabrications. I do not dispute this point, but argue simply that both of these clearly distinct experiences are real.

28. The same principle, adapted to aesthetic enjoyment, prescribes that the appreciator, while feeling pleasure, yet be personally disinterested and detached from the object. This is the Kantian legacy, which has its source in Enlightenment theory of knowledge.

29. Pioneered in the 1830s by the Milwaukee Public Museum, dioramas were state-of-the-art reproductions of authentic sites. They were often scaled-down models, in order to conserve cost and space, but were presented in realistic light and perspective behind nonreflecting glass. Technological possibility and cost have always been the limiting condition of mimetic realism.

30. Edward P. Alexander describes a "panorama craze," reproducing sound and motion, that swept Europe and America in the 1820s and 1830s. Alexander, *Museums in Motion*, 82.

31. Margaret J. King, "Instruction and Delight: Theme Parks and Education," in *The Cultures of Celebrations* (Bowling Green, Ohio: Popular Press, 1994), 228.

32. Umberto Eco, *Travels in Hyperreality: Essays,* trans. William Weaver (New York: Harcourt Brace Jovanovich, 1986), 7.

33. The substantial entry fee, once paid, allows visitors to wander freely from ride to ride and exhibit to exhibit without purchasing additional tickets or adhering to schedules. Restaurants and comfort stations are plentiful and not expensive, and despite the multitude of visitors, one does not feel crowded or harassed because of the expert management of space and subtle surveillance. The atmosphere is miraculously peaceful, yet studded with "spontaneous" diversions. Without the presence of clocks or newspapers, and with the tastefully arranged allure of unthreatening new enticements, it is no wonder that visitors are willing to spend six or eight hours, or as much as a week altogether, contentedly submitting to what Arnold Berleant calls "the sublimation of commercial culture and the desublimation of the sublime." Berleant, "The Critical Aesthetics of Disneyworld," in *Living in the Landscape: Toward an Aesthetics of Environment* (Lawrence: University Press of Kansas, 1997), 41–57.

34. Some, but not all, definitions of museums (including that of the American Association of Museums) specify their not-for-profit status.

35. As its name suggests, the U.S. Holocaust Memorial Museum has an ambigu-

ous identity as both memorial and museum. However, it has become a model for museums throughout the world, and its architects and designers are much in demand for the construction of new exhibitions.

36. This is an argument that favors artificial reproduction, but it ignores the fact that reproduction presupposes a prior reality by definition, and that without that reference the value of the reproduction would be diminished. Electronic reproduction of a Rembrandt painting, for example, would become meaningless if knowledge of the original painting ceased to exist. Thus reproduction, however accurate, can never replace preservation altogether—or rather, if it does, historical meaning will simply have come to an end.

37. Museum staff members, on the other hand, do sometimes conduct original research, and their work then merits the same notice and reward as that given to their scholarly colleagues with positions in institutions of formal education.

38. André Malraux, *Museum without Walls (Le Musée Imaginaire)*, trans. Stuart Gilbert and Francis Price (New York: Doubleday, 1967).

6. Museum Ethics: The Good Life of the the Public Servant

1. "In the allocentric mode there is objectification; the emphasis is on what the object is like; there is either no relation or a less pronounced or less direct relation between perceived sensory qualities and pleasure-unpleasure feelings . . . ; the perceiver usually approaches or turns to the object actively and in doing so either opens himself toward it receptively or, figuratively or literally, takes hold of it, tries to 'grasp' it." Ernest G. Schactel associates this perceptual mode of attention preeminently with the higher senses of sight and audition that are foremost in cognitive pursuits, such as science. Schactel, *Metamorphosis: On the Development of Affect, Perception, Attention and Memory* (New York: Basic Books, 1959), 83. Evelyn Fox Keller has suggested that poets and artists offer a more familiar model of allocentric perception, while scientists tend, regrettably, to concentrate on "objects in use." She would prefer a more "dynamic" objectivity that neither "grasps" nor seeks distance but attends to objects with erotic receptivity. Keller, *Reflections on Gender and Science* (New Haven, Conn.: Yale University Press, 1985), 120. Museums might be characterized as bound in a long-standing love affair with objects.

2. Obligations may be owed to persons in virtue of their role or station, as distinct from their individual humanity (e.g., duty to honor parents.) Obligation may also be claimed toward abstract entities or institutions (e.g., loyalty to ideals, to country); and there are obligations without specific object that simply prescribe behavior (e.g., the duty to obey the law). But, in general, moral duty devolves only upon persons to enact, and other persons are its beneficiaries. Although nonhuman animals and things are capable of causing injury, we do not regard them as morally culpable for doing so; nor, in the secular culture of the West, do we attribute moral merit to plants or objects, whatever their balm or benefit to us might be. The obligation of humans toward nonhuman things is rarely depicted as reciprocal.

3. Deep Ecologists argue that since humans count as only one among the species that inhabit the earth, they have no greater claim to its benefits than any other,

let alone to supremacy over other species. Of course it does not follow that they should have less claim or should be subordinate to others.

4. Classical Western philosophers are even more restrictive. Those who understand morality as a cognitive capacity attribute it exclusively to beings with the power of reason. This has been taken to justify the denial of moral judgment to women, children, the infirm, and the mentally incompetent, and therefore to legitimate paternalistic authority over them. It does not follow that they are to be mistreated, but only that they are not held competent to judge for themselves. To the extent that ethical discourse applies to them, their duty is obedience.

5. Christopher D. Stone argues that legal rights should be extended to nonhuman beings for the sake of their protection on grounds other than property ownership. Stone even suggests that they—trees, rivers—might be held responsible for the commission of wrongs and how they might, through intermediaries functioning as guardians or trustees, repay those whom they have injured. Stone, *Should Trees Have Standing?: and Other Essays on Law, Morals, and the Environment* (Dobbs Ferry, N.Y.: Oceana Publications, 1996). As legally constituted institutions, museums do have responsibilities and obligations, but their moral status is unspecified.

6. In its 1994 (second printing) *Code of Ethics for Museums,* the AAM affirms: "The distinctive character of museum ethics derives from the ownership, care, and use of objects, specimens and living collections representing the world's natural and cultural common wealth. This stewardship of collections entails the highest public trust and carries with it the presumption of rightful ownership, permanence, care, documentation, accessibility, and responsible disposal." *Code of Ethics for Museums* (Washington, D.C.: American Association of Museums, 1994), 8.

7. Museums are especially vulnerable to erratic and legally binding testamentary demands as well as to policy decisions taken by boards of trustees long ago and for possibly obsolete purposes.

8. In democratic societies the flourishing of the larger community is believed to follow from the aggregate of private, individual gratifications; more "organicist" social theories affirm that personal identity and well-being are achieved only derivatively, within a human or theocratic community. To my knowledge, no ethical philosopher attributed a "good life," or moral identity distinct from that of either the whole or its parts, to intermediate-level collective entities, such as museums or other public institutions.

9. The term *moral discontinuities* is taken from an essay by Thomas Nagel, "Ruthlessness in Public Life," in *Public and Private Morality,* ed. Stuart Hampshire (New York: Cambridge University Press, 1978), 75–91. Nagel is specifically concerned with the distinction between private and public life: "Institutions are not persons and do not have private lives, nor do institutional roles usually absorb completely the lives of their occupants. Public institutions are designed to serve purposes larger than those of particular individuals or families. They tend to pursue the interests of masses of people. . . . In addition, public acts are diffused over many actors and sub-institutions; there is a division of labor both in decision and in execution. All this results in a different balance between the morality of outcomes and the morality of actions.

These two types of moral constraint are differently expressed in public life, and both of them take more impersonal forms."

10. It is doubtful that any situation can be so particularized that no one, apart from the directly participating agents and those acted upon by them, is affected, because all actions have consequences beyond their immediate outcome. No one acts entirely independently of a social milieu. However, classical ethical theory typically treats moral acts as autonomous and disconnected from a larger context, thereby underscoring direct and immediate individual responsibility. In a professional context, the impact of one's actions is frequently indirect and not immediately discernible.

11. For the definition of the term *profession,* see chapter 3, note 8.

12. There should, of course, be adequate remuneration for professional work. This should be commensurate with the intensive training required and with the value of the work accomplished. However, it is not the function of the professional code of ethics to guarantee such rewards.

13. The international museum community and its representative organization, ICOM, have also articulated a code of ethics—*International Council of Museums Statutes and Code of Professional Ethics* (1990), with which the AAM code is coordinated. I confine my discussion here to the U.S. codes for the sake of simplicity.

14. *AAM Code of Ethics for Museum Workers* (New York: 1925); reprinted in *Museum News* 52 (June 1974): 26–29.

15. A session on "Stolen Art" organized for the AAM convention of 1996 left no doubt that illicit acquisition and trade in contraband art are still problems. The speakers were, however, chiefly concerned with control by legislation and enforcement, matters that lie outside the scope of ethical inquiry. Subsequent controversy over the accession of works of art diverted from Holocaust victims reveals the persistence of the problem. See also Alexander, *Museums in Motion,* 241.

16. Douglas J. Preston, *Dinosaurs in the Attic: An Excursion into the American Museum of Natural History* (New York: St. Martin's Press, 1986); Thomas Hoving, *Making the Mummies Dance: Inside the Metropolitan Museum of Art* (New York: Simon and Schuster, 1993); Aline B. Saarinen, *The Proud Possessors: The Lives, Times, and Tastes of Some Adventurous Art Collectors* (New York: Random House, 1958).

17. "Museum Ethics," report printed in *Museum News* 56 (March–April 1978), reprinted as a pamphlet in 1978 by AAM, Washington, D.C.

18. This observation puts me at odds with Foucaultian commentators, who identify museums with other instruments of social surveillance and control. I do not deny their function as tastemakers and regulators of substantive opinion (along with other educational institutions), but I believe their internal codes of ethics have less to do with the exercise of power over the public, directly or indirectly, than with the forging of a suprapersonal identity uniquely related to nonpersonal things.

19. *Museum Ethics* (Washington, D.C.: AAM, 1978), 11.

20. A correlative conviction among philosophers of value theory was that the optimal ethical judgment must be made by an impartial, detached observer, guided only by principle and from behind a "veil of ignorance" of specifics.

Likewise in aesthetic contexts, the critic must be disinterested in and emotively unconnected to the object of evaluative appreciation. But, see my discussion of the erosion of the concept of dispassionate experience in Chapter 5.

21. Many people wanted museums (and all agencies with educational responsibility) to take a stand on controversial matters such as civil rights, the Vietnam war, racism, sexism, and environmental destruction. The prevailing response given by museum leaders was that commitment to a position, and more so activism on its behalf, would be a betrayal of rational objectivity and so of the very ideals upon which museums (and all educational institutions) were founded. The pursuit of knowledge—not its implementation—was held to be the business of disinterested scholarship and so of the centers that pursued it, and to the extent that they deviated from strict neutrality, they were thought to compromise both their credibility and their integrity. Years would pass before that affirmation was seriously challenged on epistemological and not simply political grounds.

22. Stephen E. Weil, one of the first to explore the legal and ethical character of art museums in depth, pointed out in 1982 that many American museums are neither strictly public nor strictly private; they are part of the "third sector" of "charitable" institutions, which "do not operate for profit, and are devoted to serving the general welfare—not simply the welfare of their members or supporters." Despite their enormous assets, these hybrid organizations are protected from public accountability and were, until recently, rarely exposed to scrutiny under criminal and civil provisions of private law. Their jurisprudential ancestry in equity places them under the quasi-ethical constraints of "fairness, justness and right dealing," and this, as with charitable trusts, gives vague supervisory power to trustees with little public oversight. "The net effect of those factors is that under the common law [in the United States] trustees and administrators of charitable trusts have been virtually exempt from supervision." The problem, as Weil understood it at the time, was the absence of agreed-upon standards for museum conduct, and its solution, as he saw it, was "for the museum community—unless and until it is proved incapable of doing so—to undertake this task (of legislating standards) itself." Otherwise stated, this is a plea for strengthened self-oversight and professionalism. "Breaches of Trust, Remedies and Standards," in Weil, *Beauty and the Beasts.*

23. Giles W. Mead, introduction to *Museum Ethics.*

24. These reports were compiled and revised by subcommittees within the profession. They were published separately in *Museum News* and distributed as a combined package, together with the AAM's *Code of Ethics for Museums* (1994). In addition, various studies are available that deal with quasi-legal, quasi-ethical matters, such as collecting cultural property and labor relations, where museum policy is at an interface with federal, state, and local law.

25. In *Beauty and the Beasts,* Weil cites such examples as the court-supervised closing of the Harding Museum in 1982, when its assets were turned over to the Art Institute of Chicago, and the negotiated formulation of deaccessioning practices by the Metropolitan Museum of Art in 1973.

26. Robert MacDonald, "Ethics: Constructing a Code," *Museum News* (May–June 1992): 62–65. There was strong feeling within the community that the proceeds

from object sales should be used exclusively for the development of collections and not for general maintenance and operation of the museum, since this would jeopardize the very existence of museums according to the still-influential object-centered model. This issue strikes at the museum community's deepest ontological commitment. Though apparently a discussion of economic strategies, the restriction on how funds may be allocated prevents the substitution of programs and technology for the preservation and care of things.

27. See my discussion of this connection in Chapter 3.

28. Support for these developmental and educational projects also came from governmental sources such as the National Science Foundation (NSF) and the NEA and NEH, but the bulk of funding came from agencies such as the W. K. Kellogg Foundation, which prior to its "Projects in Museum Education" had shown little interest in museums, despite its long-standing concern for "continuing education." Mary Ellen Munley, *Catalysts for Change: The Kellogg Projects in Museum Education* (Washington, D.C.: Published in conjunction with the AAM, 1986).

29. "Open-ended, experiential, tied to no specific testing agenda, diffuse, qualitative rather than quantitative, centering upon individual variation rather than typical practice, de-emphasizing the authority of the expert host. . . . (A)s final authority on its own essence, the museum is beginning to disappear as emphatically as the literary text has for contemporary reader-response theorists, and for similar reasons. It is being deprivileged as throughout our entire culture the canons of taste and the assumptions of scholarship have been challenged and challenged from within. There is no reason to believe that museums can be immune from this any more than universities, libraries, or medical schools." Neil Harris, "Polling for Opinions," *Museum News* 69, no. 5 (September–October 1990): 46–55.

30. The Frankfurt Institut fur Sozialforschung played a large part in bringing institutional criticism to the foreground. Among the critical claims was the thesis that institutions are not transparent but work as mediators between individual consciousness and the grand sweep of economic and/or metaphysical history. Few theorists discussed museums directly (but see Theodor Adorno, "The Valery Proust Museum," in *Prisms,* and Walter Benjamin's autobiographical "Unpacking My Library," in *Illuminations.* The ideas of Walter Benjamin are certainly relevant to the next generation's awakened consciousness of interconnections between social theory, technology and the arts. (e.g., "The Work of Art in the Age of Mechanical Reproduction," in *Illuminations,* which places art within the social context of technological production). Most of the literature of the period, however, discusses art as institution, as distinct from the institutions in which the art is housed. For further discussion of this topic, see also *Museum Culture: Histories, Discourses, Spectacles,* ed. Daniel J. Sherman and Irit Rogoff (Minneapolis: University of Minnesota Press, 1994). Sherman suggests that an understanding of the political role of museum collection akin to that later pronounced by Walter Benjamin was already evident in the writing of the leading art theorist following the French Revolution, "Quatremere/Benjamin/Marx: Art Museums, Aura, and Commodity Fetishism"; Sherman and Rogoff, 123–43. See also Peter Vergo, ed., *The New Museology* (London: Reaktion Press, 1989).

31. Douglas Crimp, *On the Museum's Ruins* (Cambridge, Mass.: MIT Press, 1993).
32. A radical challenge to museum conservatism came from artists who organized satirical installations that parodied conventional museum displays. Marcel Broodthaers, a Belgian conceptual artist, founded an entirely fictive museum, Le Musée d'Art Modern, Département des Aigles, inaugurated by himself as director in 1968. See Crimp, "This is Not a Museum of Art," in *On the Museum's Ruins*, 200–34. See also Benjamin H. D. Buchlow, special issue of *October* on Broodthaers, no. 42 (fall 1987); also, the photographic documentaries of museum interiors by Louise Lawler.
33. Membership subscription to the code did not actually take effect on the prescribed date; it was delayed for at least one year pending further discussion (and possible revocation) of a clause that restricted the use of proceeds from the sale of collection materials to the acquisition of (other) collection materials. *Aviso* (December 1991): 3.
34. MacDonald, "Ethics: Constructing a Code," 65.
35. The most famous contemporary instance of constraint concerns the events surrounding the exhibition "Robert Mapplethorpe: The Perfect Moment" in 1989–90. The Corcoran Gallery of Art, in Washington, D.C., cancelled its scheduled showing of Mapplethorpe's photographs in anticipation of controversy over congressional reauthorization of the NEA, which had funded a prior exhibition of his work elsewhere. Despite protests, the exhibition was subsequently shown in a number of museums, including the Cincinnati Contemporary Art Center in April 1990. This museum and its director, Dennis Barrie, were tried on pornography and obscenity charges but ultimately were acquitted by a jury in October 1990. Although reauthorized, the NEA was constrained by the U.S. Senate to deny funding to work that denigrates religion and was required to reclaim funding from artists who produce work found to be criminally obscene. The U.S. Supreme Court has since ruled that the application of a "decency" standard as a condition of funding does not violate the First Amendment of the Constitution.
36. President Bush signed H.R. 5237 into law on November 16, 1990 (25 U.S. Code 3001 et seq.). The act focuses on Native American human remains, funerary objects, sacred objects, and objects of cultural patrimony, defined by negotiation among the interested parties. Federally funded museums and federal agencies were required to submit inventories of their holdings, and their disposition was reviewed by committees made up of museum specialists, scientists, and Native American representatives. Though potentially divisive, the five-year dialogue between museums and tribal representatives led to productive collaboration, revealing the complex ethical dimensions on both sides of the controversy, by and large contributing to an increase in mutual respect.
37. The 1994 *Code of Ethics* explicitly includes under its museum heading "noncollecting institutions," which use nonowned materials that they "borrow or fabricate" as the basis of "research, exhibits, and programs that invite public participation." *Code of Ethics for Museums*, 3.
38. *Code of Ethics for Museums*, 1994. See also Marie C. Malaro, *Museum Governance: Mission, Ethics, Policy* (Washington, D.C.: Smithsonian Institution

Press, 1994), which includes, as appendix B, "International Council of Museums (ICOM) Code of Professional Ethics, Paris, 1986."

39. *Arousal* is a clinical concept. It is measurable by means of physiological changes such as pupil dilation, rapid breathing, tumescence, or accelerated heartbeats. It can therefore be quantitatively compared on the same scale as other physically discernible events.

40. Hallucinations, illusions, and even aesthetic appearances have long been distinguished for their "nonreality," but this has always presupposed a primary (and referential) point of departure in terms of which the phenomenological character (as hallucination, illusion, or aesthetic appearance) is recognized. It is just this epistemic anchor that the unattached "virtually real experience" is supposed to eliminate. See my discussion of this issue in Chapter 5.

41. Unlike dissimulation, which retains a connection with a reality that it hides, simulation does away entirely with reality, erasing true or false representation and erecting in its place a utopian simulacrum:

> Such would be the successive phases of the image:
> it is the reflection of a profound reality;
> it masks and denatures a profound reality;
> it masks the *absence* of a profound reality;
> it has no relation to any reality whatsoever;
> it is its own pure simulacrum.

Jean Baudrillard, *Simulacra and Simulation,* trans. Sheila Faria Glaser (Ann Arbor: University of Michigan Press, 1994), 6. The fatal attraction of this chase from the real, to the neoreal, to the hyperreal, is that of nostalgia, described as an obscene deference to an involuted and surreal memory of reality.

42. "The true revolution of the nineteenth century, of modernity, is the radical destruction of appearances, the disenchantment of the world and its abandonment to the violence of interpretation and of history." The second revolution, that of postmodernity, strikes at meaning. Analysis is its weapon of choice, which, surfeited upon itself, collapses at last into indifference. Baudrillard, "On Nihilism," in *Simulacra and Simulation.*

43. The AAM's 1994 *Code of Ethics* expresses this concern: "Loyalty to the mission of the museum and to the public it serves is the essence of museum work, whether volunteer or paid. Where conflicts of interest arise—actual, potential, or perceived—the duty of loyalty must never be compromised." *Code of Ethics for Museums,* 4.

44. The moral prohibition against speech or spectacle that irresponsibly manipulates people's judgment and action applies to museums in the same fashion as to theater and should forbid indulgence in excessive sentimentality as much as incitement to riot or mayhem.

45. Legal incorporation does, of course, engender a fictional person, who can receive benefits and be held liable for wrongs where its incorporators explicitly cannot. That legal convenience, however, is designed to deflect the distribution of moral accountability from individuals, and not to declare a specifically institutional foundation for moral identity.

46. Intentionality does not invariably imply consciousness. The arm movement that functions as a baseball pitch or dance gesture evinces an intention inscribed by the institution that invests the movement with a specific meaning. The movement in the appropriate context discernibly has that meaning; however, the institution lacks consciousness of what it does. The agent that acts within the institutional framework (by moving an arm) is conscious; however, it is not unusual that an agent who carries out an institution's objectives is unaware of its intention. That possibility is well exploited by institutions that engage in large-scale environmental depredation. These are frequently carried out by low-level actors who "know not what they do" and are the first to suffer for it. Family, church, and nation are all institutions that realize their intentions without consciousness through individual agents who may or may not act with consciousness and often without relevant intention.

47. Institutionally naturalized properties differ in nature from those called "tertiary qualities" (such as beauty) by the philosopher John Locke. Locke believed that the latter were experienced subjectively upon perception of triggering complexes of primary and secondary qualities. Their contemporaneity with these complexes, he thought, gave them the appearance of adhering together objectively. Unlike these Lockeian qualities, museum-made qualities are constituted entirely by the museum's authority, fortified by that of other cultural agencies and the credulity of museumgoers.

48. A current demand is that curators and other museum staff members be given individual credit and take personal responsibility for the exhibitions they produce. Where previously the "museum voice" spoke with anonymous authority, now many spokespersons want to have their particular statements heard. Some museums have adopted a policy of naming exhibition producers, thereby giving credit, but simultaneously distancing themselves and informing the public that museum exhibitions are the offspring of fallible individual judgments. Ironically, this has had the effect of weakening the museums' credibility without necessarily strengthening public respect for the integrity and reliability of the individual curators and exhibition producers. The dispute over the feasibility of allocating curatorial responsibility has redirected attention to the collective nature of museum work and to what I am calling the museum's institutional moral character. See Alfred F. Young, "A Modest Proposal: A Bill of Rights for American Museums," *Public Historian* 14, no. 3 (summer 1992).

49. The exhibition foregrounded people normally left unidentified: the unnamed servants and slaves who attended the illustrious persons portrayed, and the invisible museum guards and staff, who tended also to be underclass persons of color. The exhibit also displayed whipping posts and shackles among other items of furniture and craftware in common use at that time.

50. Rectification will also not be achieved by merely strengthening the individual rights and duties of persons who work in museums. These rights should not be jeopardized by institutional command or self-censorship, but the removal of such risk does not guarantee the moral merit of museum exhibitions; neither does it directly ensure the good character of the museum.

51. *Excellence and Equity: Education and the Public Dimension of Museums* (Washington, D.C.: AAM, 1992).

52. Pearce, *Museums, Objects and Collections,* 264.

7. Museums and Education

1. Introduction, *Patterns in Practice: Selections from the Journal of Museum Education* (Washington, D.C.: Museum Education Roundtable [MER], 1992).
2. Tony Bennett, *The Birth of the Museum: History, Theory, Politics* (London and New York: Routledge, 1995), 146.
3. I exclude unconscious experience. No doubt such experiences are personally formative, but by definition they are not delivered or received with educative intention, and when discovered, if Freud is to be believed, it is often for the sake of purging their consequences.
4. Carol B. Stapp, "Defining Museum Literacy," reprinted with "Afterword" in *Patterns in Practice,* 112. Stapp's egalitarian commitment to fostering genuine public access to museums suggests a policy of open immigration that contrasts sharply with Pierre Bourdieu's account of museum literacy as tool of exclusion. Bourdieu describes a class-based skill imparted to bourgeois children and deliberately withheld from others, who are thereby encouraged to preserve their own sense of incompetence and class inequality. Pierre Bourdieu and Alain Darbel, with Dominique Schnapper, *The Love of Art: European Art Museums and Their Public* (Stanford, Calif.: Stanford University Press, 1990).
5. "Object Knowledge: Every Museum Visitor an Interpreter," *Roundtable Reports* 9, no. 1 (winter 1984): 5–9; reprinted in *Patterns in Practice,* 102.
6. My conclusion regarding the museum's intentions is confirmed by the fact that, to my regret, upon returning to this museum after its extensive renovation, I found that the exhibits I had learned from had been rearranged and partially removed. They were displaced by a video that insistently "taught" the fabric-making procedures and left no room for independent musing. What I had learned might be attributed to a "hidden curriculum," unplanned by the museum but effectively erased by its determination to clarify a "proper curriculum." I am indebted to Jane Roland Martin for distinguishing these pedagogic concepts.
7. Fred Schroeder, "Designing Your Exhibits: Seven Ways to Look at an Artifact," Technical Leaflet 91, ASLH, *History News* 31, no. 11 (November 1976). Thomas Schlereth gives an alternative, overlapping set of nine paradigmatic approaches to "reading" material objects. They are:

    (1) art history, (2) symbolism, (3) cultural history, (4) environmentalism, (5) functionalism, (6) structuralism, (7) behavioralism, (8) national character, (9) social history.

    Each of these approaches might render a "reading" of a given object. They represent parallel classification systems roughly equivalent in degree of abstraction, differing in this respect from Schroeder's typology, which moves consecutively from the least to the highest degree of abstraction. See Thomas J. Schlereth, *Material Culture Studies in America* (Nashville, Tenn.: ASLH, 1982), 32–72.
8. Elsa Feher and Karen Rice, "Development of Scientific Concepts through the Use of Interactive Exhibits in a Museum," *Curator* 28, no. 1 (1985): 35–46;

Minda Borun, "Naive Notions and the Design of Science Museum Exhibits, *Journal of Museum Education* 14, no.2 (spring–summer 1989): 16–17; Borun, ed., *What Research Says about Learning in Science Museums* (Washington, D.C.: Association of Science and Technology Centers, 1990).

9. Howard Gardner, *Frames of Mind: The Theory of Multiple Intelligences* (New York: Basic Books, 1985). See also Jessica Davis and Howard Gardner, "Open Windows, Open Doors: Museums and the New Thinking about Individually Centered Learning," *Museum News* 72, no. 1 (January–February 1993): 34. The multiple intelligence approach generates a learning typology, including the categories: narrational, quantitative, foundational, aesthetic, and experiential, which suggests a variety of educational activities that could also be fashioned into different strains of museum exhibition design. It seems that even these pluralistic design projects adhere to the faith that "all roads lead to Rome," for although they advocate different approaches, they assume that a single point of arrival, the ability to solve problems and fashion products, can be achieved and recognized by all contenders.

10. James Clifford and George E. Marcus, eds., *Writing Culture: The Poetics and Politics of Ethnography* (Berkeley and Los Angeles: University of California Press, 1986). Clifford describes a photograph taken (and "carefully posed") of the anthropologist Malinowski seated at a table in his tent, writing, as a group of Trobrianders looks on "observing the curious rite." Clifford's introduction intends to demarginalize the "making of texts," which is what anthropologists do—a curious custom of "writing culture," chiefly that of "others." Clifford is, of course, "reading an object" (the photograph) himself, which leads to his meditation on "the constructed, artificial nature of cultural accounts." Museums play a primary role in that construction and artifice, and this role is the object foregrounded by the new, critical ethnography.

11. James Clifford, "Four Northwest Coast Museums: Travel Reflections," in Karp and Lavine, *Exhibiting Cultures*. I take the terminology of *minority museum* from this source.

12. Nancy J. Fuller, "The Museum as a Vehicle for Community: The AkChin Indian Community Ecomuseum Project," in Karp, Kreamer, and Lavine, *Museums and Communities*, 328. According to Fuller, the "father" of the ecomuseum concept was the French museologist, Georges Henri Rivière (1897–1985), who stressed the cultural significance of place. Rivière's notion that museums should serve and be integrated in their local society was adopted as official policy by the ICOM in 1974.

13. "Creating a Dialogic Museum: The Chinatown History Museum Experiment," in Karp, Kreamer, and Lavine, *Museums and Communities*, 320.

14. The *Elementary and Secondary Education Act* of 1965, especially Titles I and III, made funds available to schools as part of Lyndon Johnson's Great Society program.

15. A notable group, assembled in Vermont in the summer of 1966 by Charles Blitzer, director of education and training at the Smithsonian Institution, resulted in the issuance of the *Belmont Report,* which explored how museums could apply their specific capacities to contribute to curricular development and the formal educational process. *America's Museums: The Belmont Report*

(Washington, D.C.: AAM, 1969). See also Eric Larrabee, ed., *Museums and Education* (Washington, D.C.: Smithsonian Institution Press, 1968).

16. The National Endowments were created in 1965 under the *National Foundation on the Arts and Humanities Act,* 20 U.S. Code, par. 951ff., which included the National Museums Act. In 1971, Congressman John Brademas (D-Ind.) introduced legislation through the subcommittee on education for a separate agency to support museums. The Institute for Museums Services (IMS) was finally established under the Museum Services Act in 1976. During the Reagan adminsitration, it was merged with the Institute for Library Services.

17. Initially a volunteer undertaking, this journal, renamed in 1985 the *Journal of Museum Education,* is now professionally edited and designed, and the organization that founded it, Museum Education Roundtable, has produced several books and taken an increasingly prominent place within the museum world. *Patterns in Practice: Selections from the Journal of Museum Education* (Washington, D.C.: MER, 1992.) See my discussion of professionalism in museums in Chapter 6.

18. Since the tax-exempt status of museums under the Internal Revenue Code, as well as eligibility for many foundation grants, rests on museums' educational function, this claim is of more than casual significance. Moreover, commitment to a general spirit of upliftment no longer suffices as a pedagogic credential. Under the *Elementary and Secondary Education Act,* and according to most foundation award guidelines, recipients of funds must provide programmatic evidence of their educational mission. Within the decade, granting agencies also required that formal procedures be in place to evaluate the success of educational programs, and so a professional cadre of evaluators came upon the scene as well.

19. "Excellence and Equity: Education and the Public Dimension of Museums," report of the AAM Task Force on Museum Education, *Journal of Museum Education* 16, no. 3 (fall 1991): 3–17.

20. The 1846 act of Congress that established the Smithsonian Institution provided for a library, a museum, and a gallery of art.

21. The extent of disagreement between Joseph Henry, the first secretary, and Spencer Fullerton Baird, his successor, has been disputed by museum historians. See Joel J. Orosz, "Disloyalty, Dismissal, and a Deal: The Development of the National Museum at the Smithsonian Institution, 1846–1855," *Museum Studies Journal* 2, no. 2, (spring 1986), and a critical response by S. Dillon Ripley and Wilcomb E. Washburn in *Museum Studies Journal* 2, no. 4 (spring–summer 1987). See also Gary Kulik, "Designing the Past: History-Museum Exhibitions from Peale to the Present," in *History Museums in the United States: A Critical Assessment,* ed. Warren Leon and Roy Rosenzweig (Urbana: University of Illinois Press, 1989).

22. Danielle Rice, "Our Work Is Good for People," in *Patterns in Practice,* 55.

23. *Smithsonian Institution Annual Report for 1897,* pt. 2 (Washington, D.C.: 1901), cited in Alexander, *Museums in Motion,* 11.

24. "The Idea of an Art Museum," in Lee, *Past, Present, East and West.*

25. These educational directives were aimed chiefly at schools, but they coincided well with museum pedagogy in their emphasis on the use of concrete objects

and especially the materials of everyday life. Good learning environments, therefore, need not be special places that contain expensive equipment: they are places where students find encouragement to indulge curiosity and are given the opportunity to gratify it.

26. This movement, a reaction to positivistic behaviorism, was, like its predecessor, empirically oriented. But it rejected the radical Lockean view that the uneducated mind is a tabula rasa upon which learning is inscribed by experience. Although the doctrine of innate ideas remained out of fashion, philosophical structuralists such as Jean Piaget, Noam Chomsky, Claude Lévi-Strauss, and others who intellectually nurtured the discovery method, believed that certain capacities were "natural" to the human organism. These were found as competencies or dispositions (rather than substantive ideas) that were realized performatively in the normal developmental course. Their fulfillment, it was thought, could be accelerated in an enriched environment such as that which progressive schools or museums could provide.

27. Stimulated in part by cold-war competition, scientists turned to elementary and secondary school teaching in the 1950s and 1960s. They initiated such programs as the Physical Science Study Curriculum (PSSC), headed by MIT's Jerrold Zacharias, and Elementary Science Study (ESS), an "outer Cambridge" based institution for the development of elementary science teaching. Active participants included prominent physicists and theoretical thinkers—David Hawkins, Philip Morrison, Frank Oppenheimer, and many others who went on to carry their ideas into science centers and museums. The scientists had little patience with denials of objective reality and were not prepared for the fractionating contextualizing of even the laws of nature that was soon to come. They persisted in loyalty to the belief that regardless of the conditions that lead to posing a question, its correct answer is what it is because that is how the world is—and so discovery would lead to truth.

28. The fact that many of these were also volunteer docents contributed to their low prestige. Often treated as a necessary nuisance, they were viewed as "bluehaired" ladies, wives, and mothers with time on their hands and no particular vocation, although museums relied heavily on their service; Bloom et al., *Museums for a New Century*, 61.

29. Visitor studies were rare prior to the 1950s. An analysis of the history of audience evaluation and its relation to the broad educative mission of the museum may be found in George E. Hein, *Learning in the Museum* (London and New York: Routledge, 1998). For pioneers of the field in its contemporary form, see Chandler G. Screven, *The Measurement and Facilitation of Learning in the Museum Environment: An Experimental Analysis* (Washington, D.C.: Smithsonian Institution Press, 1974); Harris H. Shettel, "An Evaluation of Existing Criteria for Judging the Quality of Science Exhibits," *Curator* 11, no. 2 (1968): 137–53 and "Exhibits: Art Form or Educational Medium?" *Museum News* 52, no. 1 (September 1973): 32–41; Robert Lakota, *Techniques for Improving Exhibit Effectiveness* (Washington, D.C.: Smithsonian Institution Press, 1976); Minda Borun, *Measuring the Immeasurable: A Pilot Study of Museum Effectiveness* (Philadelphia: Franklin Institute, ASTC, 1977).

30. John Holt, informal lecture, cited by Joan C. Madden in "To Realize Our Museums' Full Potential," *Patterns in Practice,* 39.
31. Danielle Rice, "Implications for Museum Educators," *Patterns in Practice,* 43.
32. Bloom et al., *Museums for a New Century,* 11.
33. Carol B. Stapp, "Internal Growth," *Patterns in Practice,* 47.
34. *Journal of Museum Education* 14, no. 3 (fall 1989): 11–13, reprinted in *Patterns in Practice,* 60.
35. "Informal education" achieved a measure of recognition when public and private agencies, such as the National Science Foundation and the Howard Hughes Medical Institute, began funding science education in museums. Praising reform efforts in the teaching of science, a foundation officer wrote: "The traditional 'cell and bell' system (which confines students in classrooms for 50 minutes and then hustles them off to another class) is being replaced with a more flexible learning environment that allows for connections between ideas and practical results. These new environments, which are being created inside and outside school walls, make knowledge come alive and are tremendous motivators for learning science." Joseph G. Perpich, vice president for grants and special programs, "Learning through Science Education Partnerships," *Pre-College Science Education Initiative for Science Museums,* Howard Hughes Medical Institute, Directors Meeting Proceedings, 1994. It is important to bear in mind that "informal" relates to the flexibility of the teaching environment and not to the substance of what is taught. Most learning is informal; it takes place throughout the animate world as the young observe and mimic their elders and each other. We all learn informally by doing and a great deal of teaching is informal, but there is no such thing as informal science.
36. Prejudice lives on, however, in the magic of words. Avoiding "ugly duckling" reference to "teachers" in its job solicitation, the AAM's publication *Aviso* advertises under the heading of "curator of education" positions formerly occupied by those persons called "teachers" who held forth in the shabby basement rooms of now-abolished museum departments of education.
37. Getty Center for Education in the Arts, Los Angeles, 1986.
38. "A Study of Learning in Australian Science Centers," *Journal of Museum Management* 13, no. 3 (September 1995): 317–25.
39. Doering, "Strangers, Guests or Clients?"
40. D. L. Chandler, *Boston Globe,* April 1, 1996, 33–34.
41. *Patterns in Practice,* 55.

8. The Aesthetic Dimension of Museums

1. There are, of course, other brokers—the commercial marketplace the most obvious among them. The museum intersects other mediating institutions and at some points merges with them in practice, but it remains an intellectually distinct entity.
2. Susan M. Pearce points out that museum objects are the result of a two-tiered selection process. First chosen by an individual for her or his personal reasons, the object is then collected a second time by the museum's recognition of it as having aesthetic, historic, or scientific value. There is not a necessary connection between the first and second selective processes, and, at the pleasure of

the museum, there may be many more tiers of selections. Pearce, *Museums, Objects, and Collections.*

3. People have many reasons for collecting, but at some point, aesthetic pleasure is always one of them. Aesthetic pleasure must not be confused, however, with the identification of art. That honorific designation elevates objects to a level of distinction that carries a number of social rewards, whereas aesthetic identification can be primitive and gratuitous. See Nathaniel Burt, *Palaces for the People: A Social History of the American Art Museum* (Boston: Little, Brown, 1977). Pierre Bourdieu argues that distinction as art is wholly arbitrary, and that museums are among the chief arbitrators responsible for fixing the status of art and perpetuating the cultural divisions that it represents. See Bourdieu, *Distinction: A Social Critique of the Judgement of Taste,* trans. Richard Nice (Cambridge, Mass.: Harvard University Press, 1984), and Bourdieu and Alain Darbel, with Dominique Schnapper, *The Love of Art: European Art Museums and Their Public,* trans. Caroline Beattie and Nick Merriman (Stanford, Calif.: Stanford University Press, 1990). Whatever the truth of these social claims, they are independent of the experience of aesthetic pleasure as stimulated by a variety of causes.

4. Walter Benjamin writes: "With collecting it is decisive that the object is released from all its original functions in order to enter into the closest possible relationship with its equivalents." In that context, wrested from their history and recombined independently of their material conditions, objects are fetishized by the museum as items of universal knowledge. Cited from an entry in file "H" of Benjamin's Passagen-Werk, vol. 1 (Frankfurt am Main, Suhrkamp, 1982), 280, and discussed in "This is Not a Museum of Art," in Crimp, *On the Museum's Ruins,* 203–5.

5. Through consummatory categories that designate what is need and what is luxury, shared cultures are transformed into shared natures. Combining their anthropological and economic methodologies, the team of Douglas and Isherwood examine consumption (and display) behavior as part of a complex information system that identifies people to one another and holds them by invisible chains forged by their social relations. Through accidents of history, objects are reidentified as relics or mementos, or swept out as junk. "Consider the solid silver cigarette cases of forty to fifty years ago, which, no longer carried, have not yet joined the display of Georgian snuff-boxes in the curiosity cabinet, but lie instead stacked in attics, awaiting a decision as to their value—antiques or just their weight in silver." Mary Douglas and Baron Isherwood, *The World of Goods: Toward an Anthropology of Consumption* (London: W. W. Norton, 1979), 99.

6. Paul Valery in "The Problem of Museums" is offended by the cacophany of "ten orchestras playing at the same time," and Robert Smithson focuses on the aftermath of mutual destruction, when the objects have killed each other off. See discussion in Weil, "On a New Foundation."

7. I understand *aesthetic interest* to refer to a prima facie appreciative judgment, classically called "taste," that people bring to objects in accordance with complex affective, cognitive, and socially cohesive conditions. I take the aesthetic to be situational and conventional rather than strictly private and qualitative. I am

unpersuaded by explanations of the aesthetic in terms of perceivable qualities or emotive inclinations or quasi-logical inductions because they assume constancy on the part of both judge and item judged, which is explicitly denied by the two-tiered analysis of museum collection that I am proposing. As suggested, the physical properties of museum objects remain largely unchanged (though even that is debatable), but they become aesthetically transubstantiated upon entering the museum. For a parallel ontological discussion of the aesthetic identification of artworks, see Arthur Danto, *The Transfiguration of the Commonplace* (Cambridge, Mass: Harvard University Press, 1981), and the corpus of works by Joseph Margolis, especially *Culture and Cultural Entities: Toward a New Unity of Science* (Hingham, Mass.: Kluwer Academic Publishers, 1984), and *Art and Philosophy: Conceptual Issues in Aesthetics* (Atlantic Highlands, N.J.: Humanities Press, 1980).

8. Creating an ambience is a familiar notion to graphic designers and image makers, though sometimes treated with suspicion by linearly directed intellectuals and ignored by the public that nevertheless succumbs to the atmospheric influence.

9. A species of Platonic idealism is certainly operative here, which assigns iconic status to a rarefied ideal, that, stripped of the encumbrances of materiality and practicality, implies everything that is good and beautiful.

10. Arthur Danto notes a decline of sacral aura that formerly distinguished museum architecture but is present in "weaker and weaker titrations" since the 1960s. Exaltation, Danto observes, is no longer the mental state to which museum visitors are expected to be transported. The buildings now speak in a businesslike manner of education, not edification, and of fun, but not of rapture. Deeply democratic, they speak in plain language to the ordinary individual subject, declining the use of awesome stairways and ponderous pillars. One enters without fanfare at street level, passing briskly along commodious retail stores, checkrooms, restaurants, and unpretentious meeting areas before getting down to the ostensive subject matter. Danto, *Beyond the Brillo Box: the Visual Arts in Post-Historical Perspective* (New York: Farrar Strauss Giroux, 1992).

11. Philosophy professor Marcia Eaton distinguishes between the aesthetic and the nonaesthetic by three routes:

> (1) a psychological approach, which ascribes a particular kind of experience to the perceiver; (2) an epistemological approach, which holds that a particular set of beliefs is a condition of making an aesthetic judgment; and (3) a logical approach, which claims that certain properties of objects are so related that, under special conditions, the presence of a configuration of one sort (N-properties) permits the perception of the existence of another sort (A-properties).

Eaton's view is closest to (3), but she admits the difficulty of distinguishing between Ns and As. One of the contextual tests that she employs to make the distinction asks: Has the term been used traditionally to describe works of art? This question, however, exemplifies precisely the circularity that I maintain governs the attribution of art status. See Eaton, *Aesthetics and the Good Life* (London and Ontario: Associated University Presses, Fairleigh Dickinson University, 1989).

12. Beardsley attributed to museums, among other educational institutions, the social responsibility to protect equal opportunity of "aesthetic welfare," as sanctioned by Article 27 of the Universal Declaration of Human Rights: "Everyone has the right freely to participate in the cultural life of the community, to enjoy the arts and to share in scientific advancement and its benefits." He means by the term *aesthetic welfare* to refer to the aggregate of levels of aesthetic experience of a given community at a particular time. To fulfill their obligation, museums must strive to extend and multiply access to aesthetic experience. Beardsley, "Aesthetic Welfare, Aesthetic Justice, and Educational Policy," in *Public Policy and the Aesthetic Interest: Critical Essays on Defining Cultural and Educational Relations,* ed. Ralph A. Smith and Ronald Berman (Urbana: University of Illinois Press, 1992).

13. Burt, *Palaces for the People,* 15.

14. Bourdieu, *Distinction: A Social Critique.*

15. "The Aesthetic Point of View," in *The Aesthetic Point of View: Selected Essays,* ed. Michael J. Wreen and Donald M. Callen (Ithaca, N.Y.: Cornell University Press, 1982), 22.

16. The museum is designed to concentrate attention so as to eliminate all other distractions (and pleasures) in order to produce the type of gratification that Beardsley prescribes: "The outside world must not come in, so windows are usually sealed off. Walls are painted white. The ceiling becomes the source of light. . . . The art is free . . . 'to take on its own life.'" O'Doherty, *Inside the White Cube.* For criticism of this pared-down museum model, see Carol Duncan and Alan Wallach, "The Museum of Modern Art as Late Capitalist Ritual: An Iconographic Analysis," *Marxist Perspectives* 1, no. 4 (winter 1978): 28–51. According to Duncan and Wallach, the spatial arrangement of the New York Museum of Modern Art breaks away from an earlier, communicative civic ideal and prescribes a labyrinthine journey of renunciation that the visitor follows alone and that leads to increasing alienation and aesthetic detachment poised as spiritual enlightenment.

17. The problem is that some people really do derive exquisite aesthetic pleasure from contemplating and performing vicious acts of outrageous cruelty. Regardless of their aesthetic purity, these cannot serve as paradigms and must be restricted on moral and prudential grounds.

18. John Dewey, *Experience and Education* (Toronto: Macmillan, 1963, 1969), 38.

19. Dewey, *Art as Experience,* 349.

20. According to Hannah Arendt, privacy was a privative condition in the Greek polis. Those condemned to it (women and slaves) were deprived of political participation and therefore of human fulfillment. Only in the modern period has privacy represented exclusion by choice, self-segregation permitted by class privilege, but terminating in alienation and isolation that borders on lunacy. Arendt, *The Human Condition* (Chicago: University of Chicago Press, 1958).

21. Some contemporary theories of art, notably those influenced by Arthur Danto, hold that the concept of art is itself historical and necessarily draws upon the history of art. In light of that theory, it is logically impossible for art museums to disregard art history or to insist that aesthetic quality alone serve as the criterion for the selection of works of art. Recognizing something as a

work of art entails familiarity with a tradition of historical art production and a context; perception alone cannot decry an artwork's status. Danto, "The Artworld," *Journal of Philosophy* 6 (1964): 571–84. For discussion of the analogy between artworks and jokes, see Ted Cohen, "Jokes," in *Pleasure, Preference and Value: Studies in Philosophical Aesthetics,* ed. Eva Schaper (Cambridge: Cambridge University Press, 1983).

22. In an art museum, for example, the foregrounding of the typical may count as a museological defect, guaranteed to lead to mediocrity, but the didactic needs of other museums are served by just such collection of species-typical and atypical specimens. Productive research depends on the ability to accumulate and compare instances with a standard. Even art museums are unable to exclude all but the superlative items from their collections. To do so would make comparative judgment impossible and therefore hinder the museum's educational function.

23. Plato understood the motivating power of the aesthetic very clearly. Although he banished poets from his ideal society (*Republic,* Book 10), he was perfectly willing to harness the emotive power of music to the moral education of the young (Book 2.3) and to stir their passion to military performance. Plato rebukes only the "wrongful" use of aesthetic devices in the service of what he takes to be falsehood, bad behavior, or the denigration of reason. Aesthetic sweeteners of civic indoctrination can be found in all cultures and are often employed with sophisticated self-consciousness. Consider, for example, Albert Speer's dramatic civic architecture and Leni Riefenstahl's film *Triumph of the Will,* which glorifies the consolidation of the Nazi party at its 1934 convocation in Nuremberg.

24. The linguist Kenneth Pike coined the terms *emic* and *etic* to designate, respectively, rules of practice followed by users within a society and theoretical analyses of such rules and categories inferred from the scientific perspective of an observer. Some museum presentations borrow a bit from both perspectives. Marvin Harris shows how the dual usage obviates some confusion over "objective" and "subjective" judgment, pointing out that a practitioner can be capable of observing the rules of practice objectively and that observers are not automatically free of subjectivity. Harris, *Cultural Materialism: The Struggle for a Science of Culture* (New York: Random House, 1979).

25. Arthur Danto points out that styles are identifiable only with historical hindsight. At the time that an artist first explores those gestures destined to become a personal and imitable signature, there cannot yet be the repetition and thematic variation characteristic of a style or genre. Someone, generally other than the practitioner, recognizes these only after the fact. "Narrative and Style," Journal of Aesthetics and Art Criticism" (summer 1991), reprinted in *Beyond the Brillo Box.* A museum might take a purely historical interest in comparing two artistic styles (e.g., impressionism and luminism), placing no more emphasis on the aesthetic experience evoked by the works displayed than does a natural history museum that displays specimens of organisms that may or may not be beautiful.

26. Jacques Derrida cites Benjamin's reference to glass as "without aura," a "cold and concise material," the "enemy of secrecy" and "the enemy of possession."

He also cites Blanchot and the Bauhaus, whose glass and steel "have created spaces in which it is difficult to leave traces. . . . The new environment of glass will completely change man." From Benjamin's text Derrida appeals to a "new poverty," designating a "wandering group of poor people, indeed of the 'homeless' . . . which should be 'our' future, already our present"—perhaps those very sword swallowers and fire-eaters who congregate in the plaza of Baoubourg. Derrida, "Letter to Peter Eisenman," cited in Stephen David Ross, *Art and Its Significance: An Anthology of Aesthetic Theory,* 3d ed. (New York: SUNY Press, 1994).

27. An outstanding proponent of this aspect of science was Cyril Stanley Smith, professor of materials science at MIT, who argued not only that technology was a greater impetus to science than the reverse influence, but also that technology itself was as motivated by aesthetic curiosity as by logic or need. Utilitarian and profitable development of techniques, he believed, occur only as a sequel to playful and pleasurable exploration and follow a very different dynamic. Smith, *A Search for Structure: Selected Essays on Science, Art, and History* (Cambridge, Mass.: MIT Press, 1982). See also his *From Art to Science* (Cambridge Mass.: MIT Press, 1980).

28. In "Great Science Museums," *Discover* (November 1993): 79-113, ten scientists discuss their favorite science museums. Most recall childhood experiences, describing certain aesthetic features of the museum venue with particular fondness—its serenity, its theatrical light, its ranged spaces, and the isolation the museum affords from the world outside.

29. See my discussion of dinosaur exhibition in Chapter 5.

30. Conceptually simplified maps, models, analogies, and formulas tend to be far more conducive to understanding than exact replicas, which must reproduce the same complexity that confounded the researcher to begin with. See Jorge Luis Borges's map story, in *Labyrinths: Selected Stories and Other Writings* (New York: New Directions, 1962, 1964). But there are significant exceptions. Successful artificial synthesis of an object (e.g., a molecule) is pretty good though not conclusive evidence that one understands it. For discussion of the importance of "hands-on" model building, see *Art Bulletin* (spring 1996), an entire issue on art and science, including essays by Stephen Jay Gould, Roald Hoffmann, and Gerald Holton.

31. Roald Hoffman, "Molecular Beauty," *Journal of Aesthetics and Art Criticism (JAAC)* 48, no. 3 (summer 1990): 191-204. See also Hoffman and Vivian Torrence, *Chemistry Imagined: Reflections on Science* (Washington, D.C.: Smithsonian Institution Press,1993), and Hoffman, *The Same and Not the Same,* George B. Pegram lecture series (New York: Columbia University Press, 1995).

32. In science centers, according to the bylaws of their governing association (ASTC), member institutions must be "committed to the development of participative exhibits, demonstrations, and programs in the basic sciences and their technological applications. They should enable the general public to gain a firsthand experience with natural phenomena and man-made devices." Victor Danilov, *Science and Technology Centers* (Cambridge, Mass.: MIT Press, 1982).

33. For discussion of these differences see Judith Wechsler, ed., *On Aesthetics in Science* (Cambridge, Mass.: MIT Press, 1981). James W. McAllister considers

visualizability and abstractness to be alternative aesthetic properties of scientific theories. He argues that disputes over scientific theories between scientists often reflect the difference in their aesthetic taste. McAllister, *Beauty and Revolution in Science* (Ithaca, N.Y.: Cornell University Press, 1996), 48–54.

34. "What's Going On Here: Exploring Some of the More Elusive, Subtle Signs of Science Learning," in *Science Learning in the Informal Setting: Symposium Proceedings,* ed. Paul Heltne and Linda Marquardt (Chicago: Chicago Academy of Sciences, November 12–15, 1987).

35. Attributed to David Hawkins, in Spock, "What's Going on Here," 260.

36. Mihalyi Csikszentmihalyi, "Human Behavior and the Science Center," in Heltne and Marquardt, *Science Learning.* See also Mihalyi Csikszentmihalyi and Isabella Selega Csikszentmihalyi, *Optimal Experience: Psychological Studies of Flow in Consciousness* (Cambridge: Cambridge University Press, 1988). See also Jacob W. Getzels and Mihalyi Csikszentmihalyi, *The Creative Vision: A Longitudinal Study of Problem-Finding in Art* (New York: Wiley Interscience, 1976), and Mihalyi Csikszentmihalyi, *Flow: The Psychology of Optimal Experience* (New York: Harper and Row, 1990).

37. Roald Hoffmann calls attention to the same absorption: "As for detachment, a concentration that envelops, well—the only people I've seen more detached than chemists looking at molecules are computer hackers or Pachinko players." Hoffmann, "Molecular Beauty," *JAAC:* 202. The selflessness of this devotion to objects also recalls the "allocentric" attention identified by Schachtel and Keller; see chapter 6, note 1.

9. Conclusion: The Museum in Transition

1. All of these questions are taken from the AAM newsletter, *Excellence and Equity* (winter 1996).

2. As Hamlet warns, "Thus conscience doth make cowards of us all."

3. For an alternative representation, consider the more grandiose depiction by Ivan Gaskell, curator of painting and sculpture at Harvard's Fogg Museum. In a document celebrating the one-hundredth anniversary of that institution, Gaskell describes curators as "intellectual chameleons" poised as "multi-lingual interpreters in the visual Babel of the museum." Curators, he says, are evolving into "a new kind of art scholar, at ease with both objects and critical theory, conversant with technical analysis and art history, and a mediator among chemists, conservators, philosophers, historians, artists, archaeologists, anthropologists, students and educators." James Cuno et al., *Harvard's Art Museums: 100 Years of Collecting* (Cambridge, Mass.: Harvard University Museums and New York: Harry N. Abrams, 1996), 157.

4. The popularization of museums passed through many stages, dating back essentially to their foundation, and advanced more recently by Roosevelt's New Deal initiatives of governmental support for the arts. In 1935, Frederick P. Keppel, president of the Carnegie Corporation, affirmed that, although museums had served an oligarchy ten years before, now they must be characterized as "democratic." Five years later his annual report noted that museums had "shifted in emphasis from a custodial function to educational and other services." Though not without setbacks, these social trends paved the way to the

1969 *Belmont Report* and to subsequent grassroots demands for more inclusive community participation at all ideological and decision-making levels of museum activity. See Philip D. Spiess II, Terry Zeller, and Wilcomb E. Washburn, "75th Anniversary Memorial Review," *Museum News* 75, no. 2 (March–April 1996): 38–63.

5. A significant ingredient of this development was the diversification of the board, staff, volunteers, and community, as museums sought to broaden the base of their internal structure as well as its outreach. See my discussion in chapter 3.

6. Tony Bennett, *The Birth of the Museum: History, Theory, Politics* (London: Routledge, 1995).

7. Other museums have mounted exhibitions with similar objectives; for example, the New York Center for African Art literally made the art of exhibition the subject of several exhibitions that focused on alternative ways of selecting and presenting objects according to a number of disciplinary, national, cultural, and personal perspectives. See Susan Vogel, "Always True to the Object," in Karp and Lavine, *Exhibiting Cultures.*

8. Like the *Spirit of St. Louis,* the craft that Lindburgh flew across the Atlantic Ocean, or the *Apollo 11* space capsule, the *Enola Gay* did occupy a unique place in history. Its physical reality was undisputed, and there was no doubt that it did deliver the bomb. But the why and wherefore of its exhibition depended on which of several noncongruent theories of representation were subscribed to, and the battle between veterans, historians, and other partisans centered on that issue. For an illuminating discussion of the issues that the exhibition might have raised had the Smithsonian not been forced to recant and "smooth over" genuine debate, see Edward T. Linenthal, "Between History and Memory: The *Enola Gay* Controversy at the National Air and Space Museum," *Bulletin of Concerned Asian Scholars* 27, no. 2 (April–June 1995): 16.

9. The initial proposal for the exhibition carried the ambitious title "The Crossroads: The End of World War II, the Atomic Bomb, and the Origins of the Cold War." After five turbulently disputed revisions of its script and the removal of much of its documentary content the exhibition was renamed appropriately to its diminished scope "The Last Act: The Atomic Bomb and the End of World War II." Instead of referring to the circumstances at the war's conclusion and a subsequent age of nuclear uncertainty, the exhibition simply asserted that the bomb caused the Japanese surrender, a claim that many historians deny. On exhibit, in addition to the fuselage, was a film that celebrated the training and team spirit of both the flight crew of the *Enola Gay* and the museum's restoration team.

10. Encyclopedic museums may be likened to anthologies that bring together under a single cover a collection of texts (or segments of texts) that were not designed to be part of a single whole. Their placement in combination forces a conversation among them but also tends to homogenize them, effacing radical inconsistencies and making them appear to belong to a single discourse—one that each of them, taken separately, would repudiate.

11. The curator of a small, New England ethnic museum complains of some of the difficulties encountered by his specialized museum, whose policy is to include

every member of its widely dispersed ethnic "family" as a "part owner," "at home" in the museum community. These visitors, he says, do not have a native tradition of museums and museumgoing. They "frequently climb across barriers to touch and examine the rugs (displayed in the museum) as they would in a private home." They are also put off by the presence of nonethnic, "nonfamily" persons among the trustees, supporters, and funders of "their" institution and do not wish to include them in their councils. Gary Lind-Sinanian, "The Talking Stick: Raising Issues of Diversity," *NEMA News* 19, no. 4 (summer 1996): 11.

12. An "experience economy" is already upon us, replacing earlier economies of goods and services. Economists know that experiences are real and can be commodified like any other identifiable thing. The entrepreneurial "experience merchants" will be guided by experience-design principles with the singular objective of profitability. Museums have more complicated aims, but they are not immune to the economic pressures of the marketplace and are currently exploring the adoption of similar techniques of experience management. See Joseph Pine II and James H. Gilmore, "Welcome to the Experience Economy," *Harvard Business Review* (July–August 1998): 97–105. I am indebted to George E. Hein for this reference.

13. John H. Falk and Lynn D. Dierking have devised an experiential model that builds on the interactive spheres of the visitor's personal context, meaning her private agenda, history, knowledge, and motivation; the social context, referring to the visitor's companion(s) and their social dynamic at the museum; and physical context, meaning the comfort, convenience, and memorability of the physical circumstances of the visit. These components combine with variable intensity to form the museum experience, some part of which is classifiable as a "learning experience." The authors are interested in museums' gaining control over the aspects of visitor experience that will reinforce their apprehension of the message that museums intend exhibitions to embody. Falk and Dierking, *The Museum Experience* (Washington, D.C.: Whalesback Books, 1992). Obviously museums are not entirely in control of the "before" and "after," but the more they are affiliated with a mainstream system of cultural institutions, the more reliable their anticipation of the present can be.

14. Randall Kennedy, "Teaching about Law in the Liberal Arts," in *Focus on Law Studies* 11, no. 2 (spring 1996), a publication of the American Bar Association, Chicago.

15. Hannah Arendt, *The Human Condition* (Chicago, University of Chicago Press, 1958).

16. Critics of education in the 1960s and 1970s distinguished between those strategies that were overt and intentional means to explicit learning states (e.g., mastering the multiplication tables), and those that were covertly and sometimes unconsciously introduced by school authorities, and yet conveyed by the conditions of the learning situation (e.g., rewarding the docile and subservient behavior of some, while applauding aggressiveness on the part of others). The latter "hidden curriculum" is often entirely concealed from the learner, who consequently takes it in without resistance. I am grateful to Jane R. Martin for recalling this pedagogic literature to my attention.

17. There are, of course, teaching museums, often attached to universities or other learning institutions. These often do have a formal pedagogic agenda determined by the institution of which they are a part. Even these, however, add a dimension to the teaching function that goes beyond what the primary institution is able to offer, and the best of them are able to gratify visitor interest independently of that agency.

Index

Aldrovandi, Ulisse, 24
American Association of Museums, 18, 44, 93-97, 99-100, 102-3, 106, 116, 121-22, 123
American Museum of Natural History, 136
Anacostia Museum, 46
Appelbaum, Ralph, 65
Arendt, Hannah, 148-49
Ashmole, John, 24

B

Bacon, Francis, 56
Baudrillard, Jean, 101
Baumgarten, Alexander, 57
Beardsley, Monroe, 129-31, 140
Benjamin, Walter, 134
Bennett, Tony, 144
Borges, Jorge Luis, 52-53
Boston Children's Museum, 138-39
Boston Museum of Fine Arts, 144-45
Boston Science Museum, 125
Bourdieu, Pierre, 21, 130
Brown, Claudine, 108
Bruner, Jerome, 117
Burt, Nathaniel, 130

C

Carnegie, Andrew, 30
Chicago Museum of Science and Industry, 26
Chinatown History Museum, 47, 114
Cleveland Museum of Art, 117
Code of Ethics for Museums (1992), 102, 103
Code of Ethics for Museum Workers (1925), 93, 94, 96
Colonial Williamsburg, 30, 38
Commission on Museums for a New Century, 121-22, 123
Corcoran Gallery, 103
Crews, Spencer, 61
Csikszentmihalyi, Mihali, 36, 139-40

D

Danilov, Victor, 26
Dewey, John, 116, 131
Disney Enterprises, 80-82
Dobb, Stephen M., 123-24
Duncan, Carol, 57

E

Eco, Umberto, 81
Eisner, Elliot W., 123-24

Enola Gay, 103, 145
Excellence and Equity: Education and the Public Dimension of Museums, 106
Exploratorium, 120

F
Foucault, Michel, 52–53
Frick, Henry, 30
Friere, Paolo, 114

G
Galileo, 125
Gemaldegalerie, 20
Goode, George Brown, 25, 117, 118

H
Habsburg: collection, 57; family, 20, 56
Harris, Neil, 98
Hegel, Georg Wilhelm Friedrich, 20
Hoffman, Roald, 137
Holocaust Museum. *See* U.S. Holocaust Memorial Museum

I
Imperial War Museum (London), 84
International Council of Museums, 2, 122
Institute for Museum Services, 115

J
James, Henry, 69
Johnson (Lyndon) administration, 115
J. Paul Getty Center for Education in the Arts, 123
Jurassic Park, 11, 78, 136

K
Kennedy, Randall, 148
Kinard, John, 46
Kristeva, Julia, 39
Kuo, John Wei Tchen. *See* Wei Tchen, John Kuo

L
Lee, Sherman E., 117
Louvre, 57, 113

M
Malraux, André, 86, 87
Mapplethorpe, Robert, 103
Maryland Historical Society, 104
Metropolitan Museum of Art, 113
Mona Lisa, 11

Montessori, Maria, 116
Motown Historical Museum, 45
Museum Ethics (1978), 94–96, 122
Museum of History and Technology (1964–1980), 29
Museum Services Act (1977), 2, 115
Museums for a New Century (1984), 44, 123

N
Napoleon, 22, 57
National Air and Space Museum, 103, 146
National Endowment for the Arts, 115
National Endowment for the Humanities, 115
National Museum of American History, 29
Native American Graves Protection and Repatriation Act (1990), 99
New York SONY Center, 3
New York State Museum, 114

O
O'Doherty, Brian, 58, 59
Old Sturbridge Village (Conn.), 30, 82–83
Oppenheimer, Frank, 120

P
Peale, Charles Willson, 25
Pearce, Susan, 76, 107
Piaget, Jean, 117
Plato, 70–71, 72–73, 75, 76, 81
Plimouth Plantation, 30, 82–83
Pompidou Center (Paris), 134
Professional Standards for Museum Educators, 122–23

R
Rauschenberg, Robert, 69
Rice, Danielle, 125–26
Rockefeeler, John, 30
Roundtable Reports, 115
Rousseau, Jean-Jacques, 116

S
Schlereth, Thomas J., 111
Seoul museum (temporary), 109
Shelley, Percy Bysshe, 131
Sims, James, 61
Smithson, James, 116
Smithsonian Institution, 25, 46, 61, 108, 116, 117, 145
Spielberg, Steven, 78
Spock, Michael, 138–39
Stewart, Rowena, 45–46

T

theme parks, 16, 80–8

Tradescant, John (Elder and Younger), 24

U

U.S. Holocaust Memorial Museum, 65, 84

V

Van Meergeren, Han, 74

Vermeer, Johannes, 74

Victoria and Albert Museum, 10

Vigotsky, L. V., 117

Vivant-Denon, Dominique, 22

W

Warhol, Andy, 60

Wei Tchen, John Kuo, 47, 114

Wilson, Fred, 104–5, 134–35

Woolf, Virginia, 113